AF848964

CONGRESSIONAL POLICIES, PRACTICES AND PROCEDURES SERIES

FEDERAL RULEMAKING AND REGULATIONS

Congressional Policies, Practices and Procedures Series

Congressional Misconduct
Jack Maskell
2009 ISBN 978-1-60741-117-8

The Senate's Role in Confirmation of Political Appointees
Michael K. Connor and Matthew D. Rangel (Editors)
2009. ISBN 978-1-60741-123-9

Contested Election Cases in the House of Representatives
James P. Cotton (Editor)
2009. ISBN: 978-1-60741-118-5

Federal Role in Funding Research and Development
Piper B. Collins (Editor)
2010. ISBN: 978-1-60741-486-5

Federal Role in Funding Research and Development
Piper B. Collins (Editor)
2010. ISBN: 978-1-61668-793-9 (Online Book)

War Powers Resolution after 34 Years and the Continuing Political Debate
Jeremiah E. Sanders, (Editor)
2010. ISBN: 978-1-60692-787-8

Emergency Communications: Enhancing the Safety Network
Nicolás Cohen (Editor)
2010. ISBN: 978-1-60741-517-6

Other Transaction Authority: Understanding and Examining Its Uses by Federal Agencies
Tara M. Morrison (Editor)
2010. ISBN: 978-1-60741-519-0

Other Transaction Authority: Understanding and Examining Its Uses by Federal Agencies
Tara M. Morrison (Editor)
2010. ISBN: 978-1-61668-794-6 (Online Book)

Federal Rulemaking and Regulations
Paul Lee (Editor)
2010. ISBN: 978-1-60876-069-5

Ping Pong and Conference Committees: Resolving Legislative Differences in Congress
Marcos Carvalho (Editor)
2010. ISBN: 978-1-60741-964-8

Congressional Liaison Offices and Select Advocacy and Complaint Offices
Pauline E. Veliotis (Editor)
2010. ISBN: 978-1-61668-356-6

Congressional Liaison Offices and Select Advocacy and Complaint Offices
Pauline E. Veliotis (Editor)
2010. ISBN: 978-1-61668-433-4 (Online Book)

CONGRESSIONAL POLICIES, PRACTICES AND PROCEDURES SERIES

FEDERAL RULEMAKING AND REGULATIONS

PAUL LEE
EDITOR

Nova Science Publishers, Inc.
New York

Copyright © 2010 by Nova Science Publishers, Inc.

All rights reserved. No part of this book may be reproduced, stored in a retrieval system or transmitted in any form or by any means: electronic, electrostatic, magnetic, tape, mechanical photocopying, recording or otherwise without the written permission of the Publisher.

For permission to use material from this book please contact us:
Telephone 631-231-7269; Fax 631-231-8175
Web Site: http://www.novapublishers.com

NOTICE TO THE READER

The Publisher has taken reasonable care in the preparation of this book, but makes no expressed or implied warranty of any kind and assumes no responsibility for any errors or omissions. No liability is assumed for incidental or consequential damages in connection with or arising out of information contained in this book. The Publisher shall not be liable for any special, consequential, or exemplary damages resulting, in whole or in part, from the readers' use of, or reliance upon, this material. Any parts of this book based on government reports are so indicated and copyright is claimed for those parts to the extent applicable to compilations of such works.

Independent verification should be sought for any data, advice or recommendations contained in this book. In addition, no responsibility is assumed by the publisher for any injury and/or damage to persons or property arising from any methods, products, instructions, ideas or otherwise contained in this publication.

This publication is designed to provide accurate and authoritative information with regard to the subject matter covered herein. It is sold with the clear understanding that the Publisher is not engaged in rendering legal or any other professional services. If legal or any other expert assistance is required, the services of a competent person should be sought. FROM A DECLARATION OF PARTICIPANTS JOINTLY ADOPTED BY A COMMITTEE OF THE AMERICAN BAR ASSOCIATION AND A COMMITTEE OF PUBLISHERS.

LIBRARY OF CONGRESS CATALOGING-IN-PUBLICATION DATA

Federal rulemaking and regulations / editor, Paul Lee.
p. cm.
Includes index.
ISBN 978-1-60876-069-5 (hardcover)
1. Administrative agencies--United States. 2. Administrative procedure--United States. 3. Court rules--United States. I. Lee, Paul.
KF5407.F43 2009
342.73'066--dc22

2009038389

Published by Nova Science Publishers, Inc. ✢ New York

CONTENTS

PREFACE

Federal regulation, like taxing and spending, is one of the basic tools of government used to implement public policy. Although not as frequently examined as congressional or presidential policy making, the process of developing and framing rules is viewed by some as central to the definition and implementation of public policy in the United States. Regulations generally start with an act of Congress, and are the means by which statutes are implemented and specific requirements are established. The terms "rule" or "regulation" are often used interchangeably in discussions of the federal regulatory process. This book is an overview of the federal rulemaking process and discusses the major laws and executive orders that prescribe the procedures agencies are to apply when promulgating regulations.This book consists of public documents which have been located, gathered, combined, reformatted, and enhanced with a subject index, selectively edited and bound to provide easy access.

Chapter 1 - Executive Order (E.O.) 12866 on "Regulatory Planning and Review," issued in September 1993, describes the principles and procedures by which the Office of Management and Budget's Office of Information and Regulatory Affairs (OIRA) reviews hundreds of significant proposed and final agency regulations on behalf of the President before they are published in the *Federal Register*. On January 18, 2007, President George W. Bush issued E.O. 13422, making the most significant amendments to E.O. 12866 since it was published. The changes made by this new executive order are controversial, characterized by some as a "power grab" by the White House that undermines public protections and lessens congressional authority and by others as "a paragon of common sense and good government."

The most important changes made to E.O. 12866 by E.O. 13422 fall into five general categories: (1) a requirement that agencies identify in writing the specific market failure or problem that warrants a new regulation, (2) a requirement that each agency head designate a presidential appointee within the agency as a "regulatory policy officer" who can control upcoming rulemaking activity in that agency, (3) a requirement that agencies provide their best estimates of the cumulative regulatory costs and benefits of rules they expect to publish in the coming year, (4) an expansion of OIRA review to include significant guidance documents, and (5) a provision permitting agencies to consider whether to use more formal rulemaking procedures in certain cases.

This chapter discusses each of these changes, noting areas that are unclear and the potential implications of the changes; provides background information on presidential review of rules; discusses three congressional hearings on the executive order in 2007; and notes congressional efforts to block the implementation of the order. It concludes by pointing out that the significance of the changes made to the review process by E.O. 13422 may become clear only through their implementation. The changes made by this executive order represent a clear expansion of presidential authority over rulemaking agencies. In that regard, E.O. 13422 can be viewed as part of a broader statement of presidential authority presented throughout the Bush Administration.

Executive Order (E.O.) 12866 on "Regulatory Planning and Review," issued by President William Clinton in September 1993, describes the principles and procedures by which the Office of Management and Budget's (OMB's) Office of Information and Regulatory Affairs (OIRA) reviews hundreds of significant proposed and final agency regulations on behalf of the President before they are published in the *Federal Register*.[1] As a result of these reviews, OIRA can have a significant—if not determinative—role in the development of a broad array of public policies, from the homeland security rules governing boarding of passenger aircraft to the amount of arsenic allowed in public water systems.[2]

On January 18, 2007, President George W. Bush issued E.O. 13422, making the most significant amendments to E.O. 12866 since it was published.[3] The changes made by this new executive order are controversial, characterized by some as a "power grab" by the White House that undermines public protections and lessens congressional authority,[4] and by others as "a paragon of common sense and good government."[5] This chapter describes the changes made to the regulatory planning and review process by the new order, noting the potential impact of those changes and areas that are unclear. It also describes three hearings in 2007 examining the new executive order, and notes recent congressional efforts to block the implementation of the order. The chapter ends by offering some concluding observations. First, though, the chapter provides a brief background section on the regulatory planning and review procedures established by E.O. 12866 and its predecessors.

Chapter 2 - The statutory provision known as the Congressional Review Act (CRA) (5 U.S.C. §§801-808) has not been a frequently used method for Congress to control agency rulemaking, having been used to overturn only one rule in the more than 12 years since it took effect. However, Congress has various other methods to influence agency rulemaking and regulatory activity, including the addition of provisions to agency appropriations bills that restrict federal rulemaking or regulatory activity.

The use of restrictions in appropriations legislation to control rulemaking has received relatively little attention from scholars and analysts, but these restrictions can have substantial effects on public policy. This chapter examines the Consolidated Appropriations Act for 2008 (P.L. 110-161), and identifies four types of such provisions: (1) restrictions on the finalization of particular proposed rules, (2) restrictions on regulatory activity within certain areas, (3) implementation or enforcement restrictions, and (4) conditional restrictions (e.g., preventing implementation of a rule until certain actions are taken). The chapter then examines appropriations acts in nine previous fiscal years, noting that some provisions have been included in appropriations bills everyyear, and others have appeared for several years in a row. Numerous examples of regulatory appropriations restrictions are provided in this chapter. The reasons behind these restrictions vary, with some appearing to be based on economic considerations, some requiring or preventing the implementation of rules issued at the end of a presidential administration, and some included for various other reasons.

Although none of the appropriations provisions appear designed to *reverse* agency rulemaking actions (as the CRA was intended to permit), the number and varietyof the provisions clearly illustrate that Congress's ability to overseeand affect regulatory agencies is not confined to CRA resolutions of disapproval. On the other hand, such provisions are generally applicable only for the period of time and the agencies covered by the relevant appropriations bill. Also, to the extent that agencies have independent sources of funding (e.g., user fees) or implement their regulations through state or local governments, some of the limitations may not be as restrictive as they seem. While appropriations provisions have been advocated by representatives of virtually all political parties and interest groups, some observers have questioned whether they are constitutional or conducive to sound public policy. Nevertheless, their use by Congress is likely to continue as long as appropriations bills are considered "must pass" legislation.

Chapter 3 - The Congressional Review Act ("CRA," 5 U.S.C. §§801-808) established a special set of expedited or "fast track" legislative procedures, primarily in the Senate, through which Congress may enact joint resolutions disapproving agencies' final rules. Members of Congress have 60 "days of continuous session" to introduce a resolution of disapproval after a rule has been submitted to Congress or published in the *Federal Register*, and the Senate has 60 "session days" to use CRA expedited procedures. Although the CRA was considered a reassertion of congressional authority over rulemaking agencies, only one rule has been disapproved using its procedures, and that reversal was the result of a specific set of circumstances created by a transition in party control of the presidency.

The CRA also indicates that if a rule is submitted to Congress less than 60 session days in the Senate or 60 legislative days in the House of Representatives before Congress adjourns a session *sine die*, then the rule is carried over to the next session of Congress and treated as if it had been submitted to Congress or published in the *Federal Register* on the 15th legislative day (House) or session day (Senate). This restart of the CRA process in a new session of Congress occurs even if no joint resolution of disapproval had been introduced regarding the rule during the preceding session of Congress.

A review of the House and Senate calendars from the first session of the 100th Congress to the first session of the 110th Congress indicates that the date triggering the carryover provisions of the CRA (i.e., the date after which less than 60 legislative or session days remained in a session) has usually been determined by the House of Representatives, and that the date was almost always earlier in second sessions of Congress (during which congressional elections are held) than in first sessions. The median date after which the "carryover periods" began for all sessions during this period was June 25, and the median for all second sessions was June 9. Since the CRA was enacted in March 1996, the median starting point for these carryover periods during second sessions of Congress has been somewhat earlier — June 7.

At the conclusion of most recent presidential administrations, the volume of agency rulemaking has increased noticeably. In May 2008, the White House Chief of Staff generally required federal agencies to finalize all regulations to be issued during the Bush Administration by November 1, 2008. According to press accounts and other sources, federal agencies are planning to issue a number of significant final rules by the end of 2008. If any of these "midnight rules" are submitted within the "carryover period" of the second session of the 110th Congress, then they will be subject to the carryover provisions of the CRA.

Chapter 4 - Federal regulation, like taxing and spending, is one of the basic tools of government used to implement public policy. Although not as frequently examined as congressional or presidential policy making, the process of developing and framing rules is viewed by some as central to the definition and implementation of public policy in the United States. Regulations generally start with an act of Congress, and are the means by which statutes are implemented and specific requirements are established. The terms "rule" or "regulation" are often used interchangeably in discussions of the federal regulatory process. The Administrative Procedure Act of 1946 defines a *rule* as "the whole or part of an agency statement of general or particular applicability and future effect designed to implement, interpret, or prescribe law or policy." The procedures that federal agencies are required to follow in writing regulations is called the rulemaking process, and are the subject of this chapter.

During the past 60 to 65 years, Congress and various Presidents have developed an elaborate set of procedures and requirements to guide the federal rulemaking process, often with the implicit or explicit goal of reducing the amount of regulatory burden placed on the public. Statutory rulemaking requirements applicable to a wide range of agencies include the Administrative Procedure Act, the Regulatory Flexibility Act, the Paperwork Reduction Act, the Unfunded Mandates Reform Act, and the Information Quality Act. These and other cross-cutting rulemaking requirements often require some type of analysis on the part of the rulemaking agency before issuing a covered rule, but also often give agencies substantial discretion regarding whether the requirements are applicable. Other statutorily-based rulemaking requirements are contained in agency- or program-specific laws, which provide varying levels of discretion regarding the substance of agencies' rules and may impose (or exclude) additional analytical or procedural requirements. The most important of the current set of presidential rulemaking requirements are in Executive Order 12866, which establishes presidential review of covered agencies' rulemaking within the Office of Management and Budget's Office of Information and Regulatory Affairs (OIRA). The executive order requires covered agencies to submit their significant rules to OIRA for review before they become final, and requires those rules to meet certain minimal standards. Other executive orders and presidential directives delineate other specific rulemaking requirements incumbent on covered agencies. However, these requirements also often provide substantial discretion to agencies regarding whether, and if so how, they are applied.

The purpose of this chapter is to provide Congress with an overview of the federal rulemaking process and a brief discussion of the major laws and executive orders that prescribe the procedures agencies are to apply when promulgating regulations.

Chapter 5 - This report describes how OIRA reviews covered agencies draft rules, OIRAs effects on the rules, and changes in OIRAs procedures and policies in recent years. Much of that discussion is drawn from a September 2003 report on OIRA by the General Accounting Office (GAO). First, though, this chkapter provides a history of presidential regulatory review and describe how OIRAs review process was established. Finally, the chapter describes several potential legislative issues regarding OIRAs regulatory review authority.

Chapter 6 - Negotiated rulemaking, which is a supplement to traditional rulemaking, is a process in which representatives of federal agencies and affected parties work together in a committee to reach consensus on what can ultimately become a proposed rule. Although negotiated rulemaking is not appropriate for all regulations, advocates believe that the approach can speed rule development, reduce litigation, and generate more creative and effective regulatory solutions.

The Negotiated Rulemaking Act of 1990 established the basic statutory authority for the approach while giving agencies wide latitude in its implementation, and the Clinton Administration advocated a broader application of the approach. Agencies are permitted to use "conveners" to determine whether negotiated rulemaking is appropriate and to select participants, and to use "facilitators" to chair the negotiated rulemaking committee meetings. At the end of the process, agencies must still publish proposed and final regulations for public comment, but any proposal agreed to by the negotiating committee is not binding on the agency or other parties.

Although the Negotiated Rulemaking Act gives agencies substantial discretion as to whether the approach should be employed in rulemaking, Congress has sometimes mandated its use by rulemaking agencies and established specific procedures and time frames to follow. Studies examining the implementation of negotiated rulemaking have reached different conclusions regarding the approach's effect on rulemaking timeliness, litigation, as well as other issues. Researchers also disagree regarding how the effectiveness of negotiated rulemaking should be measured.

The Administrative Procedure Act (APA) of 1946 (5 U.S.C. §551 *et seq.*) generally requires federal agencies to publish their proposed rules (also called regulations) in the *Federal Register,* to provide the public with an opportunity to comment on those proposed rules, and to publish a final rule at least 30 days before its effective date. The APA does not, however, specify how agencies are to develop their proposed rules or who should participate in that process. Consequently, agencies sometimes develop rules without discussing relevant issues with all affected interests, and there may be little or no opportunity for an informal exchange of views among affected parties or between those parties and the rulemaking agency either before or after the proposed rule is published.

Negotiated rulemaking (sometimes referred to as regulatory negotiation or "reg-neg") is a supplement to the traditional APA rulemaking process in which agency representatives and representatives of affected parties work together to develop what can ultimately become the text of a proposed rule.[1] In this approach, negotiators try to reach consensus by evaluating their priorities and making tradeoffs, with the end result being a draft rule that is mutually acceptable. Negotiated rulemaking has been encouraged (although not usually required) by both congressional and executive branch actions, and has received bipartisan support as a way to involve affected parties in rulemaking before agencies have developed their proposals. Some questions have been raised, however, regarding whether the approach actually speeds rulemaking or reduces litigation.

Chapter 7 - The Regulatory Flexibility Act (RFA) of 1980 (5 U.S.C. §§601-612) requires federal agencies to assess the impact of their forthcoming regulations on "small entities" (i.e., small businesses, small governments, and small not-for-profit organizations). For example, the act requires the analysis to describe why a regulatory action is being considered; the small entities to which the rule will apply and, where feasible, an estimate of their number; the projected reporting, recordkeeping, and other compliance requirements of the rule; and any significant alternatives to the rule that would accomplish the statutory objectives while minimizing the impact on small entities. This analysis is not required, however, if the head of the agency certifies that the rule will not have a "significant economic impact on a substantial number of small entities." The RFA does not define "significant economic impact" or "substantial number of small entities," thereby giving federal agencies substantial discretion regarding when the act's requirements are triggered. Other requirements in the RFA and elsewhere (e.g., that agencies reexamine their existing rules, develop compliance guides, and convene advocacy review panels) also depend on the whether the agencies determine that their rules have a "significant" impact on a "substantial" number of small entities.

GAO has examined the implementation of the RFA many times during the past 20 years, and has consistently concluded that the lack of clear definitions for key terms like "significant economic impact" and "substantial number of small entities" have hindered the act's effectiveness. Therefore, GAO has repeatedly recommended that Congress define those terms, or give the Small Business Administration or some other federal agency the authority and responsibility to do so.

H.R. 4458, the "Small Business Regulatory Improvement Act," was introduced on December 12, 2007, and was reported bythe House Committee on Small Business the next day. Among other things, H.R. 4458 would define "economic impact" as including indirect effects that are "reasonably foreseeable," and would clarify that agencies' reviews of existing rules should not be limited to rules for which a regulatory flexibility analysis had been conducted. The bill would also require agencies to develop a plan for the review of all existing rules within 10 years, require more details in agencies' analyses and notifications, and require annual reports to Congress on certain agency "determinations" as part of their reviews. Although some of these provisions address long-standing issues, some provisions seem unclear and some may add time and costs to the rulemaking process. Most notably, though, H.R. 4458 does not address GAO's long-standing concerns about the lack of clear definitions for key terms in the RFA.

In: Federal Rulemaking and Regulations ISBN: 978-1-60876-069-5
Editors: Paul Lee © 2010 Nova Science Publishers, Inc.

Chapter 1

CHANGES TO THE OMB REGULATORY REVIEW PROCESS BY EXECUTIVE ORDER 13422

Curtis W. Copeland

SUMMARY

Executive Order (E.O.) 12866 on "Regulatory Planning and Review," issued in September 1993, describes the principles and procedures by which the Office of Management and Budget's Office of Information and Regulatory Affairs (OIRA) reviews hundreds of significant proposed and final agency regulations on behalf of the President before they are published in the *Federal Register*. On January 18, 2007, President George W. Bush issued E.O. 13422, making the most significant amendments to E.O. 12866 since it was published. The changes made by this new executive order are controversial, characterized by some as a "power grab" by the White House that undermines public protections and lessens congressional authority and by others as "a paragon of common sense and good government."

The most important changes made to E.O. 12866 by E.O. 13422 fall into five general categories: (1) a requirement that agencies identify in writing the specific market failure or problem that warrants a new regulation, (2) a requirement that each agency head designate a presidential appointee within the agency as a "regulatory policy officer" who can control upcoming rulemaking activity in that agency, (3) a requirement that agencies provide their best estimates of the cumulative regulatory costs and benefits of rules they expect to publish in the coming year, (4) an expansion of OIRA review to include significant guidance documents, and (5) a provision permitting agencies to consider whether to use more formal rulemaking procedures in certain cases.

This chapter discusses each of these changes, noting areas that are unclear and the potential implications of the changes; provides background information on presidential review of rules; discusses three congressional hearings on the executive order in 2007; and notes congressional efforts to block the implementation of the order. It concludes by pointing out that the significance of the changes made to the review process by E.O. 13422 may become clear only through their implementation. The changes made by this executive order represent a clear expansion of presidential authority over rulemaking agencies. In that regard, E.O. 13422 can be viewed as part of a broader statement of presidential authority presented throughout the Bush Administration.

The chapter will be updated as necessary to reflect legislative or executive branch actions relevant to the implementation of the executive order.

Executive Order (E.O.) 12866 on "Regulatory Planning and Review," issued by President William Clinton in September 1993, describes the principles and procedures by which the Office of Management and Budget's (OMB's) Office of Information and Regulatory Affairs (OIRA) reviews hundreds of significant proposed and final agency regulations on behalf of the President before they are published in the *Federal Register*.[1] As a result of these reviews, OIRA can have a significant—if not determinative—role in the development of a broad array of public policies, from the homeland security rules governing boarding of passenger aircraft to the amount of arsenic allowed in public water systems.[2]

On January 18, 2007, President George W. Bush issued E.O. 13422, making the most significant amendments to E.O. 12866 since it was published.[3] The changes made by this new executive order are controversial, characterized by some as a "power grab" by the White House that undermines public protections and lessens congressional authority,[4] and by others as "a paragon of common sense and good government."[5] This chapter describes the changes made to the regulatory planning and review process by the new order, noting the potential impact of those changes and areas that are unclear. It also describes three hearings in 2007 examining the new executive order, and notes recent congressional efforts to block the implementation of the order. The chapater ends by offering some concluding observations. First, though, the chapater provides a brief background section on the regulatory planning and review procedures established by E.O. 12866 and its predecessors.

REGULATORY PLANNING AND REVIEW UNDER E.O. 12866

Centralized review of agencies' regulations within the Executive Office of the President has been an important part of the federal rulemaking process for more than 35 years. Although each of his three predecessors had some type of review process, the most significant development in the evolution of presidential review of rulemaking occurred in 1981, when President Ronald Reagan issued E.O. 12291.[6] The executive order established a set of general requirements for rulemaking, and required federal agencies (other than independent regulatory agencies) to send a copy of each draft proposed and final rule to OMB before publication in the *Federal Register*.[7] It also required covered agencies to prepare a cost-benefit analysis for each "major" rule (e.g., those with at least a $100 million impact on the economy). As a result of this order, OIRA became the central clearinghouse for covered agencies' substantive rulemaking, reviewing between 2,000 and 3,000 rules per year. In 1985, President Reagan expanded OIRA's influence further by issuing E.O. 12498, which required each covered agency to submit a regulatory plan to OMB for review each year that covered all of their significant regulatory actions underway or planned.[8] Regulatory reviews under these executive orders were highly controversial, with complaints about the lack of transparency of the review process, unlimited delays in the completion of the reviews, OIRA serving as a conduit for influence by regulated parties, and executive branch displacements of congressional delegations of rulemaking authority.[9]

On September 30, 1993, President Clinton issued E.O. 12866, which revoked E.O. 12291 and E.O. 12498 and established a new process for OIRA review of rules. The order limited OIRA's reviews to actions identified by the rulemaking agency or OIRA as "significant" regulatory actions, defined as those that were "economically significant" (e.g., those with at least a $100 million impact on the economy) or that (1) were inconsistent or interfered with an action taken or planned by another agency; (2) materially altered the budgetary impact of entitlements, grants, user fees, or loan programs; or (3) raised novel legal or policy issues. As a result of this change, the number of rules that OIRA reviewed dropped from between 2,000 and 3,000 per year to between 500 and 700 per year. For each significant draft rule, the executive order requires the issuing agency to provide to OIRA the text of the draft rule, a description of why the rule is needed, and a general assessment of the rule's costs and benefits. For draft rules that are "economically significant," the executive order requires a detailed cost-benefit analysis, including an assessment of the costs and benefits of "potentially effective and reasonably feasible alternatives to the planned regulation."

E.O. 12866 also differs from its predecessors in other respects. For example, the order requires that OIRA generally complete its reviews of proposed and final rules within 90 calendar days. It also requires both the rulemaking agencies and OIRA to disclose certain information about how the regulatory reviews were conducted. For example, agencies are to identify for the public (1) the substantive changes made to rules between the draft submitted to OIRA for review and the action subsequently announced, and (2) changes made at the suggestion or recommendation of OIRA. OIRA is required to, among other things, provide agencies with a copy of all communications between OIRA personnel and parties outside the executive branch, and to maintain a public log of all regulatory actions under review and of all the documents provided to the agencies. Finally, E.O. 12866 required all agencies (including independent regulatory agencies) to prepare a regulatory plan listing the most important regulatory actions that the agency expects to issue in the next fiscal year. Agency heads were required to approve this plan personally.

CHANGES MADE BY E.O. 13422

E.O. 13422 took effect when it was signed by the President on January 18, 2007.[10] The most important changes made to E.O. 12866 by E.O. 13422 fall into five general categories: (1) a requirement that agencies identify in writing the specific market failure or problem that warrants a new regulation, (2) a requirement that every agency head designate a presidential appointee within the agency as a "regulatory policy officer" who can control upcoming rulemaking activity in that agency, (3) a requirement that agencies provide their best estimates of the cumulative regulatory costs and benefits of rules they expect to publish in the coming year, (4) an expansion of OIRA review to include significant guidance documents, and (5) a provision permitting agencies to consider whether to use more formal rulemaking procedures in certain cases. Each of these changes is described more fully in the following sections.

Identification of Market Failure

E.O. 12866 begins with a statement of regulatory philosophy and principles that sets the tone for agency rulemaking covered by the order. The principles say that, "to the extent permitted by law and where applicable," agencies should (among other things) assess alternatives to direct regulation, design regulations in the most cost-effective manner possible, and base regulations on the best information available. As originally written, the first such principle was that "[e]ach agency shall identify the problem that it intends to address (including, where applicable, the failures of private markets or public institutions that warrant new agency action) as well as assess the significance of that problem."

E.O. 13422 changes that language somewhat, stating the following:

> Each agency shall identify in writing the specific market failure (such as externalities, market power, lack of information) or other specific problem that it intends to address (including, where applicable, the failures of public institutions) that warrant new agency action, as well as assess the significance of that problem, to enable assessment of whether any new regulation is warranted.

The new language appears to (1) elevate "market failure" to greater prominence as a rulemaking rationale (removing the "where applicable" caveat and placing it before and on par with the more general statement of problem identification); (2) more clearly define what constitutes a market failure (e.g., "externalities, market power, lack of information");[11] (3) require a more precise delineation of why the agency is issuing the rule (the "specific" market failure or the "specific" problem); (4) require that the delineation be in writing; and (5) make clear that the purpose of this requirement is to facilitate a determination of whether the rule is needed.

The general principle that a covered agency describe the need for a new regulation is procedurally established in Section 6 of E.O. 12866. For rules that are significant, but not economically significant (e.g., do not have a $100 million impact on the economy), agencies are required only to provide a "reasonably detailed description of the need for the regulatory action." For economically significant rules, however, more detailed cost-benefit analyses are required. OMB Circular A-4 (which describes how those studies should be done) says agencies "should try to explain whether the action is intended to address a significant market failure or to meet some other compelling public need such as improving governmental processes or promoting intangible values such as distributional fairness or privacy."[12] Therefore, the "market failure" language in E.O. 13422 can arguably be read to apply to all significant rules (between 500 and 700 per year) what had previously applied only to economically significant rules (about 70 per year).

Also, although the order requires agencies to make this determination in writing, E.O. 13422 does not indicate where this written determination should appear (e.g., in the *Federal Register* notice for the proposed or final rule), or, additionally, whether it should be made available to the public in the rulemaking docket. Conceivably, therefore, agencies could satisfy the requirements of the order by preparing a written determination of the need for a rule without providing it to anyone outside government.

Some commentators have criticized this provision in E.O. 13422 as an attempt to bypass Congress by establishing standards for regulatory initiation that are not consistent with statutory requirements. One such commentator, Public Citizen, said the requirement "diminishes standards Congress may have required agencies to use, such as the best control technology, by elevating a new market failure standard that Congress never required."[13] For example, some statutes (e.g., the Clean Air Act) require agencies to establish regulations based solely on what is required to protect human health. Critics of the executive order contend that requiring agencies to identify a "specific market failure" or a "specific problem" constitutes a new standard for regulatory initiation. Supporters of this provision contend, however, that market failure is not the only basis on which regulatory agencies can justify action, and that the executive order did not eliminate the requirement in E.O. 12866 that directs agencies to issue "such regulations as are required by law, [or] are necessary to interpret the law."[14]

Public Citizen has also criticized this provision as "yet another layer added to the agency analysis" that "places yet another hurdle for agencies to issue regulations in pursuit of protecting the public." Similarly, Gary Bass, executive director of OMB Watch, said that President Bush, by requiring agencies to show a market failure, "has created another hurdle for agencies to clear before they can issue rules protecting public health and safety."[15] On the other hand, supporters of this provision contend that requiring agencies to identify the specific problem being addressed in a regulation is not onerous, and can help ensure the effectiveness of the resultant rules.[16]

Finally, although stated in terms of a requirement ("[e]ach agency shall"), this and other principles of regulation in the executive order are preceded by more permissive language, stating that agencies "should" adhere to the principles "to the extent permitted by law and where applicable." Given this language, concerns about the usurpation of congressional standards for rulemaking and unnecessary delay may be exaggerated. Ultimately, though, the extent to which these changes are significant may be revealed only through how they are implemented by OIRA and the agencies.

Regulatory Policy Officers as Presidential Appointees

As originally written, E.O. 12866 required the head of each covered agency (other than independent regulatory agencies) to designate a regulatory policy officer (RPO) who reported to the agency head.[17] The RPO is required to "be involved at each stage of the regulatory process to foster the development of effective, innovative, and least burdensome regulations and to further the principles set forth in this Executive order." According to agency officials, these RPOs were commonly agency general counsels (which are usually presidential appointees with Senate confirmation) or some other presidential appointee within the agencies.

E.O. 13422 retained the above general statement of the RPO's duties, but also required each agency head to "designate one of the agency's Presidential Appointees" to be that officer, to do so within 60 days of the date of the executive order (i.e., by March 19, 2007), to advise OMB of the designation, and to "annually update OMB on the status of this designation." Although the agency head is still permitted (within the parameters of White House and OMB control) to select the individual for this position, the requirement that the individual be a presidential appointee limits the agency head's discretion (compared to the unlimited authority that agency heads enjoyed before this amendment) and strengthens the relationship of the agency policy officers with the President. Because most of the RPOs were already presidential appointees, it is not clear how this requirement will affect the regulatory process. If agencies are permitted to continue with the same officers they have always had, then the effect may be minimal. On the other hand, if agency heads are required to designate new presidential appointees to serve in this capacity, then the effect may be more significant.

The new executive order also appeared to change the RPOs' reporting relationship. As originally issued, E.O. 12866 required the policy officers to report to the agency heads who designated them, but E.O. 13422 eliminated this requirement. Although it was initially unclear to whom these presidential appointees would report, OMB's April 2007 guidance on the order states that they should continue to report to the agency heads.[18]

E.O. 13422 also appears to significantly enhance the role of the agency RPO as part of the regulatory planning process. The order states that "[u]nless specifically authorized by the head of the agency, no rulemaking shall commence nor be included on the Plan without the approval of the agency's Regulatory Policy Office."[19] This change appears to represent an elevation in the duties and responsibilities of the agency policy officer when compared to the role previously ascribed to that officer (i.e., to "be involved" in the regulatory process, to "foster the development" of sound rules, and to "further" the order's principles). Unless specifically authorized by the agency head, the presidential policy officer must approve the listing of all significant forthcoming regulatory actions in the regulatory plan and approve the initiation of all rulemaking actions. (Previously, only the agency head could approve the regulatory plan, and there was no language in the order prohibiting rulemaking in the absence of the RPO's approval.) As characterized in the *New York Times*, "[t]he White House will thus have a gatekeeper in each agency to analyze the costs and the benefits of new rules and to make sure the agencies carry out the president's priorities."[20]

The executive order's use of the word "designate" suggests that agency heads must select RPOs from among current presidential appointees within the agencies. (Neither the President nor agency heads are authorized to create presidential appointee positions; only Congress can do so.) The order is silent as to whether the designated presidential appointee would be subject to Senate confirmation. Senate confirmation of presidential appointees is generally considered a way to strengthen congressional influence over agency decision making, because (among other things) nominees often agree during the confirmation process to appear subsequently before relevant congressional committees. According to the most recent listing of "Policy and Supporting Positions" (known as the "Plum Book"), most major regulatory departments and agencies have few (and in some cases, no) presidential appointees who are not Senate confirmed.[21] Therefore, in most cases, agency heads must select presidential appointees who are subject to Senate confirmation.[22]

Even in agencies with presidential appointees who are not subject to Senate confirmation, one could argue that it is up to Congress to decide whether the position of RPO should be occupied by an appointee who is Senate confirmed. The Supreme Court has held that "any appointee exercising significant authority pursuant to the laws of the United States is an 'Officer of the United States,' and must, therefore, be appointed in the manner prescribed" in the Constitution.[23] Given the enhanced power and authority of the policy officer to control day-to-day rulemaking activities within federal agencies ("no rulemaking shall commence"), the policy officer could be considered an officer of the United States under the appointments clause of the Constitution.

Article II, Section 2, clause 2 of the Constitution states the following:

> [The President] shall nominate, and by and with the Advice and Consent of the Senate, shall appoint Ambassadors, other public Ministers and Consuls, Judges of the supreme Court, and all other Officers of the United States, whose Appointments are not herein otherwise provided for, and which shall be established by Law: but the Congress may by Law vest the Appointment of such inferior Officers, as they think proper, in the President alone, in the Courts of Law, or in the Heads of Departments.

Therefore, one could argue that it is the role of Congress to prescribe, in law, whether the RPO position should be subject to Senate confirmation. In fact, to take this argument further, even if the agency head designated a person in a Senate-confirmed position for this new position, one could argue that this person would have to undergo another confirmation process because the scope of the person's responsibilities had been changed significantly.

One other element of this process is also unclear, and may represent a change in the scope of presidential influence in rulemaking. As noted previously, the requirement that each agency head appoint one of the agency's presidential appointees as the RPO does not apply to independent regulatory agencies. However, E.O. 12866 requires independent regulatory agencies to develop regulatory plans, and the requirement in E.O. 13422 that the "Regulatory Policy Office" approve items included in the plan and the commencement of all rulemaking amends that section of E.O. 12866. Therefore, this provision could arguably be read to require that independent regulatory agencies have presidential appointees as RPOs, which would extend the reach of the President and presidential review into agencies that had not previously been subject to such scrutiny (and commensurately lessening the agencies' relationships with Congress, which created them). In guidance on the implementation of E.O. 13422, OMB said independent regulatory agencies were encouraged, but not required, to designate RPOs to meet the regulatory planning requirements.[24]

Designation of RPOs

As noted previously, agencies were required to designate their RPOs under the executive order by March 2007. In July 2007, OMB published a list of the designated RPOs in 29 cabinet departments and agencies.[25] However, because OMB did not have a list of the RPOs before the executive order was published, this listing does not indicate how many RPO changes were made through this designation process. All but two of the 29 RPOs that OMB listed were presidential appointees requiring Senate confirmation.[26] Many of the designees were general counsels, deputy secretaries, or assistant secretaries, but in some cases the agency heads designated themselves (e.g., at the General Services Administration and the Office of Personnel Management). A *Bureau of National Affairs* article noted that the RPOs had varied backgrounds, but some had previously been employed at OMB or in regulated industries. For example, the article said that the RPOs at the Environmental Protection Agency (EPA) and the Department of Agriculture (USDA) both served in high-level positions at OMB, while the RPO at the Department of Transportation (DOT) previously worked with Koch Industries, "a leading operator of oil pipelines which has been prosecuted for environmental violations."[27]

Estimate of Aggregate Regulatory Costs and Benefits

As part of the above-mentioned regulatory planning process, agencies have been required to provide a "summary of each planned significant regulatory action including, to the extent possible, alternatives to be considered and preliminary estimates of the anticipated costs and benefits." E.O. 13422 adds to this provision the requirement that each agency provide its "best estimate of the combined aggregate costs and benefits of all its regulations planned for that calendar year to assist with the identification of priorities."

At first impression, the changes established by this provision appear relatively straightforward, simply requiring agencies to tally up the costs and benefits of the individual rules listed in the regulatory plan. However, upon closer examination, some aspects of this provision appear unclear. For example, the regulatory plans that agencies develop are supposed to be published at the start of each fiscal year in October, and are required to reflect the most significant proposed and final rules that they expect to publish "in that fiscal year or thereafter." Therefore, the requirement in E.O. 13422 that agencies develop estimates of aggregate costs and benefits for regulations planned "for that calendar year" seems inconsistent with the previous focus on fiscal years.

More substantively, some critics of the order have suggested that this provision is intended to elevate the role of cost-benefit analysis in the development of regulatory priorities. They argue that cost-benefit analysis is inherently biased against regulation, particularly with regard to such issues as global warming and long-term exposure to carcinogens, so the effect of this provision would be to reduce regulatory activity.[28] Other critics have said this provision is a prelude to the development of a regulatory budget in which the costs associated with an agency's rules could be capped and no new rules could be issued unless other costs were reduced or eliminated.[29] Proponents of this provision, on the other hand, may argue that such aggregate estimates are needed to reveal the cumulative impacts of rulemaking. Individually, regulations on a particular industry may not be significant, but the aggregation of the impact of multiple rules may reveal cumulative effects that are not otherwise apparent.

Also, agencies' regulatory plans are published as part of the *Unified Agenda of Federal Regulatory and Deregulatory Actions*, and contain information about the most significant regulatory actions that agencies expect to undertake in the coming year.[30] The listed items include both proposed and final rules that the agency expects to issue during that period. For forthcoming proposed rules, agencies often have not developed cost or benefit estimates because the specifics of the proposed rules have often not been developed. Even for forthcoming final rules, agencies frequently provide only general narrative information about expected costs or benefits. Also, some items that are listed in agencies' regulatory plans are never issued as final rules, and some significant agency rules never appear in agencies' regulatory plans. Therefore, the requirement in the executive order that agencies provide aggregate cost and benefit information may prove difficult to implement in a meaningful fashion. On the other hand, as noted previously, agencies are only required to develop rule-specific and aggregate estimates of costs and benefits "to the extent possible." It is unclear whether the agencies or OIRA will ultimately determine what is "possible."

OIRA Review of Significant Guidance Documents

Another controversial provision in E.O. 13422 has been the expansion of OIRA review from agencies' draft regulations to also include significant agency guidance documents.[31] Specifically, the new executive order adds the following to E.O. 12866:

> Each agency shall provide OIRA, at such times and in the manner specified by the Administrator of OIRA, with advance notification of any significant guidance documents. Each agency shall take such steps as are necessary for its Regulatory Policy Officer to ensure the agency's compliance with the requirements of this section. Upon the request of the Administrator, for each matter identified as, or determined by the Administrator to be, a significant guidance document, the issuing agency shall provide to OIRA the content of the draft guidance document, together with a brief explanation of the need for the guidance document and how it will meet that need. The OIRA Administrator shall notify the agency when additional consultation will be required before the issuance of the significant guidance document.

E.O. 13422 defines a "guidance document" as "an agency statement of general applicability and future effect, other than a regulatory action, that sets forth a policy on a statutory, regulatory, or technical issue or an interpretation of a statutory or regulatory issue." It says a "significant" guidance document is one that is

> disseminated to regulated entities or the general public that, for purposes of this order, may reasonably be anticipated to:
>
> (A) Lead to an annual effect of $100 million or more or adversely affect in a material way the economy, a sector of the economy, productivity, competition, jobs, the environment, public health or safety, or State, local, or tribal governments or communities;
>
> (B) Create a serious inconsistency or otherwise interfere with an action taken or planned by another agency;
>
> (C) Materially alter the budgetary impact of entitlements, grants, user fees, or loan programs or the rights or obligations of recipients thereof; or
>
> (D) Raise novel legal or policy issues arising out of legal mandates, the President's priorities, or the principles set forth in this Executive order.

These categories are essentially the same as those used in E.O. 12866 to define significant rules, the only difference being the use of the prefatory phrase "may reasonably be anticipated to" instead of "is likely to result in a rule that may."

The implications of these amendments to the scope of presidential review of agency actions are potentially significant. Agencies issue thousands of guidance documents each year that are intended to clarify the requirements in related statutes and regulations.[32] Therefore, the requirement that agencies provide OIRA with advance notification of significant guidance documents may represent a major expansion of the office's (and, therefore, the President's) influence, particularly when coupled with the ability of OIRA to determine which guidance documents are "significant" and the ability of OIRA to conclude that "additional consultation will be required" before a document is issued. Also, the requirement that presidentially appointed RPOs ensure compliance with this requirement arguably represents another extension of the President's authority in regulatory agencies.

As is the case with other aspects of E.O. 13422, though, several aspects of these provisions are unclear. For example, although the order refers to guidance "documents," the definition of the term is not limited to written materials. In a related OMB bulletin on agency guidance that was issued the same day as the executive order amendments, OMB said that the bulletin's definition of a guidance document (which is the same as in the executive order)

> is not limited only to written guidance materials and should not be so construed. OMB recognizes that agencies are experimenting with offering guidance in new and innovative formats, such as video or audio tapes, or interactive web-based software. The definition of "guidance document" encompasses all guidance materials, regardless of format.[33]

Therefore, a wide range of agency communications with the public—even oral statements by agency officials and staff—may be considered guidance "documents," as long as they are statements of "general applicability and future effect."

However, given the definition provided in the executive order, it is unclear what could constitute a "significant" guidance document. Guidance documents, unlike regulations, cannot have a binding effect on the public.[34] Therefore, it is not clear how guidance can be expected to have the effects delineated in the definition (e.g., "lead to an annual effect of $100 million or more" or "materially alter the budgetary impact" of entitlements or grants). Arguably, because no guidance document can, by itself, have such an effect, the requirement that agencies provide OIRA with advance notification of any significant guidance documents could have little or no impact on regulatory agencies. On the other hand, OMB has said that "there are situations in which it may reasonably be anticipated that a guidance document could lead parties to alter their conduct in a manner that would have such an economically significant impact."[35] Ultimately, because OIRA is given the authority to determine which documents are "significant," the scope and impact of this section's requirements may be as broad as OIRA determines that it needs to be.

Also unclear is the extent to which certain transparency provisions in E.O. 12866 will apply to guidance documents that are submitted to OIRA for review. For example, will agencies be required to disclose the changes to their significant guidance documents made at the suggestion and recommendation of OIRA (just as they are with regard to rules)? Will OIRA be required to list publicly the significant guidance documents that are under its review, and to disclose its meetings with outside entities regarding those documents? Because E.O. 13422 did not change those sections of E.O. 12866, it is reasonable to presume that the transparency provisions applicable to rules are not applicable to agencies' significant guidance documents.

Supporters of the expansion of presidential review to significant guidance documents have said the change will standardize and make more transparent the process by which federal agencies develop, issue, and use guidance documents.[36] Critics contend that the potentially broad scope of this provision may result in fewer guidance documents being issued, with the policy officer or OIRA review serving as a "bureaucratic bottleneck that would slow down agencies' ability to give the public information it needs."[37] Another possible effect of this requirement, given the number of guidance documents that agencies currently issue, is that OIRA staff may be inundated with such documents to review (on top of the hundreds of significant proposed and final rules and the thousands of paperwork clearances they produce each year)—at least until it is clear to the agencies what is and is not covered.

Use of Formal Rulemaking Procedures

E.O. 13422 also amends Section 6 of E.O. 12866 by adding the following sentence: "In consultation with OIRA, each agency may also consider whether to utilize formal rulemaking procedures under 5 U.S.C. 556 and 557 for the resolution of complex determinations." Virtually all agency regulations are currently issued under informal rulemaking procedures under 5 U.S.C. 553, in which agencies publish proposed rules in the *Federal Register* for public comment, and subsequently publish a final rule reflecting any changes made as a result of those comments. Formal rulemaking, as the name implies, is a much more rigorous, trial-like, on-the-record procedure in which interested persons testify and cross-examine witnesses, and the agency may take depositions and issue subpoenas. It is generally considered a more time-consuming and expensive process than informal rulemaking. Also, according to 5 U.S.C. 556(d)(1), "[e]xcept as otherwise provided by statute, the proponent of a rule or order has the burden of proof." Formal rulemaking was criticized in the 1970s, and has fallen into disuse since then.[38] The Administrative Conference of the United States recommended that Congress should not require procedures beyond informal rulemaking, and should never require trial-type procedures for resolving questions of policy or fact.[39] One administrative law scholar has referred to formal rulemaking as a "discredited" procedure that allows regulated entities to slow down the rulemaking process.[40]

The executive order does not indicate, and OIRA has not explained, why this provision was added to E.O. 12866. Agencies have always had the ability to employ formal rulemaking when they conclude that it is in the agencies' best interest to do so. Therefore, the statement that agencies "may also consider whether to utilize formal rulemaking procedures" seems to grant discretion where discretion was already allowed. On the other hand, an agency's "consultation with OIRA" may result in greater use of formal rulemaking if OIRA can convince the agency that it is in their best interest to do so. If that occurs, agency rulemaking could become even more "ossified" than it already is.[41]

CONGRESSIONAL HEARINGS ON E.O.13422

On February 13, 2007, two House subcommittees held oversight hearings on E.O. 13422—one by the House Committee on Science and Technology's Subcommittee on Investigations and Oversight,[42] and the other by the House Committee on the Judiciary's Subcommittee on Commercial and Administrative Law.[43] On April 26, 2007, the Subcommittee on Investigations and Oversight held a second hearing on the executive order.[44]

Investigations and Oversight—February 2007

At the Investigations and Oversight Subcommittee hearing in February 2007, Chairman Brad Miller questioned whether the new executive order creates "an almost insuperable bias in favor of agency inaction," and whether the order "shift(s) to the President powers that the framers of our Constitution intended to be exercised by Congress." However, Ranking Member F. James Sensenbrenner, Jr. said "I am inclined to think that the issues that will be brought up today have less to do with their policy implications, and more to do with *who* issued them," and said he believed the executive order and the related OMB guidance bulletin simply formalize many of the principles established in previous administrations. (Emphasis in original.) Three of the four witnesses at the hearing noted areas of concern about the new executive order:

- Sally Katzen, a professor of law, OIRA Administrator during the Clinton Administration, and one of the original authors of E.O. 12866, noted three areas of concern about E.O. 13422: (1) its issuance "without any consultation or explanation," (2) its issuance "on the heels of OMB's imposing multiple mandates/requirements on the agencies when they are developing regulations," and (3) its effect of "making it more difficult for agencies to do their jobs because regulations are disfavored in this Administration."[45]
- David C. Vladeck, associate professor of law and director of the Institute for Public Representation at the Georgetown University Law Center, said the new order (1) "usurps congressional authority by directing agencies to justify regulatory actions on the basis of market failure," (2) "unwisely expands OIRA's authority to guidance," (3) "resurrect's the discredited concept of a regulatory budget," and (4) "further politicizes the regulatory process" through the new RPO designation process.[46]
- Rick Melberth, director of federal regulatory policy at OMB Watch, recommended that Congress (1) explore the legality of the executive order amendments and their implementation, (2) oversee the issuance of OIRA guidance on the market failure principle, and (3) "look at limiting agencies' and OIRA's spending on the specific elements of the amendments."[47]

The fourth hearing witness, however, welcomed the issuance of E.O. 13422. William L. Kovacs, vice president of the U.S. Chamber of Commerce, said the order was "[f]ar from being radical," and merely instructs federal agencies to (1) state the reason for the regulation, (2) identify the aggregate cost of the regulation to assist the identification of agency priorities, and (3) have an agency RPO ensure that these requirements have been followed. He also said the order "corrects the abuse of guidance documents by federal agencies seeking to avoid public participation in the rulemaking process," and that the order and the OMB guidance bulletin "are part of a long effort by Congress and several Administrations to improve the transparency and quality of government data and provide effective parameters to guide the regulatory activities of federal agencies."[48]

Commercial and Administrative Law—February 2007

At the Commercial and Administrative Law Subcommittee hearing in February 2007, Chairman Linda T. Sanchez said she was "concerned that the main thrust of this new Order appears to shift control of the regulatory process from the agencies—the entities that have the most substantive knowledge and experience—to the White House." On the other hand, Ranking Member Chris Cannon said the changes were "useful refinements" to the existing regulatory review process, and could be expected to lead to improved governance.

The first witness was Steven D. Aitken, then Acting Administrator of OIRA, who said both the new executive order and the OMB guidance bulletin "share the goal of improving the way that the federal government does business." The bulk of his testimony focused on the guidance provisions; there, he said that only some agency guidance documents would be subject to interagency review, and that many agencies may already be doing what the order requires. Mr. Aitken also said that (1) RPOs in many federal agencies were already presidential appointees, and that by requiring the designation of presidential appointees for this position the President was ensuring that, in most cases, the initiation of rulemaking would be authorized by individuals in Senate-confirmed positions; (2) the requirement that agencies aggregate the costs and benefits of their upcoming rules shifts the burden of summing up rules from the public to the agencies; and (3) the concept of market failure has always been part of E.O. 12866, is not the only basis on which agencies can justify their regulations, and does not affect other statutory provisions that may prompt the issuance of a rule.[49]

One other witness at the hearing—Paul Noe, of C&M Capitolink, LLC, and former counselor to former OIRA Administrator John Graham—indicated that E.O. 13422 comprised "important and salutary steps toward good governance," and did not represent a threat to federal rulemaking. For example, he said the provisions in the order involving RPOs "only codifies prior practice in both the Bush and Clinton Administrations," and he characterized the requirement for aggregate cost and benefit estimates as a sensible "toting up of already required information."[50]

Two other witnesses at this hearing were less sanguine about the effects of the executive order. Sally Katzen repeated the concerns that she voiced at the earlier hearing, and concluded by saying that "the message [of the executive order] is that agencies should not be doing the job that Congress has delegated to them."[51] Another witness, Peter Strauss of Columbia Law School, said that the RPO provisions in the executive order "threatens a dramatic increase in presidential control over regulatory outcomes, to an extent Congress has not authorized and in my judgement must authorize." He also said that the provisions regarding formal rulemaking "threatens redeployment of a discredited, remarkably expensive rulemaking procedure that delivers substantial controls over the timing and cost of rulemaking into the hands of private parties— notably, I fear, those whose dangerous activities proposed regulations are intended to limit." Professor Strauss, noting that the President could veto any freestanding legislation designed to undo the executive order, suggested that a "do not spend" rider on an appropriations bill was more likely to be effective in preventing the order from taking effect.[52]

Investigations and Oversight—April 2007

At the Investigations and Oversight Subcommittee hearing in April 2007, Steven D. Aitken (by then, former Acting Administrator of OIRA) testified that many of the requirements in E.O. 13422 were not new, and were sometimes misunderstood. For example, he said that the order did not require agencies to submit all significant guidance documents to OIRA for review, but only to *inform* OIRA of upcoming documents so that there could be an *opportunity* for review. He also said that agency RPOs would continue to report to agency heads even though the requirement in E.O. 12866 had been deleted. However, Chairman Miller said that the RPO provisions in the order were "especially troubling," and that given their new authority, RPOs could "smother regulatory efforts in the crib before an agency can even begin considering a regulatory action."[53] He also asked Mr. Aitken to describe how the executive order was developed, but Mr. Aitken declined to do so, citing a "deliberative process" privilege within the executive branch.

Other witnesses at the hearing offered differing perspectives on the executive order. For example, Robert W. Hahn and Robert E. Litan of the AEI-Brookings Joint Center for Regulatory Studies generally supported the issuance of E.O. 13422. Although they agreed with critics that the designation of presidentially appointed RPOs would "politicize" the rulemaking process by taking away some discretion from civil servants, they characterized that result as "a good thing" that would make the President more accountable for regulatory policies. Their one complaint about the order was that it did not go far enough, excluding independent regulatory agencies from its requirements. On the other hand, Gary Bass from OMB Watch said the executive order "threatens public protections by further centralizing executive control over the regulatory process, removing agency discretion over legislative implementation, codifies regulatory delay, and substitutes free market criteria for public values of health, safety, and environmental protections." He urged Congress to overturn the order or limit its implementation.

CONGRESSIONAL ACTIONS TO BLOCK THE IMPLEMENTATION OF E.O.13422

Congress has revoked executive orders in the past, both diresctly (e.g., declaring that a specific order shall not have any legal effect) and by reversing certain provisions in the orders.[54] However, if the President chooses to veto such legislation, enactment into law would require a two-thirds majority in both houses of Congress. Therefore, some (e.g., Professor Peter Strauss) have suggested including language prohibiting the implementation of the executive order in "must pass" legislation (e.g., an appropriations bill), thereby making a presidential veto less likely.[55]

On June 27, 2007, during House floor consideration of H.R. 2829, the Financial Services and General Government (FSGG) Appropriations Act, 2008 (which funds OMB, among other agencies), Representative Brad Miller and Representative Linda Sanchez offered a "general provision" amendment stating that "None of the funds made available by this Act may be used to implement Executive Order 13422." In introducing the amendment, Mr. Miller said the executive order "claims powers for the President over agency rulemaking that is [sic] consistent neither with statutes passed by Congress nor with the Constitution." He also said that the order "lets political appointees overrule the professionals at each agency in secret with no accountability to anyone." Representative Jose Serrano said he supported the amendment, saying that Representative Miller had "raised some very serious issues that need addressing." Representative Ralph Regula said he opposed the amendment, saying it needed additional study, but did not call for a recorded vote. The amendment was agreed to as Section 901 of H.R. 2829 as passed by the House. If this provision were part of the final FSGG appropriations act, neither OMB nor any other agency funded by the act could use its FY2008 appropriations to implement the order. However, this provision would not affect agencies that are funded by other appropriations acts.

In the wake of this action, on July 12, 2007, the Director of OMB sent a letter to the chairmen and ranking members of the House and Senate Appropriations Committees stating that "If the President were presented with a bill that contained a restriction on the implementation of Executive Order 13422, the President's Senior Advisors would recommend that he veto the bill." The Director urged the rejection of any provision that would interfere in any way with the implementation of the executive order "because it involves a matter that directly affects the operation of [OMB] and involves the President's authority to manage the Executive Branch." That same day, a group of 64 trade organizations covering a range of industries (reportedly organized by the U.S. Chamber of Commerce) sent a letter to the chairman and ranking member of the Senate Committee on Appropriations urging them to oppose any language in the FSGG appropriations bill that would bar funding for E.O. 13422.[56] The letter characterized the executive order as a "good government" measure, and said the requirements "are merely an attempt to instill principles of accountability and transparency into the regulatory process."[57]

As reported by the Senate Subcommittee on Financial Services, the FSGG appropriations bill contained a provision stating that no funds in the measure could be used to implement either E.O. 13422 or the OMB bulletin on guidance documents. However, one of the "manager's package" amendments to the legislation that was adopted when the bill was reported by the full Senate Appropriations Committee on July 12, 2007, deleted this provision from the legislation. Aides to Senator Richard Durbin were quoted as saying that the Senator would attempt to reinstate the House language inhibiting the implementation of the executive order when the bill was considered in conference.[58] However, the FSGG appropriations bill was later folded into the

Consolidated Appropriations Act for FY2008 (H.R. 2674), and congressional leaders decided to avoid conference procedures on the bill—instead reaching agreement between the House and the Senate by exchanging amendments between the two chambers. President Bush signed the bill into law on December 26, 2007.[59] The legislation did not contain any language regarding E.O. 13422.

CONCLUDING NOTES

The amendments made by E.O. 13422 to E.O. 12866 are the most significant since the latter order was issued in 1993, but the characterizations of the changes by interested parties are dramatically different. Jeffrey Rosen, general counsel at OMB, reportedly characterized the new executive order as "a classic good-government measure that will make federal agencies more open and accountable."[60] On the other hand, Gary Bass, executive director of OMB Watch said the changes made to the regulatory review process were "bad, bad, bad," and predicted that they would hamper the government's ability to respond to regulatory crises such as E.coli outbreaks on fresh vegetables.[61] One Member of Congress was quoted as saying that the order "allows the political staff at the White House to dictate decisions on health and safety issues, even if the government's own impartial experts disagree. This is a terrible way to govern, but great news for special interests."[62]

Although observers have taken very different positions on the desirability of the changes made by E.O. 13422, several things about the order are not clear. First, it is unclear why the changes to the existing regulatory review process were made. Notably, although E.O. 13422 requires agencies to provide written rationales for why they are issuing regulations, no such rationale was offered in conjunction with this or any of the other new requirements in the order. For example, it is unclear what "market failure" or other specific problem led to the issuance of the requirements that agencies have RPOs who are presidential appointees, or that agencies submit significant guidance documents to OIRA for review. Although the acting OIRA Administrator indicated that the executive order's guidance provisions were intended to "reinforce" the OMB guidance bulletin and improve the quality of agency guidance documents through interagency review, he did not describe any recent instances of poor quality guidance that led to this provision in the order. Also, his comments indicating that other parts of the executive order were consistent with existing practices (e.g., provisions regarding "market failure" and formal rulemaking) raise questions regarding why changes to the executive order were believed necessary. Neither the President nor OMB is required to explain why executive orders are issued, or why existing OIRA review processes are changed. And sound public policy rationales can be envisioned concerning why the changes were made. Providing those rationales might have gone a long way toward quieting some of the concerns that have been voiced regarding the changes.

Also unclear is the effect of the changes made by E.O. 13422 on federal rulemaking agencies, the rules that emerge from the rulemaking process, and on the transparency of that process to the public. In some cases, that lack of clarity is because of the discretion given to agencies and OIRA in the review process (e.g., that agencies take certain actions "to the extent possible" or "where applicable"). In other cases, the effects are unclear because the order does not appear to change existing practices (e.g., that agencies be allowed to use formal rulemaking). In still other cases, the new requirements seem to be based on false presumptions (e.g., that agencies' regulatory plans contain estimates of costs and benefits that can be aggregated) or seem to have an indefinite scope (e.g., what qualifies as a "guidance document" or a "significant guidance document").

Ultimately, the degree to which E.O. 13422 changes existing practices will likely depend on how the order is implemented by OIRA and the agencies. Will, for example, OIRA insist that agencies identify a "specific market failure" before issuing proposed or final rules, or will that provision be interpreted more broadly to require simply a clear statement of the rules' intentions? Will agency heads continue to have discretion in the appointment of RPOs (albeit less than before since they must now select from current presidential appointees), or will the White House direct the agency heads in those appointments? Will these policy officers continue to report to the agency heads (as OMB says they should), or will they now report to the White House or OMB? Will the requirement that agencies provide estimates of aggregate costs and benefits be used as a prelude to greater control and the development of regulatory budgets, or will such estimates be relatively easy to develop and reveal cumulative effects that have heretofore been hidden? Will the requirement that OIRA be notified of forthcoming significant agency guidance documents prove to be a major expansion of presidential influence over regulatory agencies, or will "significant guidance document," as defined in the order, be a contradiction in terms resulting in virtually no such documents being covered by the order's requirements? And finally, will OIRA require agencies to enter into more formal rulemaking procedures, or will agencies continue to have the discretion to use such procedures only in rare circumstances?

Third, it is unclear what impact the changes brought about by E.O. 13422 will have on the balance of power between the President and Congress in this area. Congress has a vested interest in the regulations that emerge from the rulemaking process, having created each regulatory agency, confirmed agency heads, and enacted the legislation underpinning each proposed and final rule. Therefore, presidentially initiated changes that may affect these congressional directives (e.g., the requirement that each agency identify a specific "market failure" or "problem" before issuing a rule) are naturally of potential interest to Congress. Another area of the executive order that may affect presidential-congressional balance of power involves the RPOs, particularly their new authority to control regulatory planning and output (unless the agency head objects), the fact that the order no longer requires them to report to the agency head, and the lack of clarity as to whether they must be reconfirmed by the Senate because of their new authorities. Finally, OMB's statements notwithstanding, it is unclear whether the executive order intended to require that independent regulatory agencies have presidential appointees as RPOs. Doing so would extend the reach of the President and presidential review into agencies that had not previously been subject to such scrutiny (and commensurately lessening the agencies' relationships with Congress, which created them to be more independent of the President).

These three areas of uncertainty notwithstanding, the issuance of these amendments to E.O. 12866 are important if for no other reason than that the President deemed them necessary. The changes made by E.O. 13422—particularly the expansion of OIRA review to guidance documents and the requirement that RPOs be presidential appointees with enhanced power—represent a clear expansion of presidential authority over rulemaking agencies. In that regard, the executive order can be viewed as part of a broader statement of presidential authority presented throughout the Bush Administration—from declining to provide access to executive branch documents and information to presidential signing statements indicating that certain statutory provisions will be interpreted consistent with the President's view of the "unitary executive."[63] In fact, in his February 2007 testimony on the order, the acting OIRA Administrator cited the "basic need of the President and his White House staff to monitor the consistency of executive agency regulations with Administration policy" as justification for the extension of OIRA review to agency guidance documents. Also, in his July 2007 letter conveying the

Administration's objections to legislation restricting the implementation of the executive order, the OMB Director said he was doing so because the legislation "involves the President's authority to manage the Executive Branch."

Cornelius M. Kerwin, author of the textbook *Rulemaking: How Government Agencies Write Law and Make Policy*,[64] was quoted as saying that this dispute between Congress and the President over E.O. 13422 appears to be a classic example of an "inter-branch conflict."[65] Similarly, Cindy Skrzycki, the author of *The Regulators*,[66] said, "The Bush administration and the Democraticcontrolled Congress are fighting over who will have the most influence over writing rules on health and safety issues. While the dispute is not as dramatic as the ones over fired prosecutors and wartime surveillance, the stakes are high."[67]

End Notes

[1] Executive Order 12866, "Regulatory Planning and Review," 58 *Federal Register* 51735, October 4, 1993.

[2] U.S. General Accounting Office, *Rulemaking: OMB's Role in Reviews of Agencies' Draft Rules and the Transparency of Those Reviews*, GAO-03-929, September 22, 2003, p. 3, available at http://www.gao.gov/new.items/d03929.pdf. See also CRS Report RL32397, *Federal Rulemaking: The Role of the Office of Information and Regulatory Affairs*, by Curtis W. Copeland; and CRS Report RL32855, *Presidential Review of Agency Rulemaking*, by T. J. Halstead.

[3] Executive Order 13422, "Further Amendment to Executive Order 12866 on Regulatory Planning and Review," 72 *Federal Register* 2763, January 23, 2007. Five years earlier, E.O. 13258 reassigned certain responsibilities from the Vice President to the President's chief of staff, but otherwise did not change the OIRA review process. See Executive Order 13258, "Amending Executive Order 12866 on Regulatory Planning and Review," 67 *Federal Register* 9385, February 28, 2002.

[4] Public Citizen, "New Executive Order Is Latest White House Power Grab," available at http://www.citizen.org/pressroom/release.cfm?ID=2361. See also Margaret Kriz, "Thumbing His Nose," *National Journal*, July 28, 2007, pp. 32-34.

[5] Attributed to William Kovacs, Vice President of Environment, Energy, and Regulatory Affairs, U.S. Chamber of Commerce, in John Sullivan, "White House Sets Out New Requirements for Agencies Developing Rules, Guidance," *Daily Report for Executives*, January 19, 2007, p. A-31.

[6] Executive Order 12291, "Federal Regulation," 46 *Federal Register* 13193, February 19, 1981.

[7] Independent regulatory agencies include the Federal Communications Commission, the Nuclear Regulatory Commission, and the Securities and Exchange Commission, and are created by Congress to be more independent of the President than other agencies (e.g., commission members may generally be removed by the President only for cause).

[8] Executive Order 12498, "Regulatory Planning Process," 50 *Federal Register* 1036, January 8, 1985.

[9] See, for example, Morton Rosenberg, "Beyond the Limits of Executive Power: Presidential Control of Agency Rulemaking Under Executive Order 12291," *Michigan Law Review*, vol. 80 (1981), pp. 193-247.

[10] Several press accounts have suggested that E.O. 13422 did not take effect until July 24, 2007. (See, for example, Cindy Skrzycki, "Fighting for the Right to the Rules," *Washington Post*, July 17, 2007, p. D2.) However, although some of the requirements of a related OMB good guidance practices bulletin took effect on July 24, 2007, OMB memorandum M-07-13 (issued April 25, 2007) states that the executive order took effect immediately. To view a copy of this memorandum, see http://www.whitehouse.gov/omb/memoranda/fy2007/m07-13.pdf.

[11] According to OMB Circular A-4, an "externality occurs when one party's actions impose uncompensated benefits or costs on another party. Environmental problems are a classic case of externality. For example, the smoke from a factory may adversely affect the health of local residents while soiling the property in nearby neighborhoods." It says "[f]irms exercise market power when they reduce output below what would be offered in a competitive industry in order to obtain higher prices," such as when a monopoly exists. Inadequate information can occur when the public is unaware of the dangers associated with the use of a product. To view a copy of this circular, see http://www.whitehouse.gov/omb/circulars/a004/a-4.pdf.

[12] To view a copy of this circular, see http://www.whitehouse.gov/omb/circulars/a004/a-4.pdf.

[13] Public Citizen, "New Executive Order Is Latest White House Power Grab."

[14] Testimony of Steven D. Aitken in U.S. Congress, House Committee on the Judiciary, Subcommittee on Commercial and Administrative Law, *Changes to OMB Regulatory Review by Executive Order 13422*, February 13, 2007, available at http://judiciary.house.gov/media/pdfs/Aitken070213.pdf.

[15] Robert Pear, "Bush Directive Increases Sway on Regulation," *New York Times*, January 30, 2007, p. A1.

[16] Testimony of Paul Noe in U.S. Congress, House Committee on the Judiciary, Subcommittee on Commercial and Administrative Law, *Changes to OMB Regulatory Review by Executive Order 13422*, February 13, 2007, available at http://judiciary.house.gov/media/pdfs/Noe070213.pdf.

[17] Although the regulatory planning sections apply more broadly, the executive order generally defines an "agency" as "any authority of the United States that is an 'agency' under 44 U.S.C. 3502 (1), other than those considered to be independent regulatory agencies, as defined in 44 U.S.C. 3502 (10)." The order does not define "agency head," but agency policy officers in Cabinet departments have typically been designated by the secretary.

[18] See OMB memorandum M-07-13, p. 11.

[19] Notably, E.O. 13422 speaks in terms of a regulatory policy "office" as opposed to a regulatory policy "officer," suggesting that agencies may provide staff to assist the policy officers in their duties within the agencies. However, the acting OIRA Administrator has said that "office" was a typographical error, and should have said "officer."

[20] Robert Pear, "Bush Directive Increases Sway on Regulation." Newspaper editorial writers have offered various opinions regarding this issue. For example, see David McNaughton, "Reverse Regulation: With Another Nonsense Order, President Bush Quashes Legitimate Rule-making by Inserting Political Overseer," *The Atlanta Journal-Constitution*, February 2, 2007, p. A10, which cited Emory University Law Professor William Buzbee as saying that this provision "makes it even more likely that regulatory decisions will be made by someone more sympathetic to political pressure and ideology than to the federal agency's legal duty." Also, see Jim Wooten, "Vouchers, Transit Alert, Sen. Obama," *The Atlanta Journal-Constitution*, February 2, 2007, p. A11, which approved of this provision and said "[t]here's nothing radical about applying cost-benefit analysis to proposed laws and regulations."

[21] U.S. Congress, House Committee on Government Reform, *United States Government Policy and Supporting Positions*, November 22, 2004. For example, the Department of Transportation had 32 positions subject to presidential appointment with Senate confirmation (PAS positions) in 2004, but none without Senate confirmation (PA positions). The Environmental Protection Agency had 14 PAS positions, but no PA positions; the Department of Labor had 19 PAS positions, but no PA positions. On the other hand, the Department of Homeland Security had 18 PAS positions, but also had six PA positions.

[22] At a February 13, 2007, hearing on E.O. 13422, the acting OIRA administrator confirmed that most RPOs are Senate-confirmed presidential appointees. For a copy of his testimony, see http://www.whitehouse.gov/omb/legislative/testimony/oira/aitken_02132007.pdf.

[23] *Buckley v. Valeo*, 424 U.S. 1, 126 (1976).

[24] See OMB memorandum M-07-13, p. 11.

[25] The OMB list can be found at http://www.whitehouse.gov/omb/inforeg/regpol/agency_reg_policy_officers.pdf.

[26] The two agencies with RPOs who were not in Senate-confirmed positions were at the United States Access Board and the National Capital Planning Commission.

[27] Ralph Lindeman, "Mix of Backgrounds Characterizes Agency Policy Officers Under Bush Executive Order," *BNA Daily Report for Executives*, July 17, 2007, p. A-23.

[28] Public Citizen, "New Executive Order Is Latest White House Power Grab."

[29] OMB Watch, "Undermining Public Protections: Preliminary Analysis of the Amendments to Executive Order 12866 on Regulatory Planning and Review," available at http://www.ombwatch.org/article/articleview/3685/1/132?TopicID=3.

[30] To view the most recent regulatory plan (published in December 2006), see http://frwebgate.access.gpo.gov/cgi-bin/getdoc.cgi?dbname=2006_unified_agenda_&docid =f:ua061002.pdf.

[31] On the same day that E.O. 13422 was issued, OMB also issued a "Final Bulletin for Agency Good Guidance Practices" that mirrored, in many respects, the provisions in this section of the executive order. Unlike the order, however, the bulletin requires agencies to include certain standard elements in their significant guidance documents, to list those documents on the agencies' websites, and to publish a notice in the *Federal Register* soliciting public comments on economically significant documents. To view a copy of this bulletin, see http://www.whitehouse.gov/omb/memoranda/fy2007/m07-07.pdf; and Office of Management and Budget, "Final Bulletin for Agency Good Guidance Practices," 72 *Federal Register* 3432, January 25, 2007.

[32] For example, the Occupational Safety and Health Administration indicated in 2000 that it had issued 3,374 guidance documents since March 1996. See U.S. Congress, House Committee on Government Reform, *Non-Binding Legal Effect of Agency Guidance Documents*, 106th Cong., 2nd sess., H.Rept. 106-1009 (Washington: GPO, 2000), p. 5.

[33] Office of Management and Budget, "Final Bulletin for Agency Good Guidance Practices," p. 3434.

[34] See, for example, *Appalachian Power Co. v. EPA*, 208 F.3d 1015 (D.C. Cir. 2000); *Chamber of Commerce v. Department of Labor*, 174 F.3d 206 (D.C. Cir. 1999); Robert A. Anthony, "Interpretive Rules, Policy Statements, Guidances, Manuals, and the Like—Should Agencies Use Them to Bind the Public?" *Duke Law Journal*, vol. 41 (1992), p. 1311.

[35] Office of Management and Budget, "Final Bulletin for Agency Good Guidance Practices," p. 3435.

[36] John Sullivan, "White House Sets Out New Requirements for Agencies Developing Rules, Guidance," citing Paul Noe, partner at C&M Capitolink, who was a counselor to former OIRA administrator John Graham.

[37] Public Citizen, "New Executive Order Is Latest White House Power Grab." Notably, in guidance on the implementation of the executive order (OMB memorandum M-07-13, p. 8), OMB said it would complete its review of agency guidance documents within 30 days "or, at that time, advise the agency when consultation will be complete."

[38] For a discussion of formal rulemaking, see Jeffrey S. Lubbers, ed., *A Guide to Federal Agency Rulemaking, Fourth Edition* (Chicago: American Bar Association, 2006), pp. 58-59.

[39] ACUS Recommendation 72-5, *Procedures for the Adoption of Rules of General Applicability,* 38 *Federal Register* 19782, 1972; Jeffrey S. Lubbers, ed., *A Guide to Federal Agency Rulemaking, Fourth Edition*, pp. 309-310.

[40] Testimony of Peter Strauss, Betts Professor of Law, Columbia Law School, in U.S. Congress, House Committee on the Judiciary, Subcommittee on Commercial and Administrative Law, hearing on Executive Order 13422, February 13, 2007, available at http://judiciary.house.gov/media/pdfs/Strauss070213.pdf.

[41] Several observers have commented on the "ossification" of the rulemaking process as a result of numerous statutory and executive order requirements. See, for example, Thomas O. McGarity, "Some Thoughts on 'Deossifying' the Rulemaking Process, *Duke Law Journal*, vol. 41 (June 1992), pp. 1385-1462; Richard J. Pierce, Jr., "Seven Ways to Deossify Agency Rulemaking," 47 *Administrative Law Review*, vol. 47, winter 1995, pp. 59-93; Paul R. Verkuil, "Rulemaking Ossification—A Modest Proposal," *Administrative Law Review*, vol. 47 (summer 1995), pp. 453-459.

[42] To view a copy of the hearing charter and the witnesses' prepared statements, see http://science.house.gov/publications/hearings_markups_details.aspx?NewsID=1269.

[43] To view this hearing and obtain copies of the witnesses' prepared statements, see http://judiciary.house.gov/oversight.aspx?ID=269.

[44] To view this hearing and obtain copies of the witnesses' prepared statements, see http://science.house.gov/publications/hearings_markups_details.aspx?NewsID=1777.

[45] For a copy of Ms. Katzen's written statement, see http://democrats.science.house.gov/Media//File/Commdocs/hearings/2007/oversight/13feb/katzen_testimony.pdf.

[46] For a copy of Mr. Vladeck's written statement, see http://democrats.science.house.gov/Media/File/Commdocs/hearings/2007/oversight/13feb/vladeck_testimony.pdf.

[47] For a copy of Mr. Melberth's written statement, see http://democrats.science.house.gov/Media/File/Commdocs/hearings/2007/oversight/13feb/Melberth_testimony.pdf.

[48] For a copy of Mr. Kovac's written statement, see http://democrats.science.house.gov/Media/File/Commdocs/hearings/2007/oversight/13feb/kovacs_testimony.pdf.

[49] For a copy of Mr. Aitken's written statement, see http://judiciary.

[50] For a copy of Mr. Noe's written statement, see http://judiciary.house.gov/media/pdfs/Noe070213.pdf.

[51] For a copy of Ms. Katzen's written statement, see http://judiciary.house.gov/OversightTestimony.aspx?ID=726.

[52] For a copy of Mr. Strauss' written statement, see http://judiciary.house.gov/media/pdfs/Strauss070213.pdf.

[53] Ralph Lindeman, "House Panels Seek Ways to Curb Impact of Executive Order on Regulatory Activity," *BNA Daily Report for Executives*, April 27, 2007, p. A-39.

[54] CRS Report RS20846, *Executive Orders: Issuance and Revocation*, by T. J. Halstead. The most recent direct congressional revocation appears to have involved E.O. 12806, an order by President George H.W. Bush to the Secretary of the Department of Health and Human Services to establish a human fetal tissue bank for research purposes. Congress revoked the order by simply stating that "the provisions of Executive Order 12806 shall not have any legal effect." See P.L. 103-43, 107 Stat. 133, 121. For other examples, see House Committee on Rules, Subcommittee on Legislative and Budget Process, 106th Cong., 1st sess., *Hearing on the Impact of Executive Orders on Lawmaking: Executive Lawmaking?* (October 27, 1999), pp. 124-127.

[55] Testimony of Peter L. Strauss, in U.S. Congress, House Committee on Science and Technology, Subcommittee on Investigations and Oversight, *Amending Executive Order 12866: Good Governance or Regulatory Usurpation? Part II*, hearings, 110th Cong., 1st sess., April 26, 2007.
[56] Ralph Lindeman, "Senate Appropriations Committee Declines To Bar Spending on Rulemaking Exec Order," *BNA Daily Report for Executives*, July 16, 2007, p. A-19.
[57] To view a copy of this letter, see http://www.uschamber.com/issues/letters/2007/070712_financial_services.htm.
[58] Rebecca Adams and Michael Crittenden, "Congress and White House: A Regulatory Rumble," *CQ Weekly*, July 23, 2007, p. 2162.
[59] For more on this legislation, see CRS Report RL34298, *Consolidated Appropriations Act for FY2008: Brief Overview*, by Robert Keith.
[60] Robert Pear, "Bush Directive Increases Sway on Regulation."
[61] John D. McKinnon, "White House Flexes Muscles Over U.S. Regulations," *Wall Street Journal (Europe)*, February 1, 2007, p. 12.
[62] Robert Pear, "Bush Directive Increases Sway on Regulation."
[63] For a discussion of the Bush Administration's use of signing statements, see CRS Report RL33667, *Presidential Signing Statements: Constitutional and Institutional Implications*, by T. J. Halstead. More generally, see Adriel Bettelheim, "Executive Authority: A Power Play Challenged," *CQ Weekly*, October 30, 2006, p. 2858. For a discussion of the unitary executive principle, see Christopher S. Yoo, Steven G. Calabresi, Anthony J. Colangelo, "The Unitary Executive in the Modern Era, 1945-2004," 90 Iowa L. Rev. 601 (January 2005); and Robert v. Percival, "Presidential Management of the Administrative State: The Not-So Unitary Executive," 51 *Duke Law Journal* 963 (December 2001).
[64] Cornelius M. Kerwin, *Rulemaking: How Government Agencies Write Law and Make Policy*, third ed., (Washington: CQ Press, 2003).
[65] Cindy Skrzycki, "Fighting for the Right to the Rules," *Washington Post*, July 17, 2007, p. D2.
[66] Cindy Skrzycki, *The Regulators: Anonymous Power Brokers in American Politics* (Lanham, MD: Rowman & Littlefield Publishers, 2003).
[67] Cindy Skrzycki, "Fighting for the Right to the Rules."

In: Federal Rulemaking and Regulations ISBN: 978-1-60876-069-5
Editors: Paul Lee © 2010 Nova Science Publishers, Inc.

Chapter 2

CONGRESSIONAL INFLUENCE ON RULEMAKING AND REGULATION THROUGH APPROPRIATIONS RESTRICTIONS

Curtis W. Copeland

SUMMARY

The statutory provision known as the Congressional Review Act (CRA) (5 U.S.C. §§801-808) has not been a frequently used method for Congress to control agency rulemaking, having been used to overturn only one rule in the more than 12 years since it took effect. However, Congress has various other methods to influence agency rulemaking and regulatory activity, including the addition of provisions to agency appropriations bills that restrict federal rulemaking or regulatory activity.

The use of restrictions in appropriations legislation to control rulemaking has received relatively little attention from scholars and analysts, but these restrictions can have substantial effects on public policy. This chapter examines the Consolidated Appropriations Act for 2008 (P.L. 110-161), and identifies four types of such provisions: (1) restrictions on the finalization of particular proposed rules, (2) restrictions on regulatory activity within certain areas, (3) implementation or enforcement restrictions, and (4) conditional restrictions (e.g., preventing implementation of a rule until certain actions are taken). The chapter then examines appropriations acts in nine previous fiscal years, noting that some provisions have been included in appropriations bills everyyear, and others have appeared for several years in a row. Numerous examples of regulatory appropriations restrictions are provided in this chapter The reasons behind these restrictions vary, with some appearing to be based on economic considerations, some requiring or preventing the implementation of rules issued at the end of a presidential administration, and some included for various other reasons.

Although none of the appropriations provisions appear designed to *reverse* agency rulemaking actions (as the CRA was intended to permit), the number and varietyof the provisions clearly illustrate that Congress's ability to overseeand affect regulatory agencies is not confined to CRA resolutions of disapproval. On the other hand, such provisions are generally applicable only for the period of time and the agencies covered by the relevant appropriations bill. Also, to the extent that agencies have independent sources of funding (e.g., user fees) or implement their regulations through state or local governments, some of the limitations may not be as restrictive as they seem. While appropriations provisions have been advocated by representatives of virtually all political parties and interest groups, some observers have questioned whether they are constitutional or conducive to sound public policy. Nevertheless, their use by Congress is likely to continue as long as appropriations bills are considered "must pass" legislation.

INTRODUCTION[1]

In March 1996, the statutory provisions commonly known as the "Congressional Review Act" (CRA) (5 U.S.C. §§801-808) were included as part of the Small Business Regulatory Enforcement Fairness Act. Under the CRA, before any final rule can take effect, it must be filed with each house of Congress and the Government Accountability Office (GAO). The act established expedited procedures by which Congress may disapprove agencies' rules by enacting a joint resolution of disapproval, with subsequent presentation to the President for signature or veto.[2]

Although initially considered a reassertion of congressional authority over rulemaking agencies, the CRA is now viewed by some observers as a far less effective check on finalizing undesirable rules than originally anticipated. Between April 1996 and April 2008, federal agencies submitted nearly 48,000 final rules to GAO (and, presumably, to Congress), and 47 CRA joint resolutions of disapproval were introduced regarding 35 rules. However, during this 12-year period, only one rule was overturned through the CRA's procedures — the Occupational Safety and Health Administration's (OSHA's) ergonomics standard in March 2001 — and that reversal was the result of a unique set of circumstances.[3]

Even though the CRA has resulted in the congressional reversal of only one agency rule, Congress influences regulatoryactivityin a variety of other ways. Those methods include specifically delineating in the underlying statutes how regulations are to be written,[4] statutory requirements delineating the analytical and procedural steps that must be followed in the development of proposed and final rules,[5] oversight hearings on particular rules or rulemaking requirements, confirmation hearings for the heads of regulatory agencies, restrictions on rulemaking in authorizing legislation,[6] and provisions included in the text of agencies' appropriations bills.[7] Compared to the other congressional methods of influence, appropriations provisions related to agency rulemaking and regulatory activity have received comparatively little attention by scholars and analysts, but those provisions can have substantial effects on public policy.[8]

This chapter focuses on appropriations provisions that affect rulemaking and regulation, particularly those that prevent or restrict agency actions. After discussing four types of such provisions in the Consolidated Appropriations Act of 2008 (P.L. 110-161), the report examines their prevalence over a longer period of time, discusses why the provisions are used, and concludes with a discussion of their perceived strengths and weaknesses. First, however, the chapter briefly discusses several other types of regulatory appropriations measures.

Regulatory Appropriations Provisions that Do Not Restrict Rulemaking

Although appropriations provisions that are designed to prevent or restrict the development, implementation, or enforcement of particular rules or types of rules are common, other types of appropriation measures are also prevalent and deserve mention. These measures include those that require agencies to develop rules in particular areas, that change the rulemaking process, that assign regulatory reporting requirements, and that control the funding and operation of a regulatory initiative.

Initiation of Rulemaking

Some appropriations provisions direct federal agencies to develop rules in particular areas, or to take particular enforcement actions. For example, a provision in the Consolidated Appropriations Act for 2008 (121 Stat. 2084) amends the Homeland Security Act of 2002 (6 U.S.C. §361 *et seq.*) and requires the Secretary of the Department of Homeland Security to "regulate the sale and transfer of ammonium nitrate by an ammonium nitrate facility in accordance with the subtitle to prevent the misappropriation or use of ammonium nitrate in an act of terrorism." The provision delineates what the regulations must contain (e.g., a registration process for owners, records that must be maintained, and an appeals process); and mandates that the Secretary "(1) shall issue a proposed rule implementing this subtitle not later than 6 months after the date of the enactment of this subtitle; and (2) shall issue a final rule implementing this subtitle not later than 1 year after such date of enactment."

In some cases, the congressional requirement for agency rulemaking is conditional upon other factors. For example, the Consolidated Appropriations Act for 2004 (P.L. 108-199, 118 Stat. 236) requires the Secretary of Labor to "re-propose aruleon respirable coal dust which incorporates the use of Personal Dust Monitors," but only after "the successful demonstration of Personal Dust Monitor technology, and if the Secretary of Labor makes a determination that Personal Dust Monitors can be effectively applied in a regulatory scheme."[9]

In other cases, particular amounts of funds are set aside for rulemaking. For example, the Consolidated Appropriations Act for 2008 (121 Stat. 2128) states that not less than $3.5 million of the funds provided in EPA's Environmental Programs and Management account "shall be provided for activities to develop and publish a draft rule not later than 9 months after the date of enactment of this Act, and a final rule not later than 18 months after the date of enactment of this Act, to require mandatory reporting of greenhouse gas emissions above appropriate thresholds in all sectors of the economy of the United States."

Rule Development Process

Other appropriations provisions affect the process by which certain types of rules are developed, and therefore the participants in that process. For example, Executive Order 12866 requires the Office of Management and Budget's (OMB's) Office of Information and Regulatory Affairs (OIRA) to review most agencies' significant rules before they are published in the *Federal Register*.[10] However, a provision within the Consolidated Appropriations Act for 2008 (121 Stat. 1982) states that "none of the funds appropriated in this Act for the Office of Management and Budget [OMB] may be used for the purpose of reviewing any agricultural marketing orders or any activities or regulations under the provisions of the Agricultural Marketing Agreement Act of 1937 (7 U.S.C. §601 *et seq.*)."[11] Another provision in the same section of the act states that "none of the funds provided in this or prior Acts shall be used, directly or indirectly, by the Office of Management and Budget, for evaluating or determining if water resource project or study reports submitted by the Chief of Engineers acting through the Secretary of the Army are in compliance with all applicable laws, regulations, and requirements relevant to the Civil Works water resource planning process."[12]

Provisions added to appropriations bills in previous years have also led to the establishment of new procedural requirements on rulemaking agencies. For example, Consolidated Appropriations Act, 2001 (P.L. 106-554, 114 Stat. 2763A-154) established what came to be known as the Information Quality Act (sometimes referred to as the Data Quality Act). The provision required OMB to issue guidance to federal agencies designed to ensure the "quality, objectivity, utility, and integrity" of information disseminated to the public.[13] It also required agencies to issue their own information quality guidelines, and to establish administrativemechanisms that allow affected persons to seek correction of information maintained and disseminated by the agencies that does not comply with the OMB guidance.[14]

Other appropriations provisions have attempted to *prevent* the establishment of certain new rulemaking procedures. For example, as passed by the House, Section 901 of the Financial Services and General Government (FSGG) Appropriations Act, 2008 (H.R. 2829, which funded OMB, among other agencies) stated that "None of the funds made available by this Act may be used to implement Executive Order 13422." That executive order, which had been issued by President Bush in January 2007, required (among other things) that agencies give OMB advance notification of any significant guidance documents, and that each agency head designate a presidential appointee as a regulatory policy officer.[15] The order also gave these officers enhanced power to control agency rulemaking.[16] Ultimately, though, this provision was not enacted. The FSGG appropriations bill was later folded into the Consolidated Appropriations Act for 2008, and the final version of the legislation did not contain any language regarding the executive order. A similar provision has reportedly been added to the FSGG bill for FY2009.[17]

OMB Reporting Requirements

Certain appropriations provisions have imposed regulatory reporting requirements on OMB. Section 645(a) of the Treasury, Postal Service and General Government Appropriations Act, 1997 (P.L. 104-208) required the Director of OMB to submit a report to Congress providing

> (1) estimates of the total annual costs and benefits of Federal regulatory programs, including quantitative and nonquantitative measures of regulatory costs and benefits; (2) estimates of the costs and benefits (including quantitative and nonquantitative measures) of each rule that is likely to have a gross annual effect on the economy of $100,000,000 or more in increased costs; (3) an assessment of the direct and indirect impacts of Federal rules on the private sector, State and local government, and the Federal Government; and (4) recommendations from the Director and a description of significant public comments to reform or eliminate any Federal regulatory program or program element that is inefficient, ineffective, or is not a sound use of the Nation's resources.

Appropriations legislation for the next several years essentially repeated these requirements, and a provision added to OMB's appropriation for FY2001 made this type of reporting requirement permanent.[18]

Electronic Rulemaking Initiative

Congress has also used appropriations provisions in an attempt to control transfers of funding and reimbursements for the Bush Administration's electronic rulemaking initiative and other e-government projects. From FY2003 through FY2007, Congress appropriated less than $20 million to the E-Government Fund for all e-government projects — much less than the $345 million authorized in the E-Government Act for that period.[19] The lack of direct appropriations for e-government has led to controversial funding mechanisms, in which at least 10 e-government projects (including electronic rulemaking) have been funded by required "contributions" from participating agencies. In response, for several years in a row, Congress has required approval by the Appropriations Committees before any transfers or reimbursements of agency appropriations are made. For example, one of the governmentwide provisions in the Consolidated Appropriations Act for 2008 (Section 737) states that "no funds shall be available for transfers or reimbursements to the E-Government initiatives sponsored by the Office of Management and Budget prior to 15 days following submission of a report to the Committees on Appropriations by the Director of the Office of Management and Budget and receipt of approval to transfer funds by the House and Senate Committees on Appropriations." The provision goes on to require justification materials for subsequent funding requests, and says that "no funds shall be available for obligation or expenditure for new E-Government initiatives without the explicit approval of the House and Senate Committees on Appropriations."[20]

APPROPRIATIONS PROVISIONS AND THE RESTRICTION OF RULEMAKING OR REGULATORY ACTION

Many other provisions in appropriations acts are intended to prevent or restrict federal agencies from taking certain rulemaking or regulatory actions. In fact, one author, writing about appropriations provisions in general, said the following:

> The classic appropriation rider is negative in its thrust and strictly pertains to the expenditure of funds. It declares that the agency may not spend anyof the monies Congress is appropriating to engage in a specific activity described in the legislation. This type of rider is often described as a "limitation rider" because it limits the executive branch from engaging in certain activity by denying the funds necessary for its undertaking. For instance, a rider may provide that an agency cannot spend money to buy equipment or to hire personnel for a particular office. More substantively, a rider may provide that the agency cannot spend money to prepare a study on a specific topic, to propose a rule on a specific topic, to make final a pending proposed rule, to implement a final rule, to make a legal argument in court, or to appeal a pending case.[21]

Some of the more high-profile appropriations restrictions regarding agency rulemaking have received attention by analysts and scholars. For example, GAO and others have written about congressional restrictions on the development of corporate average fuel economy, or "CAFE," standards.[22] For six years (FY1996 through FY2001), the Department of Transportation's (DOT's) appropriations acts stated that none of the funds in the acts could be used to prepare, propose, or promulgate regulations prescribing CAFE standards for automobiles that differed from the standards promulgated prior to the enactment of the legislation. Other regulatory-related appropriations restrictions that have garnered some attention include provisions preventing the implementation of the Delaney Clause (a provision of the Federal Food, Drug, and Cosmetic Act that banned any additive in processed food that had been shown to cause cancer in humans or laboratory animals);[23] and prohibitions on OSHA developing or issuing regulations on ergonomics (which were enacted before the adoption of the January 2001 resolution of disapproval under the CRA).[24] A "timber salvage rider" that Congress enacted in 1995 reportedly accelerated the use of restrictions in environmental appropriations legislation during the remainder of the 1990s.[25] However, many other appropriations restrictions related to rulemaking or regulatory action have not received much attention in the relevant literature.

Regulatory Restrictions in the Consolidated Appropriations Act for 2008

To determine the frequency and nature of regulatory appropriations restrictions, CRS initially searched the Consolidated Appropriations Act for 2008 for provisions that were designed to prohibit or limit the development, implementation, or enforcement of agency regulations.[26] The search revealed nearly two dozen such provisions in the act, which generally fell into four categories: (1) prohibitions on the finalization of particular proposed rules, (2) prohibitions on the development of regulations with regard to particular statutes or issues, (3) implementation or enforcement restrictions, and (4) conditional restrictions on the development or implementation of particular rules.

Prohibiting the Finalization of Particular Proposed Rules

Several provisions in the Consolidated Appropriations Act deny the use of agency funds to make particular proposed rules final. For example:

- Section 723 within Division A of the legislation (the Agriculture, Rural Development, Food and Drug Administration, and Related Agencies Appropriations Act, 2008; 121 Stat. 1878) states: "None of the funds made available by this Act may be used to issue a final rule in furtherance of, or otherwise implement, the proposed rule on cost-sharing for animal and plant health emergency programs of the Animal and Plant Health Inspection Service [APHIS] published on July 8, 2003 (Docket No. 02-062-1; 68 Fed. Reg. 40541)." As discussed in detail later in this report, the July 2003 APHIS rule would have required states and certain groups to pay a greater share of the cost of these programs.
- Section 735 within Division D of the legislation (the Financial Services and General Government Appropriations Act, 2008; 121 Stat. 2027) states that "none of the funds appropriated or made available under this Act or any other appropriations Act may be used ... to implement the proposed regulations of the Office of Personnel Management [OPM] to add sections 300.311 through 300.316 to part 300 of Title 5 of the Code of Federal Regulations, published in the Federal Register, volume 68, number 174, on September 9, 2003 (relating to the detail of executive branch employees to the legislative branch)."
- Section 559 within Division E of the legislation (the Department of Homeland Security Appropriations Act, 2008; 121 Stat. 2083) states: "None of the funds made available in this Act may be used by the Secretary of Homeland Security or any delegate of the Secretary to issue any rule or regulation which implements the Notice of Proposed Rulemaking related to Petitions for Aliens To Perform Temporary Nonagricultural Services or Labor (H-2B) set out beginning on 70 Fed. Reg. 3984 (January 27, 2005)." An H-2B alien is someone who comes to the United States to perform temporary nonagricultural labor or services, and the proposed rule would have facilitated the use of the H-2B program by creating a simplified application process.
- Section 432 within Division F of the legislation (the Department of the Interior, Environment, and Related Agencies Appropriations Act, 2008; 121 Stat. 2152) states: "None of the funds made available under this Act may be used to promulgate or implement the Environmental Protection Agency [EPA] proposed regulations published in the Federal Register on January 3, 2007 (72 Fed. Reg. 69)." The proposed rule at issue would have amended the general provisions to the

national emission standards for hazardous air pollutants, replacing a policy that had been established in 1995.

- Section 170 within Division K of the legislation (the Transportation, Housing and Urban Development, and Related Agencies Appropriations Act, 2008; 121 Stat. 2401) states: "None of the funds provided or limited under this Act may be used to issue a final regulation under section 5309 of title49, United States Code, except that the Federal Transit Administration may continue to review comments received on the proposed rule (Docket No. FTA-2006-25737)." The targeted proposed rule would have made changes in the Federal Transit Administration's "small starts" capital investment grant program.[27]

Restricting Certain Types of Regulatory Activity

Other provisions in the Consolidated Appropriations Act for 2008 are more general, prohibiting the development, issuance, amendment, implementation, or enforcement of certain types of regulations. For example:

- Section 726 within Division A of the legislation (funding, among others, the Department of Agriculture, 121 Stat. 1878) states: "None of the funds provided in this Act may be used for salaries and expenses to draft or implement any regulation or rule insofar as it would require recertification of rural status for each electric and telecommunications borrower for the Rural Electrification and Telecommunication Loans program."
- Section 511 within Division D of the legislation (121 Stat. 1998) states: "None of the funds appropriated by this Act may be used by the Federal Communications Commission to modify, amend, or change its rules or regulations for universal service support payments to implement the February 27, 2004 recommendations of the Federal-State Joint Board on Universal Service regarding single connection or primary line restrictions on universal service support payments."
- Section 617 within Division D of the legislation (121 Stat. 2015) states that "for fiscal years 2008 and 2009, neither the Board of Governors of the Federal Reserve System nor the Secretary of the Treasury may determine, by rule, regulation, order, or otherwise, for the purposes of section 4(K) of the Bank Holding Company Act of 1956, or section 5136A of the Revised Statutes of the United States, that real estate brokerage activity or real estate management activity

(which for purposes of this paragraph shall be defined to mean 'real estate brokerage' and 'property management' respectively, as those terms were understood by the Federal Reserve Board prior to March 11, 2000) is an activity that is financial in nature, is incidental to any financial activity, or is complementary to a financial activity."

- Section 823 within Division D of the legislation (within the general provisions applicable to the District of Columbia, 121 Stat. 2041) states: "None of the funds contained in this Act may be used to enact or carry out any law, rule, or regulation to legalize or otherwise reduce penalties associated with the possession, use, or distribution of any schedule I substance under the Controlled Substances Act (21 U.S.C. 801 et seq.) or any tetrahydrocannabinols derivative."[28]
- Section 433 of Division F of the legislation (121 Stat. 2152) states: "None of the funds made available by this Act shall be used to prepare or publish final regulations regarding a commercial leasing program for oil shale resources on public lands pursuant to section 369(d) of the Energy Policy Act of 2005 (P.L. 109-58) or to conduct an oil shale lease sale pursuant to subsection 369(e) of such Act."
- A portion of Division G of the legislation (providing funds for salaries and expenses at OSHA as part of the Departments of Labor, Health and Human Services, and Education, and Related Agencies Appropriations Act, 2008; 121 Stat. 2163) contains a provision stating that "none of the funds appropriated under this paragraph shall be obligated or expended to prescribe, issue, administer, or enforce any standard, rule, regulation, or order under the Act which is applicable to any person who is engaged in a farming operation which does not maintain a temporary labor camp and employs 10 or fewer employees."
- A section of the legislation within Division K of the act having to do with Federal Aviation Administration (FAA) operations (121 Stat. 2379) states that "none of the funds in this Act shall be available for the Federal Aviation Administration to finalize or implement any regulation that would promulgate new aviation user fees not specifically authorized by law after the date of the enactment of this Act."
- Section 111 within Division K (121 Stat. 2381) states: "None of the funds in this Act shall be used to pursue or adopt guidelines or regulations requiring airport sponsors to provide to the Federal Aviation Administration without cost building construction,

maintenance, utilities and expenses, or space in airport sponsor-owned buildings for services relating to air traffic control, air navigation, or weather reporting";[29] and

- Another section within Division K having to do with operations and research at the National Highway Traffic Safety Administration (NHTSA, 121 Stat. 2391) states that "none of the funds appropriated by this Act may be obligated or expended to plan, finalize, or implement any rulemaking to add to section 575.104 of title 49 of the Code of Federal Regulations any requirement pertaining to a [tire] grading standard that is different from the three grading standards (treadwear, traction, and temperature resistance) already in effect."

Restricting Implementation or Enforcement

In still other cases, language in the Consolidated Appropriations Act of 2008 prohibits the use of funds to implement or enforce a rule or set of rules, but does not appear to prohibit the development of the rules. In some cases a particular rule or set of rules is specified, but in other cases it is not clear whether any particular rules on the issues are already in place. For example:

- Section 741 within Division A of the legislation (funding the Department of Agriculture and other agencies, 121 Stat. 1881) states: "None of the funds made available in this Act may be used to pay the salaries or expenses of personnel to — (1) inspect horses under section 3 of the Federal Meat Inspection Act (21 U.S.C. 603); (2) inspect horses under section 903 of the Federal Agriculture Improvement and Reform Act of 1996 (7 U.S.C. 1901 note; P.L. 104-127); or (3) implement or enforce section 352.19 of title 9, Code of Federal Regulations."[30]
- A condition in Division D of the legislation that is associated with a nearly $118 million payment to the Postal Service Fund for revenue forgone on free and reduced-rate mail (121 Stat. 2013) states that "none of the funds made available to the Postal Service by this Act shall be used to implement any rule, regulation, or policy of charging any officer or employee of any State or local child support enforcement agency, or any individual participating in a State or local program of child support enforcement, a fee for information requested or provided concerning an address of a postal customer."
- Section 621 within Division D of the legislation (funding the Department of the Treasury and other agencies, 121 Stat. 2016) states:

"None of the funds made available by this Act may be used by the Federal Communications Commission to implement the Fairness Doctrine, as repealed in General Fairness Doctrine Obligations of Broadcast Licensees (50 Fed. Reg. 35418 (1985)), or any other regulations having the same substance."

- Title I of Division G of the legislation (funding salaries and expenses at OSHA, 121 Stat. 2163) states that "no funds appropriated under this paragraph shall be obligated or expended to administer or enforce any standard, rule, regulation, or order under the Act with respect to any employer of 10 or fewer employees who is included within a category having a Days Away, Restricted, or Transferred (DART) occupational injuryand illness rate, at the most precise industrial classification code for which such data are published, less than the national average rate as such rates are most recently published by the Secretary, acting through the Bureau of Labor Statistics, in accordance with section 24 of the Act."[31]

Some provisions in the Consolidated Appropriations Act for 2008 appeared intended to have the opposite effect—i.e., forbidding the prohibition of regulatory enforcement. For example, Section 606 within Division D of the legislation (funding the Department of the Treasury and other agencies, 121 Stat. 2013) states: "None of the funds made available by this Act shall be available for any activity or for paying the salary of any Government employee where funding an activity or paying a salary to a Government employee would result ina decision, determination, rule, regulation, or policy that would prohibit the enforcement of section 307 of the Tariff Act of 1930 (19 U.S.C. 1307)."[32]

Conditional Restrictions

Another set of provisions in the Consolidated Appropriations Act of 2008 makes the implementation of a particular rule or set of rules conditional upon certain other actions by the agencies or Congress. For example:

- A provision within Division F of the legislation (121 Stat. 2137) states: "None of the funds made available to the Indian Health Service in this Act shall be used to implement the final rule published in the Federal Register on September 16, 1987, by the Department of Health and Human Services, relating to theeligibility for the health care services of the Indian Health Service until the Indian Health Service has submitted a budget request reflecting the increased costs associated with the proposed final rule, and such request has been included in an appropriations Act and enacted into law."

- Section 110 within Division G of the legislation (funding the Departments of Labor, Health and Human Services, and Education, and related agencies, 121 Stat. 2168) states: "None of the funds made available in this or any other Act shall be available to finalize or implement any proposed regulation under the Workforce Investment Act of 1998, Wagner-Peyser Act of 1933, or the Trade Adjustment Assistance Reform Act of 2002 until such time as legislation reauthorizing the Workforce Investment Act of 1998 and the Trade Adjustment Assistance Reform Act of 2002 is enacted."[33]
- Section 305 within Division G of the legislation (121 Stat. 2198) states: "None of the funds made available in this Act may be used to promulgate, implement, or enforce any revision to the regulations in effect under section 496 of the Higher Education Act of 1965 on June 1, 2007, until legislation specifically requiring such revision is enacted."

Regulatory Restrictions in Previous Appropriations Bills

A review of appropriations legislation that was enacted from FY1999 through FY2007 indicated that many of the regulatory restrictions in the Consolidated Appropriations Act for 2008 had appeared in one or more appropriations statutes in previous years. Some were in relevant appropriations bills in all 10 years, some had been in multiple years (but not all 10), and some were present in only one year. Table 1, at the end of this report, shows which of the appropriations provisions appeared in which fiscal years.

Provisions Repeated Every Year

Some of the provisions limiting agency rulemaking or regulatory actions have appeared in one or more appropriations bills in every year during this 10-year period.[34] Those provisions included the following:

- the provision in the District of Columbia appropriation prohibiting the enactment or implementation of regulations that would legalize or reduce penalties associated with certain substances under the Controlled Substances or any tetrahydrocannabinols derivative;[35]

- the prohibition on the issuance or enforcement of any OSHA rules applicable to farming operations that do not maintain a temporary labor camp and employ 10 or fewer employees;[36]
- the provision prohibitingthepromulgation of new aviation user fees that are not specifically authorized by law;
- the provision prohibiting the use of DOT funds to plan, finalize, or implement rules that would change existing tire grading standards; and
- the prohibition on the use of funds appropriated to the Postal Service to implement any rule that would charge State or local officers or employees, or anyone in a child support enforcement program, a fee for information concerning an address of a postal customer.

Multi-year Provisions

Other regulatory appropriations restrictions have appeared in relevant appropriations bills for several years in a row, although not in every year, during the 10-year period. For example:

- the provision in the 2008 legislation prohibiting the finalization of a July 2003 APHIS rule that proposed cost sharing for animal and plan health emergency programs has been in all relevant appropriations bills since FY2004;
- the 2008 provision prohibiting the finalization of a September 2003 OPM proposed rule restricting the detail of executive branch personnel to the legislative branch has been in all relevant appropriations bills since FY2004;
- the provision prohibiting theFederal Communications Commission from changing its rules regarding universal service support payments has been in all relevant appropriations bills since FY2005;
- the prohibition on the development or finalization of a rule determining that real estate brokerage activity is "financial in nature or incidental to a financial activity" has been in all relevant appropriations bills since FY2003;
- the prohibition on the use of funds to issue regulations requiring airport sponsors to provide free building construction, maintenance, or space to the FAA for air traffic control, air navigation, or weather

reporting has been in all DOT-related appropriations bills since FY2002;

- a provision was in EPA appropriations bills from FY2000 through FY2003 stating that "none of the funds appropriated or otherwise made available by this Act shall be used to promulgate a final regulation to implement changes in the payment of pesticide tolerance processing fees as proposed at 64 Fed. Reg. 31040, or any similar proposals";[37]
- provisions were in relevant appropriations bills from at least FY1999 through FY2003 stating that "none of the funds in this Act shall be available to plan, finalize, or implement regulations that would establish a vessel traffic safety fairway less than five miles wide between the Santa Barbara Traffic Separation Scheme and the San Francisco Traffic Separation Scheme";[38]
- provisions were in multiple appropriations bills each year from at least FY1999 through FY2001 prohibiting the use of funds to implement the Kyoto Protocol (which is a protocol to the international Framework Convention on Climate Change with the objective of reducing greenhouse gases);[39]
- provisions were added to appropriations bills relevant to DOT from at least FY1999 through FY2001 preventing the Coast Guard from planning, finalizing, or implementing any regulation that would promulgate new maritime user fees that were not specifically and subsequently authorized by law;[40]
- as noted earlier in this report, for six years (FY1996 through FY2001), DOT's appropriations acts stated that none of the funds in the act could be used to prepare, propose, or promulgate regulations prescribing corporate average fuel economy, or "CAFÉ," standards for automobiles that differed from the standards promulgated prior to the enactment of the legislation;[41] and
- the appropriations bills relevant to the Department of Labor from FY2005 through FY2008 prevented the Secretary of Labor from taking any action to amend the current definition in 20 C.F.R. 667.220 for "functions and activities" under Title I of the Workforce Investment Act of 1998.[42]

Single-Year Provisions

Several other provisions appeared only in the Consolidated Appropriations Act for 2008, or in only one appropriation bill in the previous nine years examined. In some cases, it is clear why the provisions have appeared only once. For example, a provision prohibiting the use of funds to implement a January 2007 proposed rule related to the national emission standards for hazardous pollutants was only in the Consolidated Appropriations Act for 2008 (121 Stat. 2152)—the onlyappropriations legislation that has been enacted since the rule was proposed.[43]

In other cases, some investigation reveals why the provisions have not been repeated. For example, one provision appeared only in the Omnibus Consolidated and Emergency Supplemental Appropriations Act, 1999 (P.L 105-277, 112 Stat. 2681-266), and said that "None of the funds made available in this or any other Act may be expended before March 31, 1999 to publish final regulations based on the regulations proposed at 63 Fed. Reg. 3289 on January 22, 1998."[44] Because the final rule at issue was eventually published on April 12, 1999,[45] and took effect on May 12, 1999, no additional appropriations restriction of this type was required.

Reasons for Regulatory Appropriations Restrictions

In some cases, the substantive reasons that prompted the inclusion of certain appropriations restrictions seem apparent. For example, the Kyoto Protocol was (and, to some extent, remains) highly controversial, with some in the business community and elsewhere questioningits effectiveness in addressing climate change and concluding that its adoption and implementation by the United States could impose substantial cost and other burdens on regulated parties.[46] Therefore, provisions that were added to appropriations bills preventing the implementation of the Kyoto Protocol appear to have been designed to address and respond to those concerns. (Others, however, contend that the Kyoto Protocol would help address climate change and would not be extremely costly to implement.)[47] Likewise, provisions that would prevent the adoption or implementation of airport user fees, or prevent requirements that airport sponsors contribute buildings or other items to the FAA free of charge, seem designed to prevent certain costs from being imposed on certain groups.

The issues underlying other appropriations restrictions are less immediately apparent, as many of the provisions have little or no legislative history. Where such information is available, though, the reasons behind some of the provisions seem to fall into several categories or types: economic concerns, end-of-administration rules, and other reasons.

Economic Concerns

Several other appropriations restrictions appear to have been prompted by concerns about the economic ramifications of regulations on affected parties.

Animal and Plant Health

For example, as noted previously, provisions in appropriations bills from FY2004 through FY2008 prohibited the implementation of a July 2003 proposed rule on cost sharing for animal and plant health emergency programs. In that proposed rule, the Animal and Plant Health Inspection Service (APHIS) noted that the cost to the federal government of detecting and eradicating animal or plant pests or diseases had increased sharply, and the proposed regulation would provide "a better defined, more consistent approach to cost sharing and the allocation of financial responsibility among the Federal Government, State(s), and other cooperators."[48] The regulation was opposed by certain interest groups (e.g., the American Sheep Industry Association and the National Cattlemen's Beef Association), which sent letters to APHIS recommending that the rule not be made final.[49] On November 5, 2003, an amendment was added to the Department of Agriculture's appropriations bill prohibiting the use of funds to make the proposed rule final. The rationale offered for the prohibition by the amendment's sponsor was that the rule would require state governments to provide matching funds for the program, and that doing so could impose a hardship on states without sufficient funds to provide the match.[50] The language was subsequently included in the Consolidated Appropriations Act, 2004 (P.L. 108-199, 118 Stat. 39, Sec. 761). On October 31, 2005, APHIS announced that it had withdrawn the proposed rule in August 2005.[51] Nevertheless, Congress has continued to include language prohibiting the finalization of the rule in each subsequent appropriations bill funding APHIS.

Real Estate Brokerage Activity

Provisions in appropriations bills since FY2003 have prohibited the development or finalization of rules concluding that real estate brokerage activity is "financial in nature or incidental to financial activity." The provision in the Consolidated Appropriations Act for 2008 specifically referenced a January 2001 proposed rule that was jointly published by the Board of Governors of the Federal Reserve System and the Department of the Treasury.[52] That proposed rule sought comment on whether to issue a final rule declaring that real estate brokerage activity was, in fact, financial in nature, thereby allowing financial holding companies and financial subsidiaries of national banks to engage in such activity pursuant to the Gramm-Leach-Bliley Act (P.L. 106-102).[53] According to press accounts, realtors favored these appropriations restrictions and opposed the expansion of real estate activities to banks.[54] Non-appropriations legislation has been introduced in each recent Congress related to this issue, but the only legislation to be enacted has been the appropriations acts.[55]

Pesticide Tolerance Processing Fees

Appropriations provisions from FY2000 through FY2003 prohibited EPA from finalizing a June 1999 proposed rule that would have changed the fees charged for pesticide tolerance processing.[56] In that proposed rule, EPA said that a variety of factors had increased the costs associated with tolerance processing well beyond the fees that were being charged, and that the proposed fee increases would "make the tolerance processing system self-supporting" and the financial burden "borne primarily by those constituencies who directly benefit, rather than the taxpayer."[57] Although other, non-appropriations-related legislation was introduced in the 107th Congress to prohibit EPA from issuing regulations on this issue,[58] the only such legislation that was enacted between FY1999 and FY2004 were the restrictions in the various appropriations bills. In January 2004, the Consolidated Appropriations Act of 2004 (P.L. 108-199, Title V of Division G) amended the Federal Insecticide, Fungicide and Rodenticide Act (FIFRA) and created a new registration service fee system for applications of specified registration and tolerance actions. As required by FIFRA as amended, EPA subsequently published regulations replicating a fee schedule that had been published in the *Congressional Record* on September 17, 2003.[59] The appropriations restrictions have not appeared since the FIFRA amendments were enacted.

End-of-Administration Rules

Several other provisions in appropriations acts during the past 10 years appear to have been designed to slow down or prevent the issuance of certain rules issued near the end of a presidential administration (sometimes referred to as "midnight" rules), or to ensure the implementation of rules issued during that period.

Hardrock Mining

One such set of restrictions involved delays and restrictions on the issuance of rules changing 43 C.F.R. 3809, which the Bureau of Land Management (BLM) within the Department of the Interior said were designed to "protect public lands from unnecessary or undue degradation and to ensure that areas disturbed during the search for and extraction of mineral resources are reclaimed."[60] In 1997, BLM amended these "3809" or "surface management" regulations, but those rules were overturned by a federal court after being challenged by an industry association.[61] The 1998 Omnibus Consolidated and Emergency Supplemental Appropriations Act (P.L. 105-277) required that BLM pay for a study by the National Research Council (NRC) of the National Academies of Science on the adequacyof requirements to prevent unnecessary or undue degradation of federal lands in each state in which mining of locatable minerals occurs. That study (entitled "Hardrock Mining on Federal Lands") was to have been completed by July 31, 1999, but was not published until late September 1999. Meanwhile, BLM published a proposed rule in February 1999 to amend the 3809 regulations,[62] but in the Omnibus Consolidated EmergencySupplemental Appropriations Act, 1999 (P.L. 106-31, 112 Stat. 2681-258), Congress prohibited the Secretary of the Interior from issuing any final rules on this issue until at least September 30, 1999. BLM reopened the comment period on the proposed rule for 120 days in October 1999. Then, in the FY2000 Omnibus Appropriations Act (P.L.106-113, 113 Stat. 1501A-210), Congress prohibited the Secretary from using appropriated funds to issue final rules revising 43 C.F.R. 3809, but said such rules could be issued if they were "not inconsistent" with the recommendations contained in the NRC report or with existing statutory authorities. The same requirement was included in the Department of the Interior and Related Agencies Appropriations Act, 2001 (P.L. 106-291, 114 Stat. 962), which was enacted in October 2000. Shortly thereafter, in November 2000, BLM published a final rule on this issue, stating that the requirements in the rule were, in fact, "not inconsistent" with the NRC report, and making the rule effective on January 20, 2001—the last full day of the Clinton Administration.[63] In December 2000 and January 2001, four lawsuits were filed by industry groups and others asserting that BLM had improperly issued the rule. In February 2001, the governor of Nevada requested that the

Secretary of the Interior postpone the effective date and implementation of the rule. In March 2001, BLM proposed suspending the regulations, citing the need to review issues raised in the lawsuits and the governor's request.[64] In May 2001, several Democratic Members of Congress reportedly said that if the Bush Administration suspended the regulations they would stop the suspension by adding a provision to the FY2002 DOI appropriation.[65]

Arsenic

Another Clinton Administration "midnight" rule that was addressed by an appropriations restriction was an EPA rule regulating arsenic in drinkingwater. A provision added to the FY2002 appropriations bill covering EPA stated that "none of the funds appropriated by this Act may be used to delay the national primary drinking water regulation for Arsenic published on January 22, 2001, in the Federal Register (66 Fed. Reg. pages 6976 through 7066, amending parts 141 through 142 of title 40 of the Code of Federal Regulations)."[66] In that rule, EPA set a new enforceable "Maximum Contaminant Level" for arsenic of 0.01 milligrams per liter (or 10 parts per billion, down from 50 parts per billion in the previous standard), and the rule was scheduled to take effect on March 23, 2001.[67] However, on January 20, 2001 — two days before the rule was published, and on the first day of the Bush Administration — Assistant to the President and Chief of Staff Andrew H. Card Jr. sent a memorandum to the heads of all executive departments and agencies directing them to (among other things) postpone for 60 days the effective date of all regulations that had not yet taken effect.[68] EPA initially delayed the effective date of the rule until May 22, 2001, and later extended the effective date until February 2002 "to reassess the scientific and cost issues associated with this rule and to seek further public input on each of these issues."[69] Also, in May 2001, OMB's OIRA asked for suggestions from the public on specific regulations that could be rescinded or changed. One of the suggestions that OIRA received focused on the January 22, 2001, arsenic rule.

In September 2001, the National Academy of Sciences issued a report concluding that even very low concentrations of arsenic were associated with a higher incidence of cancer.[70] At the end of October 2001, the EPA Administrator announced that the 10-parts-per-billion standard for arsenic would remain.[71] However, in a December 2001 report to Congress, OIRA characterized the suggested elimination or revision of the arsenic rule as a "high priority" for future action, indicating that it was "inclined to agree and look into the suggestion." By that point, though, Congress had added the provision to the EPA appropriations bill for FY2002 prohibiting the use of associated funds to delay the January 2001 rule any further.[72]

Snowmobiles

On December 18, 2000, the National Park Service within the Department of the Interior published a proposed rule to phase out the use of snowmobiles in Yellowstone National Park and other areas, with comments requested by January 17, 2001.[73] Three days later, on December 21, 2000, the Consolidated Appropriations Act, 2001, was enacted, which said (Section 128 of Appendix D) that "None of the funds provided in this or any other Act may be used prior to July 31, 2001, to promulgate or enforce a final rule to reduce during the 2000-2001 or 2001-2002 winter seasons the use of snowmobiles below current use patterns at a unit in the National Park System." On January 22, 2001, the National Park Service published a final rule that deleted certain provisions that had been in the proposed rule "to avoid any questions about consistency with the recent statute."[74] Less than two weeks later, pursuant to the January 20, 2001, Card memorandum, the National Park Service delayed the effective date of the rule from February 21, 2001, until April 22, 2001. A series of court rulings and agency actions delayed many other actions until December 2007, when NPS issued a final rule governing the use of snowmobiles in the Yellowstone area parks.[75]

Hours of Service

A DOT rule that was published in the last year of the Clinton Administration also became the subject of an appropriations limitation. In May 2000, the Federal Motor Carrier Safety Administration (FMCSA) published a proposed rule that would have changed its "hours of service" regulations to require certain motor carriers to provide drivers with better opportunities to obtain sleep.[76] Comments were initially due by July 31, 2000, but FMSCA later extended the comment period to October 31, 2000, and later to December 15, 2000. Meanwhile, on October 23, 2000, Congress enacted the Department of Transportation and Related Agencies Appropriations, 2001 (P.L. 106-346), one provision of which prohibited FMCSA from making the proposed rule final.[77] In March 2001, separate legislation was introduced to prohibit the rule from becoming final (H.R. 1008, 107th Congress), but that legislation was not enacted. However, later that year, a provision was added to the Department of Transportation and Related Agencies Appropriations Act, 2002 (P.L. 107-87, 115 Stat. 870) stating the "sense of Congress" that DOT should not change current requirements until certain conditions were met.[78] FMSCA ultimately published a final rule on this issue on April 28, 2003, reflecting "careful consideration of the concerns expressed by Members of Congress as well as the more than 53,000 comments to the docket."[79]

Other Reasons for Regulatory Appropriations Restrictions

Other provisions prohibiting certain rulemaking or regulatory actions appear to have been added to appropriations bills for other reasons.

Tire Grading Standards

As noted earlier in this report, in each of the last 10 appropriations bills covering DOT, a provision has been included prohibiting the use of appropriated funds to "plan, finalize, or implement any rulemaking to add to section 575.104 of title 49 of the Code of Federal Regulations any requirement pertaining to a grading standard that is different from the three grading standards (treadwear, traction, and temperature resistance) already in effect." The House Appropriations Committee Print for the Consolidated Appropriations Act, 2008 states that this provision has been included in all relevant appropriations bills since 1996, but does not indicate whythe provision was included.[80] The Senate Committee on Appropriations report for the Department of Transportation and Related Agencies Appropriations Bill, 1999, stated that the prohibition would "prohibit any rulemaking that would require that passenger car tires be labeled to indicate their low rolling resistance, or fuel economy characteristics," and that the committee included the provision "because the need for such labels has not been adequately justified and the additional costs associated with this proposal would likely be prohibitive."[81]

Legislative Branch Details

Provisions have been added to relevant appropriations bills each year since FY2004 to prevent the finalization of an OPM proposed rule that was published in September 2003. Among other things, the proposed regulation would have prohibited any executive agency from detailing or otherwise assigningan employee to the legislative branch without the approval of the OPM Director. The proposed rule stated that the OPM Director was allowed approve such details only if doing so would not disclose "information within the constitutional authority of the Executive to withhold" because disclosure would impair (among other things) "the performance of the Executive's constitutional duties."[82] The appropriation provision prohibiting the finalization of the rule first appeared in the Consolidated Appropriations Act, 2004 (P.L. 108-199, 118 Stat. 360, Sec. 646). In a January 23, 2004, signing statement on this legislation, the President said that he would interpret that section "in a manner consistent with the President's constitutional authority to supervise the unitary executive branch." To date, however, OPM has not published a final rule on this issue. This conflict appears to be an example of a long-standing point of contention between the President and Congress regarding Congress' authority to obtain information from the executive branch.[83]

Vessel Traffic

The FY1999 through FY2003 prohibition on the development or implementation of rules changing the size of the vessel traffic safety fairway between Santa Barbara and San Francisco appears to have been put in place because of safety and environmental concerns. According to the House Appropriations Committee report on DOT's appropriation for FY2003 (H.Rept. 107-772), the provision was added in response to an April 27, 1989, proposed rule that "would narrow the originally proposed five-mile-wide fairway to two one-mile-wide fairways separated by a two-mile-wide area whereoffshore oil rigs could be built if Lease Sale 119 goes forward. Under this revised proposal, vessels would be routed in close proximity to oil rigs because the two-mile-wide non-fairway corridor could contain drilling rigs at the edge of the fairways. The Committee is concerned that this rule, if implemented, could increase the threat of offshore oil accidents off the California coast. Accordingly, the bill continues the language prohibiting the implementation of this regulation."

Fairness Doctrine

The FY2008 prohibition on the FCC's use of funds to implement the agency's "Fairness Doctrine" (which had required broadcasters to air both sides of controversial issues, and was repealed by the FCC in 1985) was reportedly based on concerns that the doctrine could be revived, and that doing so would inhibit current political expression over commercial airways. Others, however, said there was no indication that the FCC or Congress intended to revive the doctrine, and that the appropriations provision was unnecessary.[84]

Ending Regulatory Appropriation Restrictions

In some cases, the regulatory limitations that have been added to appropriations bills during the past 10 years appear to have ended because the underlying concern was temporal in nature. For example, one provision that was in appropriations bills for FY2001 and FY2002 prohibited the use of funds to issue a certain type of proposed rule "for which the comment period would close prior to September 30, 2002." Therefore, after FY2002, the provision was no longer needed. Another provision that appeared only in an FY1999 appropriations bill prohibited the use of funds to implement amendments to federal milk marketing orders unless the implementation took place before October 1, 1999—the end of FY1999.

In other cases, appropriations restrictions appear to have ended because of changes in the political environment. Citing a Defenders of Wildlife report that there was a significant decrease in the number of "anti-environmental riders" between the 1998 to 2000 period and 2001, one observer said that this development was not surprising given that "so many of the riders in the late 1990s resulted from policy conflicts between the Republican leadership in Congress and the Clinton Administration."[85] As noted previously, several of the regulatory restrictions were added to multiple appropriations measures for several years at the end of the Clinton Administration preventing the development or issuance of regulations implementing the Kyoto Protocols on global warming. Beginning in FY2002, however, those restrictions no longer appeared in any of the appropriations bills, perhaps because the new Bush Administration had publicly announced its opposition to the Kyoto Protocols, thereby making the development of regulations implementing its requirements unlikely.[86]

Other regulatory appropriations restrictions have continued even though the original reasons for their enactments appear to have disappeared. As noted previously, even though APHIS announced that it had withdrawn a proposed rule on cost sharing for animal and plant health emergency programs in August 2005, Congress has continued to prohibit finalizing the proposed rule.

The Scope and Effect of Regulatory Appropriations Restrictions

The regulatory restrictions in appropriations bills thathavebeen enacted during the last 10 years illustrate that Congress can have a substantial effect on agency rulemaking and regulatory activity beyond the introduction of joint resolutions of disapproval pursuant to the Congressional Review Act. These appropriations provisions can prevent an agency from developing a proposed rule, from making a proposed rule final, or from implementing or enforcing a final rule. However, unlike joint resolutions of disapproval under the Congressional Review Act, these appropriations provisions cannot nullify an existing regulation (i.e., remove it from the *Code of Federal Regulations*) or permanently prevent the agency from issuing the same or similar regulations. Therefore, any final rule that has taken effect and been codified in the *Code of Federal Regulations* will continue to be binding law — even if language in the relevant regulatory agency's appropriations act prohibits the use of funds to enforce the rule. Regulated entities are still required to adhere to applicable requirements (e.g., installation of pollution control devices, submission of relevant paperwork), even if violations are unlikely to be detected and enforcement actions cannot be taken by federal agencies.

Also, unless otherwise indicated, regulatory restrictions in appropriations acts are binding only for the period of time covered by the legislation (i.e., a fiscal year or a portion of a fiscal year).[87] Therefore, any restriction that is not repeated in the next relevant appropriations act or enacted in other legislation is no longer binding on the relevant agency or agencies. This may explain why some of the provisions in the Consolidated Appropriations Act for 2008 had been in all previous appropriations measures since FY1999. On the other hand, some appropriations provisions are worded in such a way that they have essentially become permanent or multi-year requirements. For example, the provision in the Consolidated Appropriations Act, 2001 requiring OMB to publish a report on the costs and benefits of regulations stated that the report was to be produced that year "and each year thereafter."[88] Also, the Consolidated Appropriations Act, 2008 (121 Stat. 2015) prohibits the issuance of any rule indicating that real estate brokerage activity is financial in nature "for fiscal years 2008 and 2009."

Most of the regulatory restrictions are in appropriations bills providing funds for particular agencies or groups of agencies. Therefore, the prohibitions are generally applicable only to the agencies funded by that appropriations measure. However, some of the regulatory prohibitions are in the "General Provisions—Government-wide" section of one of the appropriations measures (for FY2008, Title VII of the Financial Services and General Government Appropriations Act), and are therefore applicable to virtually all federal agencies. For example, the provision in Section 735 of the Consolidated Appropriations Act of 2008 that prohibited the use of funds to implement a proposed rule on temporary details of staff to the legislative branch was in the "General Provisions—Government-wide" section of the act.[89] Other provisions are worded in such a way that their effects are broader than the agencies funded by those particular appropriations bills (e.g., those that prohibit the use of funds in "this or any other Act" to publish or implement regulations.)[90]

On the other hand, some of the appropriations provisions restricting regulatory actions may not be as restrictive as they initially appear. Some federal regulatory agencies derive a substantial amount of their operating funds from sources other than congressional appropriations (e.g., user fees), and the use of those funds to develop, implement, or enforce rules may not be legally constrained by language preventing the use of appropriated funds.[91] Also, some federal regulations (e.g., many of those issued by EPA and OSHA) are primarily implemented or enforced by state or local governments, and those governments may have sources of funding that are independent of the federal funds that are restricted by the appropriations provisions. Some state or local governments may also have their own statutory and regulatory requirements that are the same as or similar to the federal rules at issue, or may even go beyond federal standards.[92] If state or local funds or legal authorities are used to develop, implement, or enforce regulations, those actions would not appear to be constrained by statutory provisions limiting the useof *federal* funds to restrict action on particular *federal* laws and regulations.[93]

Agencies may also find ways around provisions prohibiting the use of appropriated funds for rulemaking or other regulatory actions. For example, if an agency is not permitted to use its appropriation to issue a formal rule on a particular issue, it might attempt to achievetheend result through other means (e.g., a guidance document that, while technically not having a binding effect, may be granted great deference by affected parties).[94] More generally, if Congress restricts one agency or group of agencies from issuing a rule on a particular topic, another agency with similar or overlapping statutory authority may be assigned that responsibility. For example, in 1986, the House Appropriations Committee voted to cut off funding for OMB's OIRA on grounds that the office's review amounted to "second-guessing" congressional delegations of rulemaking authority to federal agencies.[95] In response, then-OMB Director James C. Miller III said that, if funds were cut off for OIRA, "we will do it in the White House. If [you take] the office out of the White House, we will do it in the Justice Department. If you take the office out of the Justice Department, we will do it in Commerce. This is a matter of the president's constitutional power and authority."[96]

Also, as this example suggests, it is unclear how these kinds of congressional appropriations restrictions on regulatory agencies will be viewed and implemented by the President. For example, in 2006, President Bush said the provision prohibiting OMB from reviewing agricultural marketing orders "should be deleted as inconsistent with the President's constitutional authority to supervise the unitary executive branch."[97] More recently, in his December 26, 2007, signing statement on the Consolidated Appropriations Act for 2008, President Bush said the act "contains certain provisions similar to those found in prior appropriations bills passed by the Congress that might be construed to be inconsistent with my Constitutional responsibilities. To avoid such potential infirmities, the executive branch will interpret and construe such provisions in the same manner as I have previously stated in regard to similar provisions."[98] The Bush Administration has also objected to these kinds of provisions in proposed appropriations legislation.[99] If the President views restrictions on agencies' rulemaking and regulatory authorities as unconstitutional infringements on his ability to manage the executive branch, the agencies might be directed to ignore the restrictions in the appropriations act. (To date, however, CRS is not aware of any such instructions.) On the other hand, because all agency regulations are based on some type of statutory rulemaking authority, Congress may view any failure to adhere to the appropriations restrictions as equally unconstitutional.[100] In this situation, federal courts may have to decide whether the appropriations provisions are binding on the agencies.

Support for and Concerns Regarding Appropriations Restrictions

Article I, Section 9 of the Constitution states that "no money shall be drawn from the Treasury but in consequence of appropriations made by law." Kate Stith, writing in the *Yale Law Journal*, said that the "appropriations" required by the Constitution "are not only legislative specifications of money *amounts*, but also legislative specifications of the *powers, activities,* and *purposes*—what wemaycall, simply, 'objects'—for which appropriated funds may be used."[101] She takes the view that Congress has not only the right, but "a constitutional duty to limit the amount and durations of each grant of spending authority," and that the historical concept of appropriations as adopted by the colonies "encompassed dual limitations on both amount and object."[102] Stith also said that when Congress denies appropriations for a particular activity,

> the denial is not merely a determination that the public fisc cannot afford spending any money on that activity. By such appropriations legislation, Congress decides that, under our constitutional scheme, for the duration of the appropriations denial, the specific activity is no longer within the realm of authorized government actions.[103]

Other authors have also asserted that, since Article I, Section 9 of the Constitution specifically mentions appropriations as a congressional responsibility, appropriations provisions that change or repeal statutory provisions "ought to be looked at especially charitably."[104]

Other observers, however, have expressed concerns about Congress' use of certain restrictions in appropriations bills. For example, Jacques B. LeBoeuf concluded that Congress "may not interfere with the Executive's ability to execute the law. Appropriations riders that attempt to influence executive discretion in the area of law enforcement prevent the executive branch from carrying out its constitutionally mandated activities."[105] LeBoeuf also said that the "President should refuse to abide by funding limitations he or she considers to be unconstitutional,"[106] and some Presidents have lodged these kinds of objections. For example, President Reagan, in a signing statement on a limitation provision in the Supplemental Appropriations Act of 1987, said the following:

> Article II of the Constitution assigns responsibility for executing the law to the President. While Congress is empowered to enact new or different laws, it may not indirectly interpret and implement existing laws, which is an essential function allocated by the Constitution to the executive branch. If the Congress disagrees with a statutory interpretation advanced by the executive branch ... the Congress may, of course, amend the underlying statute. The use of an appropriations bill for this purpose, however, is inconsistent with the constitutional scheme of separation of powers.[107]

As noted previously, President Bush has similarly objected to appropriations provisions as inappropriately limiting his authority.[108] Others have also raised questions about the constitutionality of certain types of appropriations provisions.[109]

Neal Devins characterized appropriations restrictions as "the constitutional equivalent of authorizations," but he also said that the addition of such provisions while on the House or Senate floor was "troublesome" and that "the appropriations process may not be conducive to sound substantive policymaking for a variety of institutional reasons," including the prevention of authorizing committees from applying their expertise.[110] Devins said that such provisions "may strain the effectiveness of other branches of government" and "are symptomatic of Congress's inability to enact authorizing legislation."[111] He also said that appropriations provisions prohibiting agencies from launching regulatory initiatives without changing the underlying authorizations "unduly limit the Executive's policymaking responsibilities," may result in a "confusing patchwork" of enforcement schemes, and are viewed by some as an unconstitutional violation of separation of powers.[112] He concluded that, "while Congress's use of limitation riders is sometimes necessary, Congress should be aware of the significant risks associated with policymaking through the appropriations process."

A somewhat different perspective on the constitutionality of appropriations restrictions on executive action was offered by Peter Raven-Hansen and William C. Banks in the context of the President's authority regarding national security.[113] The authors took a position between the advocates of unlimited congressional and presidential power, but ultimatelyasserting that narrowly constructed appropriations restrictions are appropriate.

> Contrary to ritualistic incantations by proponents of congressional power, the power of the purse is not plenary in national security law. It is always qualified by the commands of the Constitution and cannot be used to achieve ends that Congress could not constitutionally achieve by other means. But it is also not a "merely procedural" power that makes an appropriation restriction somehow less than "substantive" law. A properly enacted national security appropriation has the same force and effect as any other statute. Nor is its effect diluted by the truncated legislative process by which it is sometimes enacted ... . [T]he restrictive appropriation will rarely trespass on national security functions assigned to the President by explicit constitutional text because so few functions are. Most national security

> functions are shared. It is therefore as inaccurate to invoke the "plenary" war and foreign affairs powers of the President to challenge restrictive appropriations as it is to invoke the "plenary" power of the purse to defend them. Instead, to determine the constitutionality of a restrictive national security appropriation, we must weigh the extent to which the restriction prevents the President fromaccomplishinghis constitutionally assigned functions against the need for the restriction to promote objectives within the authority of Congress. In this weighing, the special history of the power of the purse in national security often tips the sales in favor of its expertise.

The Supreme Court has not ruled on the specific issue of whether appropriations provisions limiting executive agencies' regulatory discretion represent an unconstitutional intrusion into the President's authority. However, the Court has said that, while *implicit* appropriations limitations on authorizing legislation are questionable,[114] "Congress ... may amend substantive law in an appropriations statute, as long as it does so clearly."[115]

Appropriations Restrictions and Rulemaking

Some observers and interest groups have specifically advocated the use of appropriations provisions to stop rulemaking activity. For example, John Shanahan and Mark Wilson of the Heritage Foundation described several spending restrictions in 1995 appropriations legislation for EPA and the Department of Labor (e.g., restricting implementation of the Delaney Clause, wetlands permitting requirements, and an ergonomics standard), and said the following:

> While permanent labor and environmental policy reform should be pursued, many of the problems addressed by the House appropriations riders are so egregious that immediate relief should be granted. While these riders are an imperfect solution, Americans should view them as necessary to encourage recalcitrant federal agencies to work with Congress to reform some of the nation's most burdensome regulatory statutes.[116]

Others, however, have expressed concerns about these kinds of provisions from both a procedural and a public policy standpoint. For example, in a 2005 article entitled "Regulatory Underkill," William W. Buzbee of the Center for Progressive Reform said the following:

> During the past decade, use of legislative riders has become another particularly popular and low-visibility means of derailingprograms. Such riders are typically not freestanding bills that are subject to the congressional committee process, openly debated, and visible for all to see. Instead, they commonly appear without announcement or even an open legislative sponsor. Riders are appended to other bills, often large spending appropriations bills that have broad support and reflect hundreds of fiercely negotiated bargains. Some riders enact provisions that could not pass as free-standing legislation.... Other riders bar the use of appropriations to implement controversial policies. These "carve-outs" effectively render such policies a nullity for certain periods or in certain areas. Because these riders do not involve a frontal attack on a popular law, and their advocates may remain unknown, the public seldom knows of these proposals in time to mount an effective opposition.[117]

The Future

Congress' use of regulatory appropriations restrictions has fluctuated somewhat over time, and previous experience suggests that they may be somewhatless frequent when Congress and the President are of the same party. However, the use of such provisions has not been confined to one political party or one set of interest groups. As Richard Lazarus pointed out in 2006:

> No one political party and no particular ideology have been more likely to promote or to reject the use of appropriations riders. All appear to have willingly embraced the strategy when it has served their purposes, whether Republicans or Democrats, liberals or conservatives. Each has condemned the other for doing the same. The precise identity of the condemnor or the condemnee has turned on whose political ox is being gored at the moment rather than on the willingness of anyone to adhere to a principled approach to lawmaking over the longer haul.[118]

Although the substantive reasons leading to the adoption of these regulatory restrictions are numerous (e.g., economic interests, or to support or oppose end-ofadministration rules), their inclusion in appropriations legislation as a matter of legislative strategy appears to be prompted by two factors: (1) Congress' ability via its "power of the purse" to control agency action, and (2) the fact that appropriations bills are considered "must pass" legislation. As one observer put it, "Because everyone knows that Congress must pass such legislation, it is tempting to try and attach incidental provisions that otherwise might lack the political momentum (or even majority support) necessary for passage."[119] In that regard, several of the regulatory restrictions discussed in this report were also in separate legislation that had not moved since they were introduced. The use of regulatory restrictions in appropriations bills is also likely to continue for the foreseeable future. The examples provided in this report indicate that they are a formidable "tool" in the "toolbox" of congressional oversight and control of executive agencies.

Table 1. Appropriations Provisions Affecting Rulemaking andRegulation, Fiscal Years 1999 Through 2008

	Fiscal Year(s) in Which the Provision Appeared[a]
A. Provisions Related to the Finalization of Particular Proposed Rules	
1. None of the funds made available by this Act may be used to issue a final rule in furtherance of, or otherwise implement, the proposed rule on cost-sharing for animal and plant health emergency programs of the Animal and Plant Health Inspection Service published on July 8, 2003 (Docket No. 02-062-1; 68 Fed. Reg. 40541).	2004, 2005, 2006, 2007, 2008
2. None of the funds appropriated or made available under this Act or any other appropriations Act may be used to implement or enforce restrictions or limitations on the Coast Guard Congressional Fellowship Program, or to implement the proposed regulations of the Office of Personnel Management to add sections 300.311 through 300.316 to part 300 of title 5 of the Code of Federal Regulations, published in the Federal Register, volume 68, number 174, on September 9, 2003 (relating to the detail of executive branch employees to the legislative branch).	2004, 2005, 2006, 2007, 2008
3. None of the funds made available in this Act may be used by the Secretary of Homeland Security or any delegate of the Secretary to issue any rule or regulation	2008
which implements the Notice of Proposed Rulemaking related to Petitions for Aliens To Perform Temporary Nonagricultural Services or Labor (H-2B) set out beginning on 70 Fed. Reg. 3984 (January 27, 2005).	
4. None of the funds made available under this Act may be used to promulgate or implement the Environmental Protection Agency [EPA] proposed regulations published in the Federal Register on January 3, 2007 (72 Fed. Reg. 69).[b]	2008
5. None of the funds provided or limited under this Act may be used to issue a final regulation under section	2008
5309 of title 49, United States Code, except that the Federal Transit Administration may continue to review comments received on the proposed rule (Docket No. FTA-2006-25737).[c]	2008

Table 1. (Continued)

	Fiscal Year(s) in Which the Provision Appeared[a]
A. Provisions Related to the Finalization of Particular Proposed Rules	
6. None of the funds made available in the Act may be used to finalize, implement, administer, or enforce — (1) the proposed rule relating to the determination that real estate brokerage is an activity that is financial in nature or incidental to a financial activity published in the Federal Register on January 3, 2001 (66 Fed. Reg. 307 et seq.); or (2) the revision proposed in such rule to section 1501.2 of title 12 of the Code of Federal Regulations.	2003, 2004, 2005, 2006, 2007[d]
7. None of the funds made available under this Act may be used to issue or implement the Department of Transportation's proposed regulation entitled Parts and Accessories Necessary for Safe Operation; Certification of Compliance With Federal Motor Vehicle Safety Standards (FMVSSs), published in the Federal Register, volume 67, number 53, on March 19, 2002, relating to a phase-in period to bring vehicles into compliance with the requirements of the regulation.	2005
8. None of the funds appropriated or otherwise made available by this Act shall be used to promulgate a final regulation to implement changes in the payment of pesticide tolerance processing fees as proposed at 64 Fed. Reg. 31040, or any similar proposals. The Environmental Protection Agency may proceed with the development of such a rule.	2000, 2001, 2002, 2003
9. None of the funds made available in this or any other Act may be expended before March 31, 1999 to publish final regulations based on the regulations proposed at 63 Fed. Reg. 3289 on January 22, 1998.[e]	1999
10. None of the funds made available in this Act may be used by the Secretary of the Interior or the Secretary of Agriculture to implement a final rule for estimating fair market value land use rental fees for fiberoptic communications rights-of-way on Federal lands that amends or replaces the linear right-of-way rental fee schedule published on July 8, 1987 (43 CFR 2803.1-2(c)(1)(I)). In determining rental fees for fiberoptic rights-of-way, the Secretaries shall use the rates contained in the linear right-of-way rental fee schedules in place on May 1, 2000.	2001
11. None of the funds appropriated or made available by this Act or any other Act shall be used: (1) to adopt any proposed rule or proposed amendment to a rule contained in the Notice of Proposed Rulemaking issued on April 24, 2000 (Docket No. FMCSA-97- 2350-953); (2) to adopt any rule or amendment to a rule similar in substance to a proposed rule or proposed amendment to a rule contained in such Notice; or (3) if any such proposed rule or proposed amendment to a rule has been adopted prior to enactment of this section, to enforce such rule or amendment to a rule.[f]	2001, 2002[g]

	Fiscal Year(s) in Which the Provision Appeareda
A. Provisions Related to the Finalization of Particular Proposed Rules	
12. None of the funds made available by this or any other Act shall be used to implement Notice CRP-327, issued by the Farm Service Agency on October 26, 1998, nor shall funds be used to implement any related administrative action including implementation of such procedures published in Farm Service Agency program manuals.[h]	2004
B. Provisions Related to Regulatory Activity Within Certain Areas	
1. None of the funds provided in this Act may be used for salaries and expenses to draft or implement any regulation or rule insofar as it would require recertification of rural status for each electric and telecommunications borrower for the Rural Electrification and Telecommunication Loans program.	2006, 2007, 2008
2. None of the funds appropriated by this Act may be used by the Federal Communications Commission to modify, amend, or change its rules or regulations for universal service support payments to implement the February 27, 2004 recommendations of the Federal-State Joint Board on Universal Service regarding single connection or primary line restrictions on universal service support payments.	2005, 2006, 2007, 2008
3. For fiscal years 2008 and 2009, neither the Board of Governors of the Federal Reserve System nor the Secretary of the Treasury may determine, by rule, regulation, order, or otherwise, for the purposes of section 4(K) of the Bank Holding Company Act of 1956, or section 5136A of the Revised Statutes of the United States, that real estate brokerage activity or real estate management activity (which for purposes of this paragraph shall be defined to mean 'real estate brokerage' and 'property management' respectively, as those terms were understood by the Federal Reserve Board prior to March 11, 2000) is an activity that is financial in nature, is incidental to any financial activity, or is complementary to a financial activity.	2008[i]
4. None of the funds contained in this Act may be used to enact or carry out any law, rule, or regulation to legalize or otherwise reduce penalties associated with the possession, use, or distribution of any schedule I substance under the Controlled Substances Act (21 U.S.C. 801 et seq.) or any tetrahydrocannabinols derivative.	All years (1999 through 2008)[j]
5. None of the funds made available by this Act shall be used to prepare or publish final regulations regarding a commercial leasing program for oil shale resources on public lands pursuant to section 369(d) of the Energy Policy Act of 2005 (P.L. 109-58) or to conduct an oil shale lease sale pursuant to subsection 369(e) of such Act.	2008
6. None of the funds appropriated under this paragraph shall be obligated or expended to prescribe, issue, administer, or enforce any standard, rule, regulation, or order under the Act which is applicable to any person who is engaged in a farming operation which does not maintain a temporary labor camp and employs 10 or fewer employees.	All years (1999 through 2008)[k]

Table 1. (Continued)

	Fiscal Year(s) in Which the Provision Appeareda
B. Provisions Related to Regulatory Activity Within Certain Areas	
7. None of the funds in this Act shall be available for the Federal Aviation Administration to finalize or implement any regulation that would promulgate new aviation user fees not specifically authorized by law after the date of the enactment of this Act.	All years (1999 through 2008)
8. None of the funds in this Act shall be used to pursue or adopt guidelines or regulations requiring airport sponsors to provide to the Federal Aviation	2002, 2003, 2004, 2005, 2006, 2007, 2008
Administration without cost building construction, maintenance, utilities and expenses, or space in airport sponsor-owned buildings for services relating to air traffic control, air navigation, or weather reporting.[l]	
9. None of the funds appropriated by this Act may be obligated or expended to plan, finalize, or implement any rulemaking to add to section 575.104 of title 49 of the Code of Federal Regulations any requirement pertaining to a grading standard that is different from the three grading standards (treadwear, traction, and temperature resistance) already in effect.	All years (1999 through 2008)
10. None of the funds in this Act shall be available to plan, finalize, or implement regulations that would establish a vessel traffic safety fairway less than five miles wide between the Santa Barbara Traffic Separation Scheme and the San Francisco Traffic Separation Scheme.	1999, 2000, 2001, 2002, 2003
11. None of the funds appropriated or made available by this Act shall be used to issue a proposed rule for which the comment period would close prior to September 30, 2002, final, or interim final rule pursuant to notice and comment rulemaking in relation to any change or modification of the definition of "animal"" in existing regulations pursuant to the Animal Welfare Act.	2001, 2002
12. None of the funds appropriated or otherwise made available for the United Nations may be used by the United Nations for the promulgation or enforcement of any treaty, resolution, or regulation authorizing the United Nations, or any of its specialized agencies or affiliated organizations, to tax any aspect of the Internet or international currency transactions.	2002
13. None of the funds appropriated by this Act shall be used to propose or issue rules, regulations, decrees, or orders for the purpose of implementation, or in preparation for implementation, of the Kyoto Protocol which was adopted on December 11, 1997, in Kyoto, Japan at the Third Conference of the Parties to the United Nations Framework Convention on Climate Change.	1999, 2000, 2001[m]
14. None of the funds in this Act shall be available for the Coast Guard to plan, finalize, or implement any regulation that would promulgate new maritime user fees not specifically authorized by law after the date of the enactment of this Act:	1999, 2000, 2001

15. None of the funds in this Act shall be available to prepare, propose, or promulgate any regulations pursuant to title V of the Motor Vehicle Information and Cost Savings Act (49 U.S.C. 32901 et seq.) prescribing corporate average fuel economy standards for automobiles, as defined in such title, in any model year that differs from standards promulgated for such automobiles prior to the enactment of this section.	1999, 2000, 2001
16. None of the funds in this Act shall be available to implement or enforce regulations that would result in the withdrawal of a slot from an air carrier at O'Hare International Airport under section 93.223 of title 14 of the Code of Federal Regulations in excess of the total slots withdrawn from that air carrier as of October 31, 1993 if such additional slot is to be allocated to an air carrier or foreign air carrier under section 93.217 of title 14 of the Code of Federal Regulations.	1999, 2000
17. None of the funds made available under this title may be used to . . promulgate any regulation or other transmittal or policy directive that has the effect of imposing (or clarifying the imposition of) a restriction on the coverage of injectable drugs under section 1861(s)(2) of the Social Security Act beyond the restrictions applied before the date of such transmittal.	2000
18. None of the funds made available by this Act or in subsequent Acts may be used by the Environmental Protection Agency to issue or to establish an interpretation or guidance relating to fats, oils, and greases (as described in P.L. 104-55) that does not comply with the requirements of the Edible Oil Regulatory Reform Act.	1999
19. None of the funds appropriated or otherwise made available to the Secretary by this Act, any other Act, or any other source may be used to issue the final rule to implement the amendments to Federal milk marketing orders required by subsection (a)(1) of section 143 of the Agricultural Market Transition Act (7 U.S.C. 7253), other than during the period of February 1, 1999, through April 4, 1999, and only if the actual implementation of the amendments as part of Federal milk marketing orders takes effect on October 1, 1999, notwithstanding the penalties that would otherwise be imposed under subsection (c) of such section.	1999
20. None of such funds may be used to designate the State of California as a separate Federal milk marketing order under subsection (a)(2) of such section, other than during the period beginning on the date of the issuance of the final rule referred to in subsection (a) through September 30, 1999.	1999
21. None of the funds made available by this Act shall be used in any way to promulgate a final rule (altering 29 CFR part 103) regarding single location bargaining units in representation cases.	1999
22. None of the funds provided in this or any other Act may be used prior to July 31, 2001, to promulgate or enforce a final rule to reduce during the 2000-2001 or 2001-2002 winter seasons the use of snowmobiles below current use patterns at a unit in the National Park System.[n]	2001

Table 1. (Continued)

	Fiscal Year(s) in Which the Provision Appeareda
C. Implementation or Enforcement Restrictions	
1. None of the funds made available in this Act may be used to pay the salaries or expenses of personnel to — (1) inspect horses under section 3 of the Federal Meat Inspection Act (21 U.S.C. 603); (2) inspect horses under section 903 of the Federal Agriculture Improvement and Reform Act of 1996 (7 U.S.C. 1901 note; P.L. 104-127); or (3) implement or enforce section 352.19 of title 9, Code of Federal Regulations.	2008
2. None of the funds made available to the Postal Service by this Act shall be used to implement any rule, regulation, or policy of charging any officer or employee of any State or local enforcement agency, or any individual participating in a State or local program of child support enforcement, a fee for information requested or provided concerning an address of a postal customer.	All years (1999 through 2008)
3. None of the funds made available by this Act may be used by the Federal Communications Commission to implement the Fairness Doctrine, as repealed in General Fairness Doctrine Obligations of Broadcast Licensees (50 Fed. Reg. 35418 (1985)), or any other regulations having the same substance.	2008
4. None of the funds made available by this Act shall be available for any activity or for paying the salary of any Government employee where funding an activity or paying a salary to a Government employee would result	All years (1999 through 2008)[o]
in a decision, determination, rule, regulation, or policy that would prohibit the enforcement of section 307 of the Tariff Act of 1930 (19 U.S.C. 1307).	
5. No funds appropriated under this paragraph shall be obligated or expended to administer or enforce any standard, rule, regulation, or order under the Act with respect to any employer of 10 or fewer employees who is included within a category having a Days Away, Restricted, or Transferred (DART) occupational injury and illness rate, at the most precise industrial classification code for which such data are published, less than the national average rate as such rates are most recently published by the Secretary, acting through the Bureau of Labor Statistics, in accordance with section 24 of the Act.[p]	All years (1999 through 2008)
6. None of the funds provided in this Act may be used for salaries and expenses to carry out any regulation or rule insofar as it would make ineligible for enrollment in the conservation reserve program established under subchapter B of chapter 1 of subtitle D of title XII of the Food Security Act of 1985 (16 U.S.C. 3831 et seq.) land that is planted to hardwood trees as of the date of enactment of this Act and was enrolled in the conservation reserve program under a contract that expired prior to calendar year 2002.	2004, 2005, 2006, 2007
7. None of the funds appropriated or otherwise made available by this Act shall be used to pay salaries and expenses of personnel who implement or administer section 508(e)(3) of the Federal Crop Insurance Act (7 U.S.C. 1508(e)(3)) or any	2006, 2007

regulation, bulletin, policy or agency guidance issued pursuant to section 508(e)(3) of such Act for the 2007 reinsurance year.	
8. None of the funds appropriated or made available by this or any other Act may be used to pay the salaries and expenses of personnel to carry out section 6029 of P.L. 107-171, the Farm Security and Rural Investment Act of 2002.	2004, 2006, 2007[q]
9. No funds appropriated or otherwise made available by this Act may be used to implement or enforce any provisions of the Final Rule, issued on April 16, 2003 (Docket No. FMCSA-97-2350), with respect to either of the following: (1) The operators of utility service	2004
vehicles, as that term is defined in section 395.2 of title 49, Code of Federal Regulations. (2) Maximum daily hours of service for drivers engaged in the transportation of property or passengers to or from a motion picture or television production site located within a 100-air mile radius of the work reporting location of such drivers.	
10. None of the funds provided in this Act shall be used to implement or enforce regulations for locality pay areas in fiscal year 2004 that are inconsistent with the recommendations of the Federal Salary Council adopted on October 7, 2003.	2004
11. None of the funds made available by this or any other Act shall be used to implement Notice CRP-338, issued by the Farm Service Agency on March 10, 1999, nor shall funds be used to implement any related administrative action including implementation of such procedures published in Farm Service Agency program manuals.[r]	2000
12. None of the funds made available by this or any other Act shall be used to implement Notice CRP-327, issued by the Farm Service Agency on October 26, 1998, nor shall funds be used to implement any related administrative action including implementation of such procedures published in Farm Service Agency program manuals.[s]	2000
13. None of the funds made available in this Act may be used to implement, administer, or enforce any guidelines of the Equal Employment Opportunity Commission covering harassment based on religion, when it is made known to the Federal entity or official to which such funds are made available that such guidelines do not differ in any respect from the proposed guidelines published by the Commission on October 1, 1993 (58 Fed. Reg. 51266).	2000, 2001
14. None of the funds made available in this Act may be used to implement or administer the interim guidance issued on February 5, 1998 by the Environmental Protection Agency relating to title VI of the Civil Rights Act of 1964 and designated as the ``Interim Guidance for Investigating Title VI Administrative Complaints Challenging Permits'' with respect to complaints filed under such title after the date of the enactment of this Act and until guidance is finalized.	1999, 2001
15. None of the funds appropriated by this Act may be used to delay the national primary drinking water regulation for Arsenic published on January 22, 2001, in the Federal Register (66 Fed. Reg. pages 6976 through 7066, amending parts 141 through 142 of title 40 of the Code of Federal Regulations).	2002

Table 1. (Continued)

	Fiscal Year(s) in Which the Provision Appeareda
C. Implementation or Enforcement Restrictions	
1. None of the funds made available to the Indian Health Service in this Act shall be used to implement the final rule published in the Federal Register on September 16, 1987, by the Department of Health and Human Services, relating to the eligibility for the health care services of the Indian Health Service until the Indian Health Service has submitted a budget request reflecting the increased costs associated with the proposed final rule, and such request has been included in an appropriations Act and enacted into law.	2000, 2001, 2002, 2003, 2005, 2008
2. None of the funds made available in this or any other Act shall be available to finalize or implement any proposed regulation under the Workforce Investment Act of 1998, Wagner-Peyser Act of 1933, or the Trade Adjustment Assistance Reform Act of 2002 until such time as legislation reauthorizing the Workforce Investment Act of 1998 and the Trade Adjustment Assistance Reform Act of 2002 is enacted.	2008
4. None of the funds made available by this Act may be used by the Administrator of the Environmental Protection Agency to accept, consider or rely on third-party intentional dosing human toxicity studies for pesticides, or to conduct intentional dosing human toxicity studies for pesticides until the Administrator issues a final rulemaking on this subject.[t]	2006, 2007
5. None of the funds provided in this Act or any other Act may be used by the Environmental Protection Agency (EPA) to publish proposed or final regulations pursuant to the requirements of section 428(b) of division G of P.L. 108-199 until the Administrator of the Environmental Protection Agency, in coordination with other appropriate Federal agencies, has completed and published a technical study to look at safety issues, including the risk of fire and burn to consumers in use, associated with compliance with the regulations.[u]	2006, 2007
6. The Secretary of Labor shall take no action to amend, through regulatory or administration action, the definition established in 20 CFR 667.220 for functions and activities under title I of the Workforce Investment Act of 1998, or to modify, through regulatory or administrative action, the procedure for redesignation of local areas as specified in subtitle B of title I of that Act (including applying the standards specified in section 116(a)(3)(B) of that Act, but notwithstanding the time limits specified in section 116(a)(3)(B) of that Act), until such time as legislation reauthorizing the Act is enacted.	2005, 2006, 2007, 2008[v]
7. Section 1310.12(a) of title 45 of the Code of Federal Regulations (October 1, 2004) shall not be effective until June 30, 2006, or 60 days after the date of the enactment of a statute that authorizes appropriations for fiscal year 2006 to carry out the Head Start Act, whichever date is earlier.	2006, 2007
8. None of the funds in title I of this Act may be used to adopt rules or regulations concerning travel agent service fees unless the Department of Transportation publishes in the Federal	2004

Register revisions to the proposed rule and provides a period for additional public comment on such proposed rule for a period not less than 60 days.	
9. The Secretary of Commerce "shall not prepare or publish proposed or final regulations for the implementation of" a fishing capacity reduction program for the West Coast groundfish fishery until a referendum is conducted on the industry fee system.	2003
10. None of the funds in this Act may be expended to issue, implement, or enforce a regulation that diminishes or revokes an exemption authorized under section 345 of the National Highway System Designation Act of 1995 (P.L. 104-59; 109 Stat. 613; 49 U.S.C. 31136 note) before the Secretary of Transportation determines by a rulemaking proceeding that the exemptions granted are not in the public interest and adversely affects the safety of commercial motor vehicles with respect to such exemption that is required under subsection (c) of such section and, as under subsection (d), if a result of monitoring the safety performance of drivers of commercial vehicles that are subject to an exemption	2003
under section 345, the Secretary determines that public safety has been severely affected by an exemption under this section, the Secretary shall report to Congress that determination.	
11. No funds appropriated in this Act may be used to apply or enforce a regulatory requirement for strengthening of flight deck doors on classes of aircraft not specifically required to take such action under P.L. 107-71, section 104(a)(1), unless and until the Under Secretary of Transportation for Security, after opportunity for notice and comment, determines that such strengthening is necessary for aviation security purposes.	2003
12. The Environmental Protection Agency may not use any of the funds appropriated or otherwise made available by this Act to implement the Registration Fee system codified at 40 Code of Federal Regulations Subpart U (sections 152.400 et seq.) if its authority to collect maintenance fees pursuant to FIFRA section 4(i)(5) is extended for 1 year beyond September 30, 2002.	2002, 2003
13. None of the funds made available under this Act or any other Act, may be used to implement, carry out, or enforce any regulation issued under section 41705 of title 49, United States Code, including any regulation contained in part 382 of title 14, Code of Federal Regulations, or any other provision of law (including any Act of Congress, regulation, or Executive order or any official guidance or correspondence thereto), that requires or encourages an air carrier (as that term is defined in section 40102 of title 49, United States Code) to, on intrastate or interstate air transportation (as those terms are defined in section 40102 of title 49, United States Code) — (1) provide a peanut-free buffer zone or any other related peanut- restricted area; or (2) restrict the distribution of peanuts, until 90 days after submission to the Congress and the Secretary of a peer-reviewed scientific study that determines that there are severe reactions by passengers to peanuts as a result of contact with very small airborne peanut particles of the kind that passengers might encounter in an aircraft.	1999, 2000

Table 1. (Continued)

	Fiscal Year(s) in Which the Provision Appeareda
C. Implementation or Enforcement Restrictions	
14. None of the funds made available by this Act shall be used to issue a notice of final rulemaking with respect to the valuation of crude oil for royalty purposes until March 15, 2000. The rulemaking must be consistent with existing statutory requirements.	1999, 2000
15. None of the funds in this Act or any other Act shall be used by the Secretary of the Interior to promulgate final rules to revise 43 CFR subpart 3809, except that the Secretary, following the public comment period required by section 3002 of P.L. 106-31, may issue final rules to amend 43 CFR Subpart 3809 which are not inconsistent with the recommendations contained in the National Research Council report entitled ``Hardrock Mining on Federal Lands'' so long as these regulations are also not inconsistent with existing statutory authorities.	2000, 2001

Notes: The provisions that are listed in this table may not include all provisions limiting rulemaking or regulatory activity during this period. They were drawn from the appropriations legislation that was enacted from FY1999 through FY2008, which may be found on the CRS website at [http://www.crs.gov/products/appropriations/WA00001.shtml].

a. The final continuing resolution for FY2007 (the Revised Continuing Appropriations Resolution, 2007, P.L. 110-5) did not include many of the provisions restricting regulatory actions, but Section 104 of the legislation stated that, "Except as otherwise expressly provided in this division, the requirements, authorities, conditions, limitations, and other provisions of the appropriations Acts referred to in section 101(a) shall continue in effect through the date specified in section106." Section 101(a) lists nine FY2006 appropriations acts, and Section 106 states that the funds made available were for the period ending September 30, 2007. All of the provisions in effect for FY2006 were in one of those nine appropriations acts. Therefore, this report considers the requirements that were in effect in FY2006 to also have been in effect for FY2007.

b. The proposed rule at issue would have amended the general provisions to the national emission standards for hazardous air pollutants, replacing a policy that had been established in 1995.

c. Section 5309 of Title 49 involves "capital investment grants." The proposed rule was issued on August 3, 2007, and proposed changes in the Federal Transit Administration's "small starts" capital investment grant program.

d. A similar provision appeared in the Consolidated Appropriations Act for 2008 prohibiting regulatory activity in this area by the Board of Governors of the Federal Reserve System or the Secretary of the Treasury, but not referencing this particular rule. (See item B.3. in this table.)

e. U.S. Department of the Interior, Bureau of Indian Affairs, "Class III Gaming Procedures," 63 Federal Register 3289, January 22, 1998. Class III gaming primarily includes slot machines, casino games, banking card games, dog racing, horse racing, and lotteries. In the proposed rule, the bureau said that the Department had determined that " the Secretary may promulgate Class III gaming procedures under certain specified circumstances," and that the rule "sets forth the process and standards pursuant to which any procedures would be adopted."

f. The provision went on to say the following: "Provided, That nothing in this section shall apply to issuing and proceeding, through all stages of rulemaking other than adoption of a final rule, under subchapter II of chapter 5 of title 5, United States Code on a supplemental notice of proposed rulemaking to be issued in Docket No. FMCSA-97-2350-953 that contains proposed rules and proposed amendments to rules that take appropriate account of the information received for filing in the docket on the Notice of Proposed Rulemaking (Docket No. FMCSA-97-2350-953)." The proposed rule was actually published in the Federal Register on May2, 2000. U.S. Department of Transportation, Federal Motor Carrier SafetyAdministration, "Hours of Service of Drivers; Driver Rest and Sleep for Safe Operations; Proposed Rule," 65 Federal Register 25539, May 2, 2000.

g. The language for FY2002 was different than that used for FY2001, but had the same effect.

h. U.S. Department of the Treasury, Internal Revenue Service, "Reductions of Accruals and Allocations Because of the Attainment of Any Age; Application of Nondiscrimination Cross-Testing Rules to Cash Balance Plans," 67 Federal Register 76123, December 11, 2002. The rule would affect retirement plan sponsors and administrators, and participants in and beneficiaries of retirement plans.

i. Similar provisions appeared in previous years, but did not focus on the Board of Governors of the Federal Reserve or the Secretary of the Treasury. (See item A.6 in this table.)

j. In FY2001, this provision was in P.L. 106-522 and P.L. 106-553 (both related to the District of Columbia). In FY1999, P.L. 105-277 stated that "None of the funds contained in this Act may be used to conduct any ballot initiative which seeks to legalize or otherwise reduce penalties associated with the possession, use, or distribution of any schedule I substance under the Controlled Substances Act (21 U.S.C. 802) or any tetrahydrocannabinols derivative."

k. This "farming rider" has been in appropriations legislation as far back as 1991. See, for example, title I of the Departments of Labor, Health and Human Services, and Education, and Related Agencies Appropriations Act, 1992 (P.L. 102-170).

l. This provision went on to say that "the prohibition of funds in this section does not apply to negotiations between the agency and airport sponsors to achieve agreement on 'below-market' rates for these items or to grant assurances that require airport sponsors to provide land without cost to the FAA for air traffic control facilities." In FY2005, the provision appeared in both the Consolidated

Appropriations Act, 2005 (P.L. 108-447, Division D — the Transportation, Treasury, Independent Agencies, and General Government Appropriations Act, 2005); and the Department of Homeland Security Appropriations Act, 2005 (P.L. 108-334).

m. In FY2000, this provision was in P.L. 106-69 (related to the Department of Transportation), P.L. 106-74 (related to the Environmental Protection Agency), P.L. 106-78 (related to the Department of Agriculture), and P.L. 106-113 (the Consolidated Appropriations Act, 2000). In FY2001, this provision was in numerous appropriations bills, including P.L. 106-291 (related to the Department of the Interior), P.L 106-346 (related to the Department of Transportation), Appendixes A and B of P.L. 106-377 (related to the Departments of Veterans Affairs and Housing and Urban Development and Independent Agencies), P.L. 106-387 (related to the Department of Agriculture), and P.L. 106-429 (related to foreign operations).

n. The provision went on to say the following: "Provided, That nothing in this section shall be interpreted as amending any requirement of the Clean Air Act: Provided further, That nothing in this section shall preclude the Secretary from taking emergencyactions related to snowmobile use in any National Park based on authorities which existed to permit such emergency actions as of the date of enactment of this Act."

o. This provision was in both the Consolidated Appropriations Act, 2004 (P.L. 108-189 — Division F, the Department of Transportation and Treasury, and Independent Agencies Appropriations Act, 2004); and in the Department of Homeland Security Appropriations Act, 2004 (P.L. 108-90).

p. The provision went on to provide certain exceptions (e.g., "to provide, as authorized by the Act, consultation, technical assistance,educational and training services, and to conduct surveys and studies"). In FY2004 and earlier years, the reference to DART was replaced with "an occupational injury lost workday case rate".

q. In FY2004, this provision (section 759 of P.L. 108-199) went on to say that "this section shall not apply to activities related to the promulgation of regulations or the receipt and review of applications for the Rural Business Investment Program." Therefore, it prohibited the enforcement, but not the promulgation, of regulations. In FY2005, the appropriation bill did not prohibit enforcement, but a provision (section 753 of P.L. 108-447) said that no more than $10 million could be used to carry out section 6029.

r. This provision also provided that "rental payments for any lands enrolled in the Conservation Reserve Program under this section shall be reduced by an amount equal to the Federal cost of any remaining value of a federally cost-shared conservation practice as determined by the Secretary."

s. This provision also provided that "this section shall not apply to any lands for which there is not full compliance with the conservation practices required under terms of the CRP contract."

t. The provision went on to say that "The Administrator shall allow for a period of not less than 90 days for public comment on the Agency's proposed rule before issuing a final rule. Such rule shall not permit the use of pregnant women, infants or children as subjects; shall be consistent with the principles proposed in the 2004 report of the National Academy of Sciences on intentional human dosing and the principles of the Nuremberg Code with respect to human experimentation; and shall establish an independent Human Subjects Review Board. The final rule shall be issued no later than 180-days after enactment of this Act."

u. The provision went on to say that "Not later than 6 months after the date of enactment of this Act, the Administrator shall complete and publish the technical study."

v. The provision in the Consolidated Appropriations Act, 2005 (P.L. 108-447) did not contain the language "or to modify, through regulatory or administrative action, the procedure for redesignation of local areas as specified in subtitle B of title I of that Act (including applying the standards specified in section 116(a)(3)(B) of that Act, but notwithstanding the time limits specified in section 116(a)(3)(B) of that Act)".

End Notes

[1] Morton Rosenberg, Specialist in American National Law in the American Law Division; and Stuart Carmody, reference assistant in the Knowledge Services Group, collaborated in the preparation of this report.

[2] Foa detailed discussion of CRA procedures, see CRS Report RL31160, *Disapproval of Regulations by Congress: Procedure Under the Congressional Review Act*, by Richard S. Beth.

[3] In this case, the incoming President (George W. Bush) did not veto the resolution disapproving the outgoing President's (William J. Clinton's) rule. See CRS Report RL30116, *Congressional Review of Agency Rulemaking: An Update and Assessment of the Congressional Review Act After a Decade*, by Morton Rosenberg, for a description of several possible factors affecting the law's use. Although the CRA has been used to disapprove only one rule, it may have other, less discernable effects (e.g., keeping Congress informed and preventing the publication of rules that may be disapproved).

[4] All regulations start with an act of Congress, and are the means by which statutes are implemented and specific requirements are established. The specificity of the statutory basis for a regulation can vary significantly, from broad grants of rulemaking authority that state the general intent of the legislation to very specific requirements delineating exactly what regulatory agencies should do and how they should do it. For examples of both general and specific statutory authorities, see U.S. General Accounting Office, *Regulatory Burden: Some Agencies' Claims Regarding Lack of Rulemaking Discretion Have Merit*, GAO/GGD-99-20, January 8, 1999.

[5] These statutory rulemaking requirements include the Administrative Procedure Act (5 U.S.C. §551 et seq.), the Paperwork Reduction Act (44 U.S.C. §§3501-3520), the Regulatory Flexibility Act (5 U.S.C. §§601-612), Title II of the Unfunded Mandates Reform Act (2 U.S.C. §§1532-1538), and the Information Quality Act (44 U.S.C. §§3504(d)(1) and 3516).

For a discussion of these and other requirements, see CRS Report RL32240, *The Federal Rulemaking Process: An Overview*, by Curtis W. Copeland.

[6] For example, Section 206 of the Medicare, Medicaid, and SCHIP Extension Act of 2007 (P.L. 110-173, 121 Stat. 2514) prohibited the Secretary of the Department of Health and Human Services from taking any action (including "through promulgation of regulation") to restrict coverage or payment under Title XIX of the Social Security Act for rehabilitation services or school-based administration and school-based transportation. More recently, H.R. 6660 in the 110th Congress (introduced July 30, 2008) would prohibit the Secretary of Labor from "issuing, administering, or enforcing any rule, regulation, or requirement derived from the proposal submitted to the Office of Management and Budget entitled `Requirements for DOL Agencies' Assessment of Occupational Health Risks' (RIN:1290-AA23)." This draft proposed rule had not been published in the *Federal Register*, but was characterized in the press as requiring "all recipients of federal aid under federal health programs to certify that they would not refuse to hire nurses and other providers who object to abortion and even certain types of birth control." Robert Pear, "Abortion Proposal Sets Condition on Aid," *nytimes.com*, available at [http://www.nytimes.com/2008/07/15/washington/15rule.html?_r=1&ref=us&].

[7] Limitations on the expenditure of funds may be in the text of appropriations legislation, or in committee reports, conference reports, or managers' statements. Only provisions in the text of the legislation are legally binding. See CRS Report 98-518 GOV, *Earmarks and Limitations in Appropriations Bills*, by Sandy Streeter. In this report, all of the provisions mentioned were in the text of the appropriations legislation.

[8] Some authors have discussed congressional mechanisms of executive agency control in general or appropriations provisions specifically, and have mentioned restrictions on regulatory activity as one element of those issues. See, for example, Frederick M. Kaiser, "Congressional Control of Executive Actions in the Aftermath of the *Chadha* Decision,"*Administrative Law Review*, vol. 36 (Summer 1984), pp. 258-259.

[9] In July 2000, the Department of Labor issued a proposed rule on coal dust monitoring. See U.S. Department of Labor, Mine Safety and Health Administration, and U.S. Department of Health and Human Services, Centers for Disease Control and Prevention, "Determination of Respirable Coal Mine Dust," 65 *Federal Register* 42068, July 7, 2000.

[10] For more information on OIRA and this review process, see CRS Report RL32397, *Federal Rulemaking: The Role of the Office of Information and Regulatory Affairs*, by Curtis W. Copeland.

[11] This restriction on the review of agricultural marketing orders has been attached to OMB's appropriation every year since 1983, and was reportedly enacted "at the insistence of agricultural interests that were angryatOMB's application of [Executive Order 12291's] economic principles to modify or disapprove their marketing orders." Christopher C. DeMuth and Douglas H. Ginsburg, "WhiteHouse Review of Agency Rulemaking," *Harvard Law Review*, vol. 99 (March 1986), p. 1087. For background on this action, see Jeffrey H. Birnbaum, "Farm, Budget Officials Clash on Supply Curbs by Marketing Boards," *Wall Street Journal*, December 7, 1982, p. 1.

[12] This provision has been attached to OMB's appropriation every year since 2005.

[13] OMB published final guidelines (with a request for further comments on certain points) on September 28, 2001 (66 *Federal Register* 49718), and later republished the guidelines (after making changes pursuant to public comments) on February 22, 2002 (67 *Federal Register* 8452).

[14] For more on this issue, see CRS Report RL32532, *The Information Quality Act: OMB's Guidance and Initial Implementation*, by Curtis W. Copeland.

[15] See [http://www.whitehouse.gov/news/releases/2007/01/20070118.html] for a copy of this executive order.

[16] For more on this issue, see CRS Report RL33862, *Changes to the OMB Regulatory Review Process by Executive Order 13422*, by Curtis W. Copeland.

[17] Ralph Lindeman, "House Panel Again to Block Spending on Bush-Appointed Regulatory Policy Officers," *BNA Daily Report for Executives*, July 1, 2008, p. A-17.

[18] Section 624 of the Consolidated Appropriations Act, 2001 (P.L. 106-554, 114 Stat. 2763A-161, codified at 31 U.S.C. §1105 note), also called the "Regulatory Right-to-Know Act." The provision required OMB to submit an "accounting statement and associated report" for FY2002 "and each year thereafter" that included "(1) an estimate of the total annual costs and benefits (including quantifiable and nonquantifiable effects) of Federal rules and paperwork, to the extent feasible — (A) in the aggregate; (B) by agency and agency program; and (C) by major rule; (2) an analysis of impacts of Federal regulation on State, local, and tribal government, small business, wages, and economic growth; and (3) recommendations for reform."

[19] Section 101 of the E-Government Act (which added a new Chapter 36 to Title 44 of the United States Code) established an "E-Government Fund" that was to be used to support projects "that enable the Federal Government to expand its ability, through the development and implementation of innovative uses of the Internet or other electronic methods, to conduct activities electronically."

[20] For more on e-rulemaking and this funding issue, see CRS Report RL34210, *Electronic Rulemaking in the Federal Government*, by Curtis W. Copeland.

[21] Richard J. Lazarus, "Congressional Descent: The Demise of Deliberative Democracy in Environmental Law," *Georgetown Law Journal*, vol. 94 (March 2006), p. 635. Although legislative provisions in annual appropriations acts are often referred to as "riders," the use of the term "rider" is avoided in this report because it is slang and because there is no common agreement as to whether it should apply to limitation provisions as well as legislative provisions. See CRS Report RL30619, *Examples of Legislative Provisions in Omnibus Appropriations Acts*, by Robert Keith.

[22] See, for example, U.S. General Accounting Office, *Department of Transportation, National Highway Traffic Safety Administration: Light Truck Average Fuel Economy Standard, Model Year 2000*, GAO/OGC-98-42, April 17, 1998; and U.S. Government Accountability Office, *Vehicle Fuel Economy: Reforming Fuel Economy Standards Could Help Reduce Oil Consumption by Cars and Light Trucks, and Other Options Could Complement These Standards*, GAO-07-921, August 2, 2007.

[23] The Food Quality Protection Act of 1996 (P.L. 104-170) eliminated the distinction between raw and processed food tolerances so that all pesticide residues will be regulated under an amended Federal Food, Drug, and Cosmetic Act, which requires all tolerances to be "safe," ensuring a "reasonable certainty of no harm" from pesticides. See CRS Report96-759 ENR, *Pesticide Legislation: Food Quality Protection Act of 1996 (P.L. 104-170)*,by Linda-Jo Schierow.

[24] For example, Section 104 of the Department of Labor's appropriation legislation forFY1998 (P.L. 105-78) stated that "None of the funds made available in this Act may be usedby the Occupational Safety and Health Administration to promulgate or issue any proposedor final standard regarding ergonomic protection before September 30, 1998." However, the legislation expressly did not prohibit OSHA from issuing voluntary guidelines onergonomic protection or from developing a proposed standard regarding ergonomicprotection.

[25] Richard J. Lazarus, "Congressional Descent," pp. 643-644.

[26] CRS electronically searched the act using words and phrases such as "regulations," "final rule," "proposed rule," and "none of the funds." Although this approach revealed the regulatory appropriations restrictions discussed in this report, other restrictions may have been in this and other appropriations bills that did not contain those words or phrases.

[27] U.S. Department of Transportation, Federal Transit Administration, "Major Capital Investment Projects," 72 *Federal Register* 43327, August 3, 2007.

[28] Tetrahydrocannabinol (also known as THC) is the active chemical in cannabis, or marihuana.

[29] The provision goes on to say that "the prohibition of funds in this section does not apply to negotiations between the agency and airport sponsors to achieve agreement on 'below-

market' rates for these items or to grant assurances that require airport sponsors to provide land without cost to the FAA for air traffic control facilities."

[30] Section 3 of the Meat Inspection Act covers the inspection of meat and meat food products. Section 903 of the Federal Agriculture Improvement and Reform Act of 1996 involves the regulation of commercial transportation of equine for slaughter. 9 C.F.R. 352.19 concerns ante-mortem inspections at establishments that slaughter horses.

[31] The provision went on to provide certain exceptions (e.g., "to provide, as authorized by the Act, consultation, technical assistance, educational and training services, and to conduct surveys and studies").

[32] That section of the Tariff Act prohibits the importation of products produced in foreign countries by convict or forced labor, including indentured child labor.

[33] This provision also appeared in the Revised Continuing Appropriations Resolution, 2007 (P.L. 110-5, 121 Stat. 29).

[34] The final continuing resolution for FY2007 (P.L. 110-5) did not include provisions restricting regulatory actions, but Section 104 of the legislation (121 Stat. 9) stated that, "Except as otherwise expressly provided in this division, the requirements, authorities, conditions, limitations, and other provisions of the appropriations Acts referred to in section 101(a) shall continue in effect through the date specified in section 106." Section 101(a) lists nine FY2006 appropriations acts, and Section 106 states that the funds made available were for the period ending September 30, 2007. All of the provisions in effect for FY2006 were in one of those nine appropriations acts. Therefore, unless otherwise indicated, this report considers the requirements in those nine appropriations bills that were in effect in FY2006 to also have been in effect for FY2007.

[35] For more on this issue, see CRS Report RL33563, *District of Columbia: Appropriations for 2007*, by Eugene Boyd and David P. Smole, pp. 14-15. This provision was originally designed to counteract a District of Columbia initiative on medical marijuana, and has been challenged in court several times. In 2007, the District of Columbia city council adopted a resolution prohibiting the use of federal, but not District, funds from implementing the initiative.

[36] This "farming rider" has been in appropriations legislation as far back as 1991. See, for example, Title I of the Departments of Labor, Health and Human Services, and Education, and Related Agencies Appropriations Act, 1992 (P.L. 102-170).

[37] In FY2003, the provision was in the Consolidated Appropriations Resolution, 2003 (P.L. 108-7, 117 Stat. 513).

[38] In FY2003, the provision was in the Consolidated Appropriations Resolution, 2003 (P.L. 108-7, 117 Stat. 409).

[39] For example, this provision was in several appropriations bills for FY2001, includingP.L. 106-291 (related to the Department of the Interior, 114 Stat. 996); P.L 106-346 (related to the Department of Transportation, 114 Stat. 1356A-33); Appendixes A and B of P.L. 106-377 (related to the Departments of Veterans Affairs and Housing and Urban Development and Independent Agencies, 114 Stat. 1441A-41 and 114 Stat. 1441A-85); P.L. 106-387 (related to the Department of Agriculture, 114 Stat. 1549A-33); and Appendix A of P.L. 106-429 (related to foreign operations, 114 Stat. 1900A-54).

[40] In FY2001, this provision was in the Appendix of the Department of Transportation and Related Agencies Appropriations Act, 2001 (P.L. 106-346, 114 Stat. 1356A-2).

[41] In FY2001, this provision was in the Appendix of the Department of Transportation and Related Agencies Appropriations Act, 2001 (P.L. 106-346, 114 Stat. 1356A-28).

[42] In 2008, this provision was in the Consolidated Appropriations Act, 2008 (P.L. 110-161, 121 Stat. 2167). 20 C.F.R. 667.220 describes the permissible costs of administration under Workforce Investment Act grants under Title I of the statute that are subject to administrative cost limits.

[43] The January 3, 2007, proposed rule at issue (published at 72 *Federal Register* 69) would have amended the general provisions to the national emission standards for hazardous air pollutants, replacing a policy that had been established in 1995.

[44] U.S. Department of the Interior, Bureau of Indian Affairs, "Class III GamingProcedures," 63 *Federal Register* 3289, January 22, 1998. Class III gaming primarily includes slot machines, casino games, banking card games, dog racing, horse racing, and lotteries. In the proposed rule, the bureau said that the department had determined that "the Secretary may promulgate Class III gamingproceduresunder certain specified circumstances," and that the rule "sets forth the process and standards pursuant to which any procedures would be adopted."

[45] U.S. Department of the Interior, Bureau ofI ndian Affairs, "Class III Gaming Procedures," 64 *Federal Register* 17535, April 12, 1999.

[46] See, for example, U.S. Chamber of Commerce, "Reality Check: Straight Talk About the Kyoto Protocol," available at [http://www.uschamber.com/publications/reports/reality_check_kyoto.htm].

[47] See, for example, Natural Resources Defense Council, "Bush Administration Errs on Kyoto Global Warming Agreement," at [http://www.nrdc.org/globalwarming/akyotoqa.asp].

[48] U.S. Department of Agriculture, Animal and Plant Health Inspection Service, "Cost-Sharing for Animal and Plant Health Emergency Programs," 68 *Federal Register* 40541, July 8, 2003. In this rule, APHIS said that the total amount of emergency funding provided by the federal government had increased from $136 million in the FY1993 - FY1998 period to $1,234 million in the FY1999 - FY2003 period.

[49] To view a copy of the American Sheep Industry Association's comments, see [http://www.sheepusa.org/index.phtml?page=site/text&nav_id=ce39162b34e4b689b407 5adf5b559d08&ps_session=f652586ec6000ff9459bf3c04def5290]. To view a copy of comments from the National Cattlemen's Beef Association on this proposed rule, see [http://www.beefusa.org/NEWSCattlemensCapitolConcernsNovember6200310921.aspx]. For example, the American Sheep Industry Association characterized the cost-sharing proposal as "arbitrary" and "prescriptive," and not "in the best interests of the agricultural or public sector." It also said "we believe that the federal cost associated with executing this mission has been an excellent investment."

[50] Sen. Robert F. Bennett, et al., remarks in the Senate proposing Amendment No. 2096, *Congressional Record*, vol. 149 (November 5, 2003), p. S14007.

[51] See 70 *Federal Register* 64336, October 31, 2005.

[52] U.S. Department of the Treasury and the Board of Governors of the Federal Reserve System, "Bank Holding Companies and Changein Bank Control," 66 *Federal Register* 307, January 3, 2001.

[53] The Gramm-Leach-Bliley Act amended the Bank Holding Company Act (12 U.S.C. §1841 et seq.) to allow a bank holding company or qualifying foreign bank to engage in a broad range of activities that are financial in nature. The act also permitted financial holding companies to engage in other activities that the board determines (in consultation with the Secretary of the Treasury) to be financial in nature or incidental to a financial activity.

[54] Todd Davenport, "OCC Caught in the Middle of Bank-Realtor Fight," *American Banker*, June 2, 2004.

[55] For example, in the 110th Congress, the "Community Choice in Real Estate Act" (H.R. 111 and S. 413) would have amended the Bank Holding Company Act to prohibit financial holding companies and national banks from engaging in real estate brokerage or real estate management activities. The legislation has not moved since being assigned to congressional committees.

[56] U.S. Environmental Protection Agency, "Pesticides: Tolerance Processing Fees," 64 *Federal Register* 31040, June 8, 1999.

[57] Ibid.

[58] For example, in the 107th Congress, S. 1474 would have prohibited the issuance of regulations making substantive changes to pesticide tolerance processing fees until the end of FY2006. The proposed legislation was not enacted.

[59] U.S. Environmental Protection Agency, "Pesticides: Fees and Decision Times for Registration Applications," 69 *Federal Register* 12771, March 17, 2004. See also U.S. Environmental Protection Agency, "Pesticides; Revised Fee Schedule for Registration Applications," 70 *Federal Register* 32327, June 2, 2005. For more on this issue, see CRS Report RL32218, *Pesticide Registration and Tolerance Fees: An Overview*, by Robert Esworthy. The Pesticide Registration Improvement Renewal Act (P.L. 110-94), enacted October 9, 2007, reauthorized and revised these fee provisions, which would have expired at the end of FY2008. The act also prohibits EPA from collecting any tolerance fees under the authority of Section 408(m) of the Federal Food, Drug, and Cosmetics Act (21 U.S.C. 346a(m)). In each fiscal year budget request since 2004, EPA has included proposals to further increase pesticide fees beyond those authorized. These proposals were not adopted by Congress in each year through FY2008. The FY2009 request included similar proposals.

[60] U.S. Department of the Interior, Bureau of Land Management, "Mining Claims Under the General Mining Laws; Surface Management; Final Rule," 65 *Federal Register* 69998, November 21, 2000.

[61] See *Northwest Mining Association v. Babbitt*, No. 97-1013 (D.D.C. May 13, 1998).

[62] U.S. Department of the Interior, Bureau of Land Management, "Mining ClaimsUnder the General Mining Laws; Surface Management; Proposed Rule," 64 *Federal Register* 6422, February 9, 1999.

[63] U.S. Department of the Interior, Bureau of Land Management, "Mining Claims Under the General Mining Laws; Surface Management; Final Rule," 65 *Federal Register* 69998, November 21, 2000.

[64] U.S. Department of the Interior, Bureau of Land Management, "Mining Claims Under the General Mining Laws; Surface Management," 66 *Federal Register* 16162, March 23, 2001.

[65] Pamela Najor, "Democrats Support Mining Regulations as Bush Considers Suspending Clinton Rule," *BNA Daily Report for Executives*, May 10, 2001, p. A-34. Ultimately, in October 2001, the Bush Administration issued a final hardrock mining rule that retained certain requirements in the 2000 rule, but dropped certain other requirements. Also in October 2001, the Administration issued a proposed rule containing additional changes to the hardrock mining regulations.

[66] Departments of Veterans Affairs and Housing and Urban Development, and Independent Agencies Appropriations Act, 2002 (P.L. 107-73, 115 Stat. 697).

[67] The Safe Drinking Water Act Amendments of 1996 set a January 1, 2000, deadline for EPA to publish a final rule, but Congress extended that deadline until June 22, 2001, in language contained in the final conference report of the EPA spending bill for FY2001.

[68] For more on this memorandum, see U.S. General Accounting Office, *Regulatory Review: Delay of Effective Dates of Final Rules Subject to the Administration's January 20, 2001, Memorandum* (GAO-02-370R, February 15, 2002).

[69] U.S. Environmental Protection Agency, "National Primary Drinking Water Regulations; Arsenic and Clarifications to Compliance and New Source Contaminants Monitoring," 66 *Federal Register* 20579, April 23, 2001.

[70] To view a copy of this report, see [http://books.nap.edu/catalog.php?record_id=10194].

[71] "EPA Sets 10 PPB Arsenic Standard, Based on Best Science, Says Whitman," *BNA Daily Report for Executives*, November 1, 2001, p. A-46.

[72] The legislation funding EPA (P.L. 107-73) was enacted on November 26, 2001.

[73] U.S. Department of the Interior, National Park Service, "Special Regulations, Areas of the National Park System," 65 *Federal Register* 79024, December 18, 2000.

[74] U.S. Department of the Interior, National Park Service, "Special Regulations, Areas of the National Park System,"66 *Federal Register* 7260, January 22, 2001.

[75]U.S. Department of the Interior, National ParkService, "Special Regulations; Areas of the National Park System," 72 *Federal Register* 70781, December 13, 2007. The preamble to this rule contains a history of actions relative to this issue during the previous seven years.

[76] U.S. Department of Transportation, Federal Motor Carrier Safety Administration, "Hour of Service of Drivers; Driver Rest and Sleep for Safe Operations; Proposed Rule," 65 *Federal Register* 25539, May 2, 2000.

[77] 114 Stat. 1356A-30.

[78] One of the conditions was that the Secretary of Transportation determine by rulemaking proceedings that the exemptions granted previously in statute "are not in the public interest and adversely affect the safety of commercial motor vehicles." The Secretary was also required to monitor the safety performance of drivers of commercial motor vehicles who are subject to the exemption and report to Congress prior to the rulemaking proceedings.

[79] U.S. Department of Transportation, Federal Motor Carrier Safety Administration, "Hour of Service of Drivers; Driver Rest and Sleep for Safe Operations; Final Rule," 68 *Federal Register* 22455, April 28, 2003.

[80] House Appropriations Committee Print, Consolidated Appropriations Act, 2008 (H.R. 2764; P.L. 110-161), Division K — Transportation, Housing and Urban Development, and Related Agencies Appropriations Act, 2008, pp. 2363-2364.

[81] U.S. Congress, Senate Committee on Appropriations, Department of Transportation and Related Agencies Appropriations Bill, committee print, 105th Cong., 2ndsess., June 15, 1998, S.Rept. 105-249 (Washington: GPO, 1998), p. 104. However, in 2006, the National Research Council of the National Academies of Science reported that information on rolling resistance should be made available to the public, and that Congress should provide NHTSA with resources to allow it to gather and report information on the influence of passenger tires on vehicle fuel consumption. The report also stated (on pp. 3-4) that "consumers now have little, if any,practical way of assessing howtire choices can affect vehicle economy"; a 10% reduction in rolling resistance is "technically and economically feasible"; and that such a reduction could "save about 1 billion to 2 billion gallons of fuel per year". See National Research Council, *Tires and Passenger Vehicle Fuel Economy: Informing Consumers, Improving Performance*, Transportation Research Board Special Report 286, 2006, available at [http://onlinepubs.trb.org/Onlinepubs/sr/sr286.pdf]. Nevertheless, since 2006, Congress has continued to prohibit regulatory changes to the tire grading standards. Section 111 of the Energy Independence and Security Act of 2007 (P.L. 110-140, 121 Stat. 1506) requires the Secretary of Transportation to issue rules establishing a "national tire fuel efficiency consumer information program," but specifically prohibits the Secretary from requiring "permanent labeling of any kind on a tire for the purpose of tire fuel efficiencyinformation." Legislation has been introduced in the Senate during the 110th Congress (S. 298) that would, among other things, require that all passenger automobile tires sold in the United States meet low rolling resistance standards prescribed by the administrator of NHTSA. The legislation has not moved since being referred to the Senate Committee on Finance in January 2007.

[82] U.S. Office of Personnel Management, "Employment (General)," 68 *Federal Register* 53054, September 9, 2003.

[83] See, for example, Jack L. Goldsmith, III, "Authority of Agency officials to Prohibit Employees from Providing Information to Congress," Letter Opinion for the General Counsel, Department of Health and Human Services, available at [http://www.usdoj.gov/olc/crsmemoresponsese.htm].

[84] Alexander Bolton, "Fairness Doctrine Hammered 309-115," *The Hill*, June 28, 2007. Cheryl Bolen, "FCC Spending Bill Would Prohibit Revival of Defunct Fairness Doctrine," *BNA Daily Report for Executives*, June 29, 2007, p. A-24.

[85] Richard J. Lazarus, "Congressional Descent," pp. 646-647. According to the Defenders of Wildlife study, the number of such provisions fell an average of nearly 50 per year between 1998 and 2000 to 23 in 2001.

[86] For example, at a March 21, 2001, press conference, the White House press secretary said"The President has been unequivocal. He does not support the Kyoto treaty. It exempts thedeveloping nations around the world, and it is not in the United States' economic bestinterest." [http://www.whitehouse.gov/news/briefings/20010328.html#KyotoTreaty] Seealso William H. Glaze, "Kyoto is dead," *Environmental Science & Technology*, vol. 35(May 1, 2001), p. A177, in which EPA Administrator Christine Whitman was quoted assaying that the "Kyoto Protocol was dead as far as the administration was concerned."

[87] See U.S. General Accounting Office, *Principles of Appropriations Law, Third Edition, Volume I*, GAO-04-261SP, (January 2004), p. 2-34, which states that "Since an appropriation act is made for a particular fiscal year, the starting presumption is that everything contained in the act is effective only for the fiscal year covered. Thus, the rule is: A provision contained in an annual appropriation act is not to be construed to be permanent legislation unless the language used therein or the nature of the provision makes it clear that Congress intended it to be permanent."

[88] Section 624 of the Treasury and General Government Appropriations Act of 2001 (P.L. 106-554, 31 U.S.C. §1105 note). GAO and the courts have concluded that these types of construction make appropriations provisions permanent law. See, for example, U.S. Government Accountability Office, *Bureau of Alcohol, Tobacco, Firearms, and Explosives— Prohibition in the 2008 Consolidated Appropriations Act*, B-316510 (July 15, 2008). There, GAO said (on page 3), that "the clearest indication that Congress intended a provision to be permanent is the presence in the provision of 'words of futurity' clearly indicating such intent." GAO noted that the U.S. Court of Appeals for the Second Circuit concluded that the phrase "and each fiscal year thereafter" represented "unambiguous language of permanence." *Auburn Housing Authority v. Martinez*, 277 F.3d 138, 146 (2nd Cir. 2002).

[89] Although these general provisions are applicable government-wide, they are often written in such a way that, in practice, only certain agencies are actually affected (in this case, OPM).

[90] See U.S. General Accounting Office, *Principles of Appropriations Law*, p. 2-33, which says that a general provision "may apply solely to the act in which it is contained ('No part of any appropriation contained in this Act shall be used ...'), or it may have general applicability ('No part of any appropriation contained in this or any other Act shall be used ...')."

[91] Others, however, take the view that even these non-appropriated funds must be at least figuratively deposited into the Treasury, and that "all spending in the name of the United States must be pursuant to legislative appropriation." Kate Stith, "Congress' Power of the Purse," *The Yale Law Journal*, vol. 97 (1988), p. 1345.

[92] For example, under the Occupational Safety and Health Act, states may set standards for hazards such as ergonomic injury for which no federal standard has been established. See U.S. General Accounting Office, *Regulatory Programs: Balancing Federal and State Responsibilities for Standard Setting and Implementation*, GAO-02-495, March 2002.

[93] See U.S. Government Accountability Office, *Principles of Federal Appropriations Law, Third Edition, Volume II*, GAO-06-382, February 2006, which says that, unless stated otherwise, expenditures by recipients of federal grants "are not subject to all the same restrictions and limitations imposed on direct expenditures by the federal government. For this reason, grant funds in the hands of a grantee have been said to largely lose their character and identity as federal funds."

[94] See Office of Management and Budget, "Final Bulletin for Agency Good Guidance Practices," 72 *Federal Register* 3432, January 25, 2007. OMB issued bulletin, in part, because of concerns that agencies were treating guidance documents as binding rules. Nevertheless, as OMB points out, guidance documents can have significant effects on regulated entities.

[95] Judith Havemann, "'Defunding' OMB's Rule Reviewers," *Washington Post*, July 18, 1986, p. A17. See also, Judith Havemann, "Lawmakers Want to Dethrone OMB Rule Reviewers," *Washington Post*, May 22, 1986, p. A17; Judith Havemann, "No 'Shade-Drawn' Dealings

for OMB," *Washington Post*, June 17, 1986, p. A21; and Judith Havemann, "House Moves to Wipe Out OMB Unit," *Washington Post*, July 31, 1986, p. A23.

96 Ibid. Ultimately, an agreement was reached to fund OIRA, but only after OMB agreed to institute new procedures to make OIRA's review process more transparent.

97 "Statement of Administration Policy, H.R. 5576 — Transportation, Treasury, Housing, the Judiciary, and the District of Columbia Appropriations Bill, FY2007," June 14, 2006, available at [http://www.whitehouse.gov/omb/legislative/sap/109-2/hr5576sap-h.pdf].

98 To view a copy ofthissigningstatement, see [http://www.whitehouse.gov/news/releases/2007/12/20071226-1.html]. For more information on signing statements, see CRS Report RL33667, *Presidential Signing Statements: Constitutional and Institutional Implications*, by T.J. Halstead. For information on how signing statements have been implemented, see U.S. Government Accountability Office, *Presidential Signing Statements Accompanying the Fiscal Year 2006 Appropriations Acts*, B-308603, June 18, 2007; and U.S. Government Accountability Office, *Presidential Signing Statements — Agency Implementation of Ten Provisions of Law*, B-309928, December 20, 2007.

99 See, for example, U.S. Office of Management and Budget, Executive Office of the President, "Statement of Administration Policy: H.R. 3043 — Departments of Labor, Health and Human Services, and Education, and Related Agencies Appropriation Act, 2008," July 17, 2008, in which the Administration said it "opposes the prevention of regulations to improve the Workforce Investment Act and Trade Adjustment Assistance (TAA) programs." The provision at issue was ultimately enacted as part of the Consolidated Appropriations Act of 2008 (P.L. 110-161, 121 Stat. 2168).

100 For more on the perspective of federal rulemaking agencies as extensions of Congress,and regulations as extensions of legislative activity, see David H. Rosenbloom, *Building aLegislative-Centered Public Administration: Congress and the Administrative State, 1946-1999* (Tuscaloosa, AL: The University of Alabama Press, 2000).

101 Kate Stith, "Congress' Power of the Purse," *The Yale Law Journal*, vol. 97 (1988), p.1352.

102 Ibid., p. 1343, 1353.

103 Ibid., p. 1361.

104 Matthew D. McCubbins and Daniel B. Rodriguez, "Canonical Construction and Statutory Revisionism: The Strange Case of the Appropriations Canon," *Journal of Contemporary Legal Issues*, vol. 14 (2005), pp. 669-715.

105 Jacques B. LeBoeuf, "Limitations on the Use of Appropriations Riders by Congress to Effectuate Substantive Policy Changes," *Hastings Constitutional Law Quarterly*, vol. 19 (Winter 1992), p. 493.

106 Ibid.

107 Statement on signing H.R. 1827 into law, 23 *Weekly Comp. Pres. Doc.* 800 (July 11, 1987).

108 For example, in his signing statement regarding the Consolidated Appropriations Act of 2008, available at [http://www.whitehouse.gov/news/releases/2007/12/20071226-1.html]. See also, [http://www.whitehouse.gov/omb/legislative/sap/109-2/hr5576sap-h.pdf] for "Statement of Administration Policy, H.R. 5576 — Transportation, Treasury, Housing, the Judiciary, and the District of Columbia Appropriations Bill, FY2007," June 14, 2006.

109 See, for example, J. Gregory Sidak, "How Congress Erodes the Power of the Presidency—Appropriations Muzzle," *Wall Street Journal*, Feb. 6, 1989, p. 1, who asserts that provisions like the prohibition on OMB review of agricultural marketing orders unconstitutionally inhibits the President's responsibility in Article II, Section 3, to "recommend" to Congress "such Measures as he shall judge necessary and expedient." By prohibiting the OMB to review marketing orders, Sidak argues, Congress is inhibiting the President's ability to carry out this recommendation function.

110 Neal E. Devins, "Regulation of Government Agencies Through Limitation Riders," *Duke Law Journal*, vol. 1987 (June 1987), pp. 456-500.

111 Ibid., pp. 458-459.

[112] Ibid., p. 472. See also Archie Parnell, *The Yale Law Journal*, vol. 89 (June 1980), pp. 1360-1394, where the author says (p. 1379) that "If the power to execute the laws means anything, it is that neither Congress nor individual congressmen may interfere with the executive decisions of administrative agencies as to how they interpret laws already in force."

[113] Peter Raven-Hansen and WilliamC.Banks, "Pullingthe Purse Strings of the Commander in Chief," *Virginia Law Review*, vol. 80 (May 1994), pp. 833-944.

[114] *Tennessee Valley Authority v. Hill*, 437 U.S. 153 (1978). In this case, the Tennessee Valley Authority asserted that Congress implicitly exempted actions related to the construction of the Tellico Dam project from the scope of the Endangered Species Act because it continued to appropriate funds for the construction of the dam.

[115] *Robertson v. Seattle Audubon Society*, 503 U.S. 429 (1992). See also U.S. General Accounting Office, *Principles of Federal Appropriations Law*, p. 2-32.

[116] John Shanahan and Mark Wilson, "Using Appropriations Riders to Curb Regulatory Excess," Heritage Issue Bulletin No. 218, October 16, 1995, available at [http://author.heritage.org/Research/Regulation/IB218.cfm]. According to its website, the Heritage Foundation's mission is "to formulate and promote conservative public policies based on the principles of free enterprise, limited government, individual freedom, traditional American values, and a strong national defense."

[117] William W. Buzbee, "Regulatory Underkill," available at [http://www.progressiveregulation.org/perspectives/underkill.cfm]. According to its website, the Center for Progressive Reform is "a 501(c)(3) nonprofit research and educational organization with a network of Member Scholars working to protect health, safety, and the environment through analysis and commentary."

[118] Richard J. Lazarus, "Congressional Descent," p. 637.

[119] Richard J. Lazarus, "Congressional Descent," p. 635.

In: Federal Rulemaking and Regulations
Editors: Paul Lee
ISBN: 978-1-60876-069-5
© 2010 Nova Science Publishers, Inc.

Chapter 3

CONGRESSIONAL REVIEW ACT: DISAPPROVAL OF RULES IN A SUBSEQUENT SESSION OF CONGRESS

Curtis W. Copeland and Richard S. Beth

SUMMARY

The Congressional Review Act ("CRA," 5 U.S.C. §§801-808) established a special set of expedited or "fast track" legislative procedures, primarily in the Senate, through which Congress may enact joint resolutions disapproving agencies' final rules. Members of Congress have 60 "days of continuous session" to introduce a resolution of disapproval after a rule has been submitted to Congress or published in the *Federal Register*, and the Senate has 60 "session days" to use CRA expedited procedures. Although the CRA was considered a reassertion of congressional authority over rulemaking agencies, only one rule has been disapproved using its procedures, and that reversal was the result of a specific set of circumstances created by a transition in party control of the presidency.

The CRA also indicates that if a rule is submitted to Congress less than 60 session days in the Senate or 60 legislative days in the House of Representatives before Congress adjourns a session *sine die*, then the rule is carried over to the next session of Congress and treated as if it had been submitted to Congress or published in the *Federal Register* on the 15th legislative day (House) or session day (Senate). This restart of the CRA process in a new session of Congress occurs even if no joint resolution of disapproval had been introduced regarding the rule during the preceding session of Congress.

A review of the House and Senate calendars from the first session of the 100th Congress to the first session of the 110th Congress indicates that the date triggering the carryover provisions of the CRA (i.e., the date after which less than 60 legislative or session days remained in a session) has usually been determined by the House of Representatives, and that the date was almost always earlier in second sessions of Congress (during which congressional elections are held) than in first sessions. The median date after which the "carryover periods" began for all sessions during this period was June 25, and the median for all second sessions was June 9. Since the CRA was enacted in March 1996, the median starting point for these carryover periods during second sessions of Congress has been somewhat earlier — June 7.

At the conclusion of most recent presidential administrations, the volume of agency rulemaking has increased noticeably. In May 2008, the White House Chief of Staff generally required federal agencies to finalize all regulations to be issued during the Bush Administration by November 1, 2008. According to press accounts and other sources, federal agencies are planning to issue a number of significant final rules by the end of 2008. If any of these "midnight rules" are submitted within the "carryover period" of the second session of the 110th Congress, then they will be subject to the carryover provisions of the CRA.

INTRODUCTION

The Congressional Review Act ("CRA," 5 U.S.C. §§801-808) requires federal agencies to submit all of their final rules to both houses of Congress and the Government Accountability Office (GAO) before they can take effect. The act also establishes a special set of expedited or "fast track" legislative procedures, primarily in the Senate, through which Congress may enact joint resolutions disapproving agencies' final rules. Although the general powers of Congress permit it to overturn agency rules by legislation, the CRA is unique in permitting the use of expedited procedures for this purpose. If a rule is disapproved through the CRA procedures, the act specifies not only that the rule "shall not take effect" (or shall not continue, if it has already taken effect), but also that the rule may not be reissued in a "substantially" similar form without subsequent statutory authorization.[1]

The CRA was initially considered a reassertion of congressional authority over rulemaking agencies, but thus far it has had little direct effect on agency rules.[2] After enactment, a CRA joint resolution of disapproval must be presented to the President for signature or veto. Under most circumstances, it is likely that the President would veto the resolution to protect rules developed under his own administration, and it may also be difficult for Congress to muster the two-thirds vote in both houses needed to overturn the veto. Of the nearly 50,000 final rules that have been submitted to Congress since the legislation was enacted in March 1996, the CRA has been used to disapprove only one rule — the Occupational Safety and Health Administration's November 2000 final rule on ergonomics.[3]

The March 2001 rejection of the ergonomics rule was the result of a specific set of circumstances created by a transition in party control of the presidency. The majority party in both houses of Congress was the same as the party of the incoming President (George W. Bush). When the new Congress convened in 2001 and adopted a resolution disapproving the rule published under the outgoing President (William J. Clinton), the incoming President did not veto the resolution. Congress may be most able to use the CRA to disapprove rules in similar, transition-related circumstances.[4]

This chapter addresses some of the implications of the CRA with regard to agency rulemaking in the final months of a presidential administration. It first notes the practice of increased rulemaking activity during this period, and describes how this practice has been addressed by two White House memoranda issued during the current Bush Administration. The chapter then briefly identifies key elements of the complex set of time periods established by the CRA — elements that define points during the disapproval process at which various actions may occur. This discussion focuses on the CRA provisions for carrying over the disapproval process into a subsequent session of Congress, and indicates how rules submitted at the end of a Congress may be affected by these provisions. Then, the chapter identifies the dates in previous sessions of Congress after which rules have (since the enactment of the CRA) been subject to these carryover provisions, and identifies some of the rules that may be issued in the final months of the current Bush Administration.

BUSH ADMINISTRATION MEMORANDA REGARDING "MIDNIGHT" RULES

At the conclusion of most recent presidential administrations, the volume of agency rulemaking has increased noticeably—a phenomenon that has been characterized as "midnight rulemaking."[5] As one observer stated, putting rules into effect before the end of a presidency is "a way for an administration to have life after death,"[6] for the only way that a subsequent administration can change or eliminate the rule is by going back through the often lengthy rulemaking processes that are required by the Administrative Procedure Act (5 U.S.C. §551 et seq.) and various other statutes and executive orders.[7] The current Bush Administration has responded to this situation by delaying and ultimately reducing the volume of effective rules issued in the last months of the Clinton Administration, and by protecting rules issued in its own last months from the possibility of similarly being rendered ineffective.

Card Memorandum

During the final months of the Clinton Administration, federal agencies issued hundreds of final rules—a number of which were considered "major" under the CRA.[8] In response to this action, on January 20, 2001, the Chief of Staff and Assistant to the new President, Andrew H. Card, Jr., sent a memorandum to the heads of all executive departments and agencies generally directing them to (1) not send proposed or final regulations to the Office of the Federal Register (OFR), (2) withdraw regulations that had been sent to the OFR but not published in the *Federal Register*, and (3) postpone for 60 days the effective date of regulations that had been published in the *Federal Register* but had not yet taken effect.[9] The memorandum cited the desire to "ensure that the President's appointees have the opportunity to review any new or pending regulations." In 2002, GAO reported that 90 final rules had their effective dates delayed as a result of the Card memorandum, and 15 rules still had not taken effect one year after the memorandum was issued.[10]

Bolten Memorandum

The Bush Administration has also taken action in anticipation of possible "midnight rules" at the end of the current President's term. On May 9, 2008, White House Chief of Staff Joshua B. Bolten issued a memorandum to the heads of executive departments and agencies stating that the Administration needed to "resist the historical tendency of administrations to increase regulatory activity in their final months." Therefore, Bolten said that, except in "extraordinary circumstances, regulations to be finalized in this Administration should be proposed no later than June 1, 2008, and final regulations should be issued no later than November 1, 2008."[11] He also said that the Administrator of the Office of Information and Regulatory Affairs (OIRA) within the Office of Management and Budget would "coordinate an effort to complete Administration priorities in this final year," and the OIRA Administrator would "report on a regular basis regarding agency compliance with this memorandum."[12]

CRA Time Periods and Their Potential Effect on Rules Proposed Late in a Session

The CRA is a complex statute, and among the act's chief complexities is its use of at least four different ways to measure the passage of time, each for different purposes:

- *calendar days*;
- *days of continuous session*, which excludes all days when either the House of Representatives or the Senate is adjourned for more than three days;
- *session days*, which include only calendar days on which a chamber is in session; and
- *legislative days*, which end each time a chamber adjourns and begin each time it convenes after an adjournment.

The following sections describe how the CRA uses each of these measures of time, focusing especially on the way in which they affect Congress's ability to use the CRA disapproval process for rules submitted toward the end of a session of Congress, and especially toward the end of a presidential term.

Effective Dates

Section 801(a)(3) of the CRA generally requires that the effective dates of all "major" rules be delayed for 60 *calendar* days after the date they are provided to Congress or published in the *Federal Register*, whichever is later. This delay in the effective dates helps to ensure that Congress has an opportunity to review and, if necessary, disapprove these major rules before they take effect. All non-major rules are allowed to take effect as stipulated in the rules themselves.[13] Nevertheless, even if a rule has already taken effect, the CRA can still be used to disapprove it if time remains in the periods established for congressional proceedings.

Initiation and Action Periods

Section 802(a) of the CRA states that a joint resolution of disapproval may be introduced as soon as a rule is received by Congress, but the resolution must be introduced no later than 60 days after that date, "excluding days either House of Congress is adjourned for more than 3 days during a session of Congress." This 60 *days of continuous session* defines the "initiation period" for CRA resolutions of disapproval. For example, if the House of Representatives and the Senate adjourn on a Friday and both reconvene on the following Monday or Tuesday, the 60-day "clock" for the introduction of resolutions of disapproval continues to run throughout the weekend because neither house was out of session for more than three days. On the other hand, if the House is in recess for a month but the Senate continues in session, then the 60-day "clock" for this "initiation period" stops until the House comes back into session.

Once introduced, resolutions of disapproval are referred to the committees of jurisdiction in each house of Congress. The House of Representatives would consider the resolution under its general procedures, very likely as prescribed by a special rule reported from the Committee on Rules. In the Senate, however, if the committee has not reported a disapproval resolution within 20 *calendar* days after the regulation has been submitted and published, then the committee may be discharged of its responsibilities and the resolution placed on the Senate calendar if 30 Senators submit a petition to do so.

Once the Senate committee has reported or been discharged, the CRA makes consideration of the measure privileged, prohibits various other dilatory actions, disallows amendment, and limits floor debate to 10 hours. Section 802(e) of the CRA states that the Senate has 60 *session days* from the date a rule is submitted to Congress or published in the *Federal Register* to use these expedited procedures and act on a joint resolution of disapproval.[14] This "action period" for the Senate includes only the calendar days on which the Senate is actually in session, in contrast to the "days of continuous session" for the initiation period, which includes all days other than those when either house is in adjournment lasting more than three days. Because of this difference in which days are counted, the "action period" will normally last longer than the "initiation period."

Carryover Period

Section 801(d) of the CRA provides that, if Congress adjourns its annual session *sine die* less than 60 *legislative days* in the House of Representatives or 60 *session days* in the Senate after a rule is submitted to it, then the rule is subject, during the following session of Congress, to (1) a new initiation period in *both* chambers and (2) a new action period in the Senate.[15] The purpose of this provision is to ensure that *both* houses of Congress have sufficient time to consider disapproving rules submitted during this end-of-session "carryover period." In any given year, the carryover period begins after the 60th legislative day in the House or session day in the Senate before the *sine die* adjournment, whichever date is *earlier*. The renewal of the CRA process in the following session occurs even if no resolution to disapprove the rule had been introduced during the session when the rule was submitted.

For purposes of this new initiation period and Senate action period, a rule originally submitted during the carryover period of the previous session is treated as if it had published in the *Federal Register* on the 15th legislative day (House) or session day (Senate) after Congress reconvenes for the next session. In each chamber, resolutions of disapproval may be introduced at any point in the 60 days of continuous session of Congress that follow this date, and the Senate may act on the resolution during the 60 days of session that follow the same date.

STARTING POINTS FOR CRA CARRYOVER PERIODS

In light of the CRA's requirement that major rules be delayed for 60 calendar days, the May 2008 Bolten memorandum's requirement that final rules be published in the *Federal Register* by November 1, 2008, indicates that these rules will have taken effect before the 111th Congress begins and the next President takes office in January 2009. As a result, the Bolten memorandum may also have the effect of preventing the next presidential administration from doing what was done via the Card memorandum — directing federal agencies to extend the effective dates of any rules that had been published during the Bush Administration but had not taken effect (since the rules would have already taken effect by the time the next President takes office). However, many rules submitted before the Bolten memorandum deadline will remain subject to congressional disapproval in the 111th Congress because they will not have been submitted before the starting point of the carryover period, and because the CRA permits Congress to enact resolutions of disapproval regarding rules that have already taken effect.

Although the exact starting point for the CRA carryover period in the second session of the 110th Congress can be determined only after sine die adjournment has taken place, the likely date or range of dates may be illuminated by examining congressional activity in prior years. To identify these earlier starting points, CRS examined the calendars of the House and the Senate for all sessions of Congress during the previous 20 years (i.e., from the 100th Congress, which began in 1987, through the first session of the 110th Congress in 2007). Counting backwards from the end of each session, we determined the date after which there were either less than 60 days of session in the Senate or less than 60 legislative days in the House. Although some of these sessions of Congress predate the enactment of the CRA, the starting points for those sessions were included to better understand the trends in these dates.

Table 1 below presents these data. For each session of Congress, the earlier of the House or Senate starting point dates is shown in the table in **bold face**. Since the CRA was enacted in March 1996, any rule submitted after the specified date in that session was available for disapproval under the CRA process during the following session of Congress. As the table indicates, the starting points for the CRA carryover periods varied between the two houses of Congress in each session, and across the sessions within each chamber. The data also show the following:

- In all but two sessions of Congress during this period (i.e., the first and second sessions of the 101st Congress), the starting point date for the House of Representatives occurred earlier than the starting point date for the Senate. In every session since the CRA was enacted in March 1996, the House starting point has determined the relevant date for CRA carryovers to the next session of Congress.
- Across all of these sessions of Congress, the earliest starting point for the carryover period was May 12 (second session of the 108th Congress), and the latest date was September 9 (first session, 100th Congress). However, it has been unusual for the starting point to be before June or after July. The median relevant starting point (i.e., half occurring before, half after) for all of these sessions of Congress was June 25.
- The starting points for the CRA carryover periods were almost always earlier during the second sessions of Congress (i.e., during election years) than the starting points in the first sessions.[16] The median starting point during all second sessions was June 9; the median during first sessions was July 19. This difference in median starting points is explained by the fact that both houses often adjourn or recess just prior to and/or after congressional elections.
- Since the CRA was enacted in March 1996, the starting points for the carryover periods during second sessions of Congress have been even earlier than for the full period, ranging from May 12 to June 23, with the median starting point being June 7.

Any rule that was submitted to Congress after the relevant starting point date in any session since the CRA was enacted in March 1996 would not have had 60 days of session in both houses, and Congress' ability to introduce and act on CRA resolutions of disapproval regarding the rule carried over to the next session of Congress. A new initiation period and a new action period for the rule began on the 15th session (Senate) or legislative (House) day of that new session of Congress.

Table 1. Starting Points for "Carryover Periods" During the 100th Congress Through the First Session of the 110th Congress

Congress	Session	House of Representatives — 60th legislative day from the end of the session	Senate — 60th session day from the end of the session
100th	1st	**September 9, 1987**	September 10, 1987
	2nd	**June 9, 1988**	June 20, 1988
101st	1st	July 25, 1989	**July 24, 1989**
	2nd	July 11, 1990	**June 27, 1990**
102nd	1st	**July 17, 1991**	July 25, 1991
	2nd	**June 4, 1992**	June 10, 1992
103rd	1st	**July 19, 1993**	July 27, 1993
	2nd	**June 16, 1994**	June 30, 1994
104th	1st	**August 2, 1995**	September 25, 1995
	2nd	**May 28, 1996**	June 4, 1996
105th	1st	**June 25, 1997**	July 11, 1997
	2nd	**June 18, 1998**	June 26, 1998
106th	1st	**July 15, 1999**	July 21, 1999
	2nd	**June 22, 2000**	July 12, 2000
107th	1st	**July 30, 2001**	September 6, 2001
	2nd	**June 18, 2002**	July 10, 2002
108th	1st	**June 26, 2003**	July 28, 2003
	2nd	**May 12, 2004**	June 8, 2004
109th	1st	**July 19, 2005**	July 27, 2005
	2nd	**May 23, 2006**	June 15, 2006
110th	1st	**July 25, 2007**	September 10, 2007

Source: CRS analysis of House of Representatives and Senate *Calendars*.

Note: The earlier of the House or Senate dates within each session, set in **boldface**, determines the date after which submitted rules would be carried over to the next session of Congress under the CRA. Dates prior to the enactment of the CRA in March 1996 (i.e., prior to the second session of the 104th Congress) are included for illustration only.

Second Session of the 110th Congress

Whether the patterns discussed above will hold true in the second session of the 110th Congress is currently unclear. The targeted adjournment date in the House of Representatives is September 26, 2008, but no targeted adjournment has been set in the Senate. It is possible that the House and the Senate could have so many days in session late in the year that the starting point for the carryover period (determining which rules would be eligible for new CRA initiation and action periods in the 111th Congress) would fall later than any of the above dates. However, doing so would require both houses of Congress to be in session for more days at the end of the session than has occurred during the past 20 years.

FINAL RULES THAT MAY BE ISSUED LATE IN THE SECOND SESSION OF THE 110TH CONGRESS

Another way to understand the significance of the starting point dates for CRA carryover periods is to identify some of the rules that may be issued late in the second session of the 110th Congress (and that therefore may be subject to disapproval during the first session of the 111th Congress). According to press accounts and other sources, federal agencies are reportedly planning to make a number of controversial proposed rules final by the end of calendar year 2008,[17] including

- an Environmental Protection Agency (EPA) revision of the definition of "solid waste" that, if consistent with the October 2003 proposed rule, would exclude certain types of sludge and byproducts (referred to in the proposed rule as "hazardous secondary waste") from regulation under the Resource Conservation and Recovery Act.[18]
- a Department of Transportation (DOT) rule updating existing standards for roof-crush resistance in passenger vehicles. Several Members of Congress have criticized the August 2005 proposed rule, and after a June 4, 2008, Senate oversight hearing and a bipartisan letter from several Senators, DOT asked Congress to extend the statutory deadline for the issuance of the final rule until October 2008.[19]
- an EPA "new source review" rule that, if made final, would alter current requirements for when upgrades at older power plants would require the installation of modern anti-pollution equipment.[20] EPA said that the change would balance environmental protection with the "economic need of sources to use existing physical and operating capacity." However, environmental groups contend that the change

would weaken existing protections and is counter to a recent decision of the Supreme Court related to this issue.[21]

- an EPA rule that is expected to change how pollution levels are measured under certain parts of the Clean Air Act, and that some contend will change emissions standards for industrial facilities operating near national parks.[22]
- a National Park Service rule that, if consistent with the April 2008 proposal, would change the agency's current policy and permit state laws to determine whether concealed firearms could be carried in national parks.[23]
- a Department of Justice (DOJ) proposed rule that would "clarify and update" the policies governing criminal intelligence systems that receive federal funding, but that some contend would make it easier for state and local police to collect, share, and retain sensitive information about Americans, even when no underlying crime is suspected.[24]
- a National Highway Traffic Safety Administration rule on how automakers are to meet stricter fuel economy standards for cars and light trucks pursuant to the Energy Independence and Security Act of 2007, which requires the agency to raise fuel economy standards to a fleet wide average of at least 35 miles per gallon by 2020.[25]
- a Food and Drug Administration (FDA) rule that, if consistent with the proposal, would prohibit pharmaceutical companies and manufacturers of medical devices from changing the labeling of an approved drug, biologic, or medical device unless there is "evidence of a causal association" between the product and a safety concern.[26] Several committee and subcommittee chairmen in the House and Senate have written to FDA expressing concern that this standard, if made final, would "inevitably result in fewer company-initiated warnings."[27]
- an Employment Standards Administration (ESA) rule that, if made final, would change the implementation of the Family and Medical Leave Act of 1993.[28] ESA and others defended the rule at an April 2008 congressional hearing, while other participants in the hearing (including the chairwoman of the subcommittee) said it would make it more difficult for workers to exercise their rights under the act.[29] The proposed rule is expected to be made final in November 2008.
- a Department of the Interior (DOI) rule that, in the words of the proposal, requires that surface coal mining operations "minimize the

creation of excess spoil and the adverse environmental impacts of fills," but that some observers have said would allow deposits of waste mountaintop material within 100 feet of certain streams.[30]

- a proposed amendment to the Federal Acquisition Regulation to require certain contractors and subcontractors to use the E-Verify system to confirm that certain of their employees are eligible to work in the United States, but which the U.S. Chamber of Commerce and others said contravenes the intent of Congress and raises numerous practical difficulties.[31]
- a Housing and Urban Development (HUD) rule that would amend disclosure regulations under the Real Estate Settlement and Procedures Act (RESPA), and that some Members of Congress have requested that HUD withdraw.[32]
- a Department of Health and Human Services proposed rule that would protect medical providers' right to choose whether they would help perform abortions and other medical procedures, but that some have said could affect the ability of women to obtain certain forms of contraception and other health services.[33]
- a Department of Labor proposed rule that would change the way that occupational health risk assessments are conducted within the department. Legislation has been introduced in the 110th Congress (H.R. 6660) that would prohibit the issuance or enforcement of this rule.[34]
- a DOI proposed rule that would, among other things, give federal agencies greater responsibility in determining when and how their actions may affect species under the Endangered Species Act.[35] Several Members of Congress have expressed concerns about the draft rule, and congressional hearings are expected.[36]

Potential Effect of Carryover Period on Rules Issued Late in the Second Session of the 110th Congress

The foregoing information suggests the following observations:

- Federal departments and agencies are likely to issue a number of significant final rules during the last months of the current Bush

Administration, as has been done at the conclusion of most recent presidential administrations. Some Members of Congress have already expressed concerns about several of those Bush Administration "midnight" rules, should they be issued.

- All of the final rules that are submitted to Congress during the second session of the 110th Congress with less than 60 session days left in the Senate or less than 60 legislative days left in the House will be automatically be carried over to the 111th Congress. Starting on the 15th legislative day (House) or session day (Senate) of the new session, each rule will have a new CRA initiation period (60 days of continuous session of Congress) and a new action period in the Senate (60 days of session) for resolutions of disapproval.
- House and Senate calendars from previous sessions of Congress, particularly sessions that occurred during election years (second sessions), suggest that any final rule submitted to Congress after June 2008 may be carried over to the first session of the 111th Congress, and may be subject to a resolution of disapproval during that session. However, the starting point for the carryover period could slip to late September or early October if an unprecedented level of congressional activity occurs late the session.
- Expedited procedures in the Senate and special rules in the House can help ensure that such resolutions are acted upon in each chamber. However, the enactment of any resolution of disapproval will still depend heavily on the action of the new President. If the resolution of disapproval is vetoed, it will require a two-thirds vote in both houses of Congress for the targeted rule to be rejected.

The memorandum issued by White House Chief of Staff Bolten directing agencies to issue most final rules by November 1, 2008, would, if fully implemented, ensure that most of the rules — even those considered "major" under the CRA and whose effective dates must be delayed for 60 days — would take effect before the 111th Congress begins and the next President takes office in January 2009. As noted earlier in this report, the Bolten memorandum may also have the effect of preventing the next presidential administration from doing what was done via the Card memorandum — directing federal agencies to extend the effective dates of any rules that had been published during the Bush Administration but had not taken effect (since the rules would have already taken effect by the time the next President takes office). In addition, some believe that the memorandum may be cited as a reason why certain rules will not be issued before the end of the Bush Administration.[37]

However, as also pointed out earlier, the Bolten memorandum will have no impact on the next Congress's ability to overturn agency rules that are submitted within the last 60 legislative or session days in each house of Congress, since the CRA permits Congress to enact resolutions of disapproval regarding rules that have already taken effect. Also, once a rule is disapproved, the CRA prevents the agency from proposing a substantially similar rule without subsequent statutory authorization.

Even without the CRA, though, Congress can stop rulemaking in other ways. For example, each year, Congress includes provisions in appropriations legislation prohibiting rulemaking within particular policy areas, preventing particular proposed rules from becoming final, and prohibiting or affecting the implementation or enforcement of rules.[38] However, unlike disapprovals under the CRA, the regulatory requirements that have been put into effect are not rescinded, and the agency is not prohibited from issuing a substantially similar regulation in the future.

End Notes

[1] It is unclear how "substantially" similar a rule must be to be covered by this prohibition. For as discussion of this issue, see CRS Report RL30116, Congressional Review of Agency Rulemaking: An Update and Assessment of the Congressional Review Act After a Decade, by Morton Rosenberg.

[2] See CRS Report RL30116, Congressional Review of Agency Rulemaking: An Update and Assessment of the Congressional Review Act After a Decade, by Morton Rosenberg, for a discussion of how the CRA has been implemented.

[3] U.S. Department of Labor, Occupational Safety and Health Administration, "Ergonomics Program," 65 Federal Register 68261, November 14, 2000. Although the CRA has been used to disapprove only one rule, it may have other, less direct or discernable effects (e.g., keeping Congress informed about agency rulemaking and preventing the publication of rules that may be disapproved).

[4] See, for example, Susan E. Dudley, "Reversing Midnight Regulations," Regulation, vol. 24 (Spring 2001), p. 9, who noted that the "veto threat is diminished [after a transition], since the president whose administration issued the regulations is no longer in office." See also testimony of Curtis W. Copeland, in U.S. Congress, House Committee on Government Reform, Subcommittee on Regulatory Affairs, The Effectiveness of Federal Regulatory Reform Initiatives, 109th Cong., 1st sess., July 27, 2005, p. 13. See CRS Report RL30116, Congressional Review of Agency Rulemaking: An Update and Assessment of the Congressional Review Act After a Decade, by Morton Rosenberg, for a description of this and several other possible factors affecting the law's use.

[5] See, for example, Jay Cochran, III, "The Cinderella Constraint: Why Regulations Increase Significantly During Post-Election Quarters," Mercatus Center, George Mason University, March 8, 2001. Cochran determined that, in election years since 1948 with complete

executive branch turnover, the volume of rulemaking during the post-election quarter (measured by the number of pages in the Federal Register) increased by an average of 27% when compared to the same periods in non-election years. See also Jason M. Loring and Liam R. Roth, "After Midnight: The Durability of the 'Midnight' Regulations Passed by the Two Previous Outgoing Administrations," Wake Forest Law Review, vol. 40 (2005), pp. 1441-1465, which indicated that the George H.W. Bush and William J. Clinton Administrations issued numerous "midnight rules."

[6] John M. Broder, "A Legacy Bush Can Control," New York Times, September 9, 2007, p. 4.1, quoting Phillip Clapp, president of the National Environmental Trust.

[7] For more information on these statutes and executive orders, see CRS Report RL32240, The Federal Rulemaking Process: An Overview, by Curtis W. Copeland.

[8] The CRA defines a rule as "major" if, among other things, it has a $100 million impact on the economy. According to GAO, federal agencies issue an average of about 60 major rules each year. Major rules issued by federal agencies in January 2001 included those (1) prohibiting road construction and harvesting in certain roadless areas of National Forest Service land, (2) establishing energy conservation standards for clothes washers and central air conditioners, (3) implementing requirements for the State Children's Health Insurance Program, (4) restricting use of snowmobiles in Yellowstone and Grand Teton National Parks, (5) setting maximum contaminant levels for arsenic in community water systems.

[9] See [http://www.whitehouse.gov/omb/inforeg/regreview_plan.pdf] for a copy of this memorandum. Federal courts have generally considered any delay in a rule's effective date to require notice and comment rulemaking. See Natural Resources Defense Council, Inc. v. EPA, 683 F.2d 752, 761 (3d Cir. 1982); and Council of the Southern Mountains v. Donovan, 653 F.2d 573 (D.C. Cir. 1981). Although some agencies used notice and comment rulemaking to delay effective dates pursuant to the Card memorandum, most agencies simply published the changes and invoked the Administrative Procedure Act's "good cause" exception. One such action was rejected by the court. See Natural Resources Defense Council v. Abraham, 355 F.3d 179, 204-05 (2d Cir 2004).

[10] U.S. General Accounting Office, Regulatory Review: Delay of Effective Dates of Final Rules Subject to the Administration's January 20, 2001, Memorandum, GAO-02-370R, February 15, 2002.

[11] Between June 1 and August 8, 2008, however, federal agencies sent more than 40 proposed rules to the Office of Management and Budget for review prior to publication in the Federal Register. Ralph Lindeman, "Agencies Continue to Proposed New Rules After White House-Imposed June Deadline," BNA Daily Report for Executives, August 11, 2008, p. A-9.

[12] OIRA reviews all significant rules before they are published in the Federal Register, and is the President's chief representative in the rulemaking process. See CRS Report RL32397, Federal Rulemaking: The Role of the Office of Information and Regulatory Affairs, by Curtis W. Copeland.

[13] The Administrative Procedure Act (5 U.S.C. §553(d)) generally requires agencies to publish their rules 30 days before their effective dates, but exempts certain categories of rules from this requirement (e.g., interpretative rules and statements of policy), and allows agencies to make rules effective in less than 30 days for "good cause." Also, the CRA (5 U.S.C. §808) states that "(1) any rule that establishes, modifies, opens, closes, or conducts a regulatory program for a commercial, recreational, or subsistence activity related to hunting, fishing, or camping, or (2) any rule which an agency for good cause finds (and incorporates the finding and a brief statement of reasons therefore in the rule issued) that notice and public procedure thereon are impracticable, unnecessary, or contrary to the public interest, shall take effect at such time as the Federal agency promulgating the rule determines."

[14] The action period applies only to initial consideration in the Senate because the CRA establishes no expedited procedures for initial House consideration.

[15] It is typically appropriate that the House component of the carryover period is measured in legislative days, because the House usually adjourns at the end of each daily session, so that

its legislative days and session days generally coincide. The Senate, on the other hand, sometimes continues a single legislative day through several actual days of session by using daily recesses rather than adjourning. For this reason , it is generally appropriate that the Senate component of the "carryover period" is measured directly by days of session.

[16] The starting points for carryover periods in second sessions most commonly occurred in June, with the dates ranging from May 12 to June 27. The starting points in first sessions most commonly occurred in July, with the dates ranging from June 25 to September 9.

[17] A number of these rules were identified in Ralph Lindeman, "White House Deadline on Agency Rulemaking May See Significant Slippage, Experts Say," BNA Daily Report for Executives, June 6, 2008, p. C-1; and Cindy Skrzycki, "Bush Wants Sun to Set on Midnight Regulations," Washington Post, June 3, 2008, p. D-3.

[18] For the proposed rule, see U.S. Environmental Protection Agency, "Revisions to the Definition of Solid Waste," 68 Federal Register 61557, October 28, 2003. The final rule has been under review at OIRA since April 2008. For more information on this rule and the perspectives of various parties, see Charlotte E. Tucker, "EPA Completing Last Steps for Regulation to Redefine Waste to Encourage Recycling," BNA Daily Report for Executives, July 17, 2008, p. C-1.

[19] "DOT Secretary Peters Seeks Extension to Oct. 1 of Roof Crush Final Rule Deadline," BNA Daily Report for Executives, July 2, 2008, p. A-12.

[20] For the proposed rule, see U.S. Environmental Protection Agency, "Supplemental Notice of Proposed Rulemaking for Prevention of Significant Deterioration and Nonattainment New Source Review: Emission Increases for Electric Generating Units," 72 Federal Register 26201, May 8, 2007.

[21] American Lung Association, EarthJustice, Environmental Defense, Natural Resources Defense Council, and Sierra Club; "Comments on EPA's Proposed 'Supplemental Notice of Proposed Rulemaking for Prevention of Significant Deterioration and Nonattainment New Source Review: Emission Increases for Electric Generating Units,'" available at [http://www.regulations.gov/fdmspublic/component/main?main=DocumentDetail&o=09 00006480273d62].

[22] Juliet Eilperin, "Clean-Air Rules Protecting Parks Set to Be Eased," Washington Post, May 16, 2008, p. A-1; and Mark Clayton, "Why National Parks, Coal-Fired Power Plants May Be Neighbors," Christian Science Monitor, April 24, 2008, p. 13. For the proposed rule, see U.S. Environmental Protection Agency, "Prevention of Significant Deterioration New Source Review: Refinement of Increment Modeling Procedures," 72 Federal Register 31371, June 6, 2007. In an April 2008 letter responding to questions posed by the Chairman of the House Committee on Oversight and Government Reform, EPA said it was "unable to conclusively confirm or deny" suggestions from the National Park Service that the proposed rule would make it easier to build power plants near national parks. See [http://oversight.house.gov/documents/20080514180808.pdf].

[23] U.S. Department of the Interior, National Park Service, "General Regulations for Areas Administered by the National Park Service and the Fish and Wildlife Service," 73 Federal Register 2338, April 30, 2008.

[24] For the proposed rule, see U.S. Department of Justice, Office of Justice Programs, "Criminal Intelligence Systems Operating Procedures," 73 Federal Register 44673, July 31, 2008. For a characterization of the rule, see Spencer S. Hsu and Carrie Johnson, "U.S. May Ease Police Spy Rules," Washington Post, August 16, 2008, p. A-1.

[25] For the proposed rule, see U.S. Department of Transportation, National Highway Traffic Safety Administration, "Average Fuel Economy Standards, Passenger Cars and Light Trucks; Model Years 2011-2015," 73 Federal Register 24351, May 2, 2008.

[26] U.S. Department of Health and Human Services, Food and Drug Administration, "Supplemental Applications Proposing Labeling Changes for Approved Drugs, Biologics, and Medical Devices," 73 Federal Register 2848, January 16, 2008.

[27] See [http://www.speaker.gov/blog/?p=1068] for a copy of this letter and related materials.

[28] For the proposed rule, see U.S. Department of Labor, Employment Standards Administration, "The Family and Medical Leave Act of 1993," 73 Federal Register 7875, February 11, 2008.

[29] Derrick Cain, "Witnesses Say DOL Should Scrap FMLA Rule, Call on Congress to Expand Leave Benefits," BNA Daily Labor Report, April 11, 2008, p. A-1.

[30] For the proposed rule, see U.S. Department of the Interior, Office of Surface Mining Reclamation and Enforcement, "Excess Spoil, Coal Mine Waste, and Buffers for Waters of the United States," 72 Federal Register 48889, August 24, 2007. For characterizations of the rule, see John M. Broder, "Rule to Expand Mountaintop Coal Mining," New York Times, August 23, 2007, p. A-1.

[31] For the proposed rule, see U.S. Department of Defense, General Services Administration, and National Aeronautics and Space Administration, "Federal Acquisition Regulation; FAR Case 2007-013, Employment Eligibility Verification," 73 Federal Register 33374, June 12, 2008. See [http://www.uschamber.com/assets/labor/080811_fed_Ks.pdf] for the views of the U.S. Chamber of Commerce. The day after this proposed rule was published, the Department of Homeland Security announced it was requiring its contractors to use the Everify program. U.S. Department of Homeland Security, Office of the Secretary, "Designation of the Electronic Employment Eligibility Verification System Under Executive Order 12989, as Amended by the Executive Order Entitled 'Amending Executive Order 12989, as Amended' of June 6, 2008," 73 Federal Register 33837, June 13, 2008.

[32] Mike Ferullo, "House Members Circulate Letter to HUD Urging Withdrawal of Proposed RESPA Rule," BNA Daily Report for Executives, July 22, 2008, p. A-28. For the proposed rule, see U.S. Department of Housing and Urban Development, "Real Estate Settlement Procedures Act (RESPA): Proposed Rule to Simplify and Improve the Process of Obtaining Mortgages and Reduce Consumer Settlement Costs," 73 Federal Register 14029, March 14, 2008.

[33] See [http://www.hhs.gov/news/press/2008pres/08/20080821reg.pdf] for a copy of the proposed rule. For characterizations of the rule, see Rob Stein, "Protections Set for Antiabortion Health Workers," Washington Post, August 22, 2008, p. A-1; and Robert Pear, "Abortion Proposal Sets Condition on Aid," New York Times, July 15, 2008, p. A-1.

[34] For the proposed rule, see U.S. Department of Labor, Office of the Secretary, "Requirements for DOL Agencies' Assessment of Occupational Health Risks," 73 Federal Register 50909, August 29, 2008. For characterizations of the rule, see Carol D. Leonnig, "U.S. Rushes to Change Workplace Toxin Rules," Washington Post, July 23, 2008, p. A-1; and Gayle Cinquegrani, "Miller Introduces House Bill to Prohibit DOL 'Secret Rule' on Workplace Toxin Exposure," BNA Daily Report for Executives, August 1, 2008, p. A-7. On August 18, 2008, a Washington Post editorial recommended that the Department of Labor withdraw its proposed rule ("A Toxic Proposal: The Labor Department Politicizes a Regulation of Workplace Health," Washington Post, August 18, 2008, p. A-10).

[35] For the proposed rule, see U.S. Department of the Interior, Fish and Wildlife Service, and U.S. Department of Commerce, National Oceanic and Atmospheric Administration, National Marine Fisheries Service, "Interagency Cooperation Under the Endangered Species Act," 73 Federal Register 47868, August 15, 2008. See also Juliet Eilperin, "Endangered Species Act Changes Give Agencies More Say," Washington Post, August 12, 2008, p. A-1.

[36] For in-depth information about this rule, see CRS Report RL34641, Proposed Changes to Regulations Governing Consultation Under the Endangered Species Act (ESA), by Kristina Alexander and M. Lynne Corn.

[37] Charlie Savage and Robert Pear, "Administration Moves to Avert a Late Rules Rush," New York Times, May 31, 2008, p. A-1.

[38] CRS Report RL34354, Congressional Influences on Rulemaking Through Appropriations Provisions, by Curtis W. Copeland.

In: Federal Rulemaking and Regulations
Editors: Paul Lee
ISBN: 978-1-60876-069-5
© 2010 Nova Science Publishers, Inc.

Chapter 4

THE FEDERAL RULEMAKING PROCESS: AN OVERVIEW

Curtis W. Copeland

SUMMARY

Federal regulation, like taxing and spending, is one of the basic tools of government used to implement public policy. Although not as frequently examined as congressional or presidential policy making, the process of developing and framing rules is viewed by some as central to the definition and implementation of public policy in the United States. Regulations generally start with an act of Congress, and are the means by which statutes are implemented and specific requirements are established. The terms "rule" or "regulation" are often used interchangeably in discussions of the federal regulatory process. The Administrative Procedure Act of 1946 defines a *rule* as "the whole or part of an agency statement of general or particular applicability and future effect designed to implement, interpret, or prescribe law or policy." The procedures that federal agencies are required to follow in writing regulations is called the rulemaking process, and are the subject of this chapter.

During the past 60 to 65 years, Congress and various Presidents have developed an elaborate set of procedures and requirements to guide the federal rulemaking process, often with the implicit or explicit goal of reducing the amount of regulatory burden placed on the public. Statutory rulemaking requirements applicable to a wide range of agencies include the Administrative Procedure Act, the Regulatory Flexibility Act, the Paperwork Reduction Act, the Unfunded Mandates Reform Act, and the Information Quality Act. These and other cross-cutting rulemaking requirements often require some type of analysis on the part of the rulemaking agency before issuing a covered rule, but also often give agencies substantial discretion regarding whether the requirements are applicable. Other statutorily-based rulemaking requirements are contained in agency- or program-specific laws, which provide varying levels of discretion regarding the substance of agencies' rules and may impose (or exclude) additional analytical or procedural requirements. The most important of the current set of presidential rulemaking requirements are in Executive Order 12866, which establishes presidential review of covered agencies' rulemaking within the Office of Management and Budget's Office of Information and Regulatory Affairs (OIRA). The executive order requires covered agencies to submit their significant rules to OIRA for review before they become final, and requires those rules to meet certain minimal standards. Other executive orders and presidential directives delineate other specific rulemaking requirements incumbent on covered agencies. However, these requirements also often provide substantial discretion to agencies regarding whether, and if so how, they are applied.

The purpose of this chapter is to provide Congress with an overview of the federal rulemaking process and a brief discussion of the major laws and executive orders that prescribe the procedures agencies are to apply when promulgating regulations. This report will be updated when new requirements are put in place or when the requirements in this report change.

INTRODUCTION

Federal regulation, like taxing and spending, is one of the basic tools of government used to implement public policy. In fact, the development and framing of a rule has been described as "the climactic act of the policy making process."[1] Another observer described the rulemaking process as "absolutely central to the definition and implementation of public policy in the United States," and said that "no significant attempt to alter the direction of a public program can succeed without effective management of the rulemaking process."[2] Regulations generally start with an act of Congress, and are the means by which statutes are implemented and specific requirements are established. Federal agencies issue more than 4,000 final rules each year on topics ranging from the timing of bridge openings to the permissible levels of arsenic and other contaminants in drinking water. The costs and benefits associated with all federal regulations have been a subject of great controversy, with the costs estimated in the hundreds of billions of dollars and the benefits estimates even higher. The costs federal regulations impose on regulated entities to accomplish policy goals are not reflected in the federal budget process, and some view these off- budget regulatory costs as greater than all federal domestic discretionary spending. Estimates of the benefits of federal regulations are even higher.

The terms "rule" or "regulation" are often used interchangeably in discussions of the federal regulatory process. The Administrative Procedure Act (APA) of 1946 defines a rule as "the whole or part of an agency statement of general or particular applicability and future effect designed to implement, interpret, or prescribe law or policy."[3] The process by which federal agencies develop, amend, or repeal rules is called "rulemaking," and is the subject of this chapter.

Figure 1 illustrates in a general manner the process that most federal agencies are generally required to follow in writing or revising a significant rule. However, we should be quick to point out that some aspects of **Figure 1** do not apply to all rulemaking. For example, as discussed later in this chapter, an agency may, in certain circumstances, issue a final rule without issuing a notice of proposed rulemaking, thereby skipping several steps depicted in the figure. On the other hand, some rules may be published for public comment more than once. Also, independent regulatory agencies[4] are not required to submit their rules to the Office of Management and Budget's (OMB) Office of Information and Regulatory Affairs (OIRA) for review, and no agency is required to do so for rules that are not "significant."

Note at the top of **Figure 1** that the rulemaking process begins when Congress passes a statute either requiring or authorizing an agency to write and issue certain types of regulations. An initiating event (e.g., a recommendation from an outside body or a catastrophic accident) can prompt either legislation or regulation (where regulatory action has already been authorized). For example, in response to lethal chemical releases by plants in Bhopal, India, and West Virginia, Congress enacted section 313 of the Emergency Planning and Community Right-to-Know Act of 1986 (42 U.S.C. §§1 1001-11050, 11023).

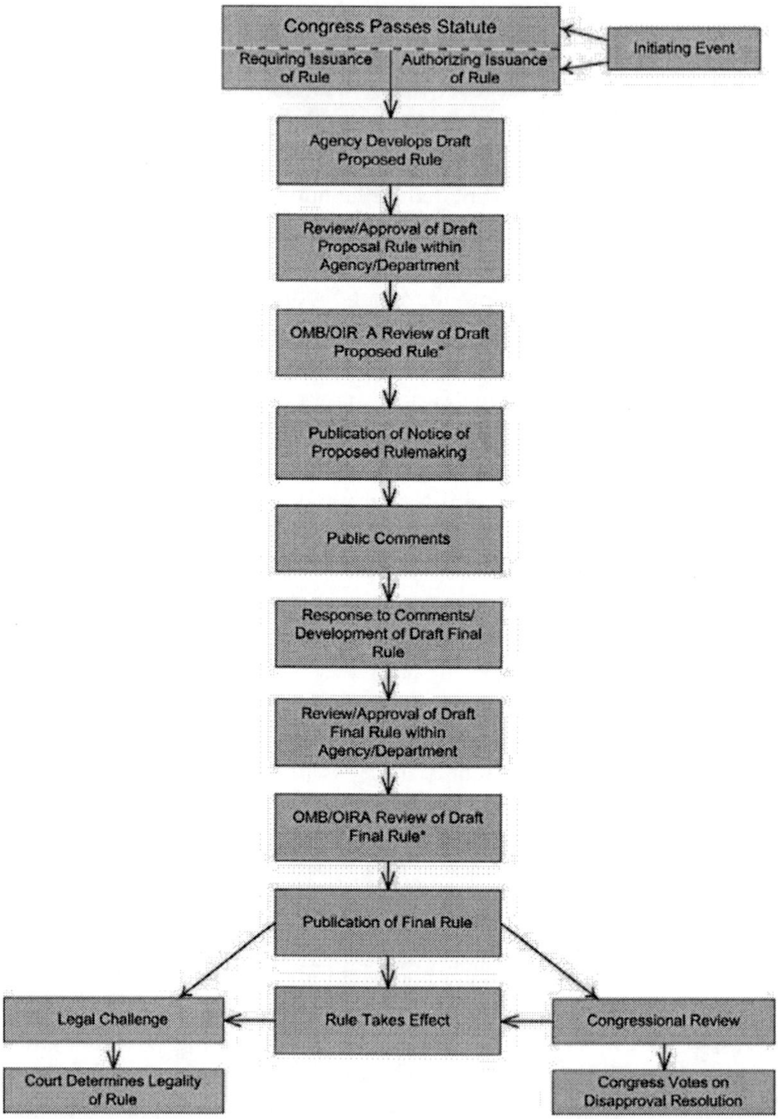

Source: CRS.

* The Office of Management and Budget's (OMB) office of Information and Regulatory Affairs (OIRA) reviews only significant rules, and does not review any rules submitted by independent regulatory agencies.

Figure 1. Federal Rulemaking Process

The act required the owners and operators of certain types of facilities to report the amounts of various toxic chemicals that the facilities release to the environment above certain thresholds, and requires the Environmental Protection Agency (EPA) to make this information available to the public. EPA subsequently issued detailed regulations implementing these requirements and, using the authority provided to it through the statute, has required reporting for more than 300 toxic substances in addition to those delineated in the law.

As this example illustrates, the authority to regulate rests with Congress, and is delegated, through law, to an agency. The statutory basis for a regulation can vary greatly in terms of its specificity, from (1) very broad grants of authority that state only the general intent of the legislation and leave agencies with a great deal of discretion as to how that intent should be implemented, to (2) very specific requirements delineating exactly what regulatory agencies should do and how they should take action. Note also in **Figure 1** the roles that Congress and the courts can play at the end of the rulemaking process, which may result in a rule being returned to an earlier point in the process or being vacated by the reviewing body. Congress may also play a role at other stages in the process through its oversight and appropriations responsibilities.

Implicit within the steps depicted in **Figure 1** is an elaborate set of procedures and requirements that Congress and various Presidents have developed during the past 60 to 65 years to guide the federal rulemaking process. Some of these rulemaking requirements apply to virtually all federal agencies, some apply only to certain types of agencies, and others are agency-specific. Collectively, these rulemaking provisions are voluminous and require a wide range of procedural, consultative, and analytical actions on the part of rulemaking agencies. Some observers contend that the requirements have resulted in the "ossification" of the rulemaking process, causing agencies to take years to develop final rules.[5] For example, the National Advisory Committee on Occupational Safety and Health noted that it takes the Occupational Safety and Health Administration (OSHA) within the Department of Labor an average of 10 years to develop and promulgate a health or safety standard.[6] On the other hand, while these congressional and presidential rulemaking requirements are numerous, it is not clear whether they or some other factors (e.g., lack of data, congressionally imposed delays, court challenges, etc.) are the primary cause of the long time-frames that are sometimes required to develop and publish final rules.

STATUTORY RULEMAKING REQUIREMENTS

Statutory rulemaking requirements can be generally categorized into two groups—those that are specific to an individual agency or program and those that are more cross-cutting in nature, and therefore applicable to a wider range of agencies or programs. Agency- or program-specific rulemaking requirements may be in authorizing or appropriating statutes, and can have a significant or even determinative effect on an agency's rules and rulemaking procedures. As noted previously, these statutes sometimes specifically delineate what the agency's rules should require. For example, the Employee Retirement Income Security Act (29 U.S.C. § 1001 *et seq.*) gives the Pension Benefit Guaranty Corporation no discretion in drafting rules that establish minimum pension insurance premium rates, specifying to the dollar what those rates should be.[7] Also, for a number of years the Department of Transportation (DOT) concluded that it had no discretion in setting the average fuel economy standards for light trucks, and was required to keep the standard at 20.7 miles per gallon.[8] Agency-specific statutes may also impose specific procedural requirements on their rulemaking processes (e.g., the conduct of public hearings, the publication of a notice of proposed rulemaking by a particular date, or the coordination of rulemaking with another agency). In other cases, though, the statutes give rulemaking agencies substantial discretion in how rules are developed and what they require. For example, the Agricultural Adjustment Act provides a broad grant of rulemaking authority to the Secretary of Agriculture, stating only that agricultural marketing should be "orderly" but providing little guidance regarding which crops should have marketing orders or how to apportion the market among growers.[9]

Agency rulemaking is also often significantly influenced by court decisions interpreting these agency- or program-specific statutory requirements. For example, in 1980 the Supreme Court ruled that, before promulgating new health standards, OSHA must demonstrate that the particular chemical to be regulated poses a "significant risk" under workplace conditions permitted by current regulations.[10] The court also said that OSHA must demonstrate that the new limit OSHA proposes will substantially reduce that risk. This decision effectively requires OSHA to evaluate the risks associated with exposure to a chemical and to determine that these risks are "significant" before issuing a regulatory standard. Other court decisions have required OSHA rulemaking to demonstrate the technical and economic feasibility of its requirements.[11] Still other decisions have required agencies to permit meaningful public participation in rulemaking and to fully explain what they considered and why they did and did not take particular actions.[12]

The following discussion of statutory rulemaking requirements focuses solely on the cross-cutting requirements that are applicable to more than one agency. The discussion provides descriptions of some of the major rulemaking-related statutes and is not intended to be a catalogue of all such requirements. Some of these rulemaking requirements have been in place for more than 70 years, but most have been implemented within the past 25 years. Some of these statutory requirements apply to Cabinet departments and independent agencies; others apply to those agencies as well as the independent regulatory agencies.

Federal Register Act

With the surge of New Deal legislation enacted in the 1930s, Congress made federal agencies responsible for issuing detailed regulations on a variety of complex social and economic issues. However, no central regulatory publication system existed, so there was no efficient way for citizens to know about regulations that affected them. Therefore, Congress enacted the Federal Register Act, which became law in July 1935 (44 U.S.C. Chapter 15). The act established a uniform system for handling agency regulations by requiring (1) the filing of documents with the Office of the Federal Register, (2) the placement of documents on public inspection, (3) publication of the documents in the *Federal Register*, and (4) (after a 1937 amendment) permanent codification of rules in the *Code of Federal Regulations*. Publication of a rule in the *Federal Register* provides official notice of its existence and contents. Other documents that are generally published in the Federal Register include presidential proclamations and executive orders, notices, and documents that the President or Congress require to be published.

Regulations for carrying out the Federal Register Act deal with, among other things, the format and distribution of the *Federal Register* and how documents are prepared, transmitted, and processed.[13] The Office of the Federal Register is responsible for printing and distributing the Federal Register, and the Office has published a guide and a drafting handbook explaining how Federal Register documents are to be prepared. The Federal Register is published each business day, and is now available electronically.[14]

Administrative Procedure Act

The most long-standing and broadly applicable federal rulemaking requirements are in the Administrative Procedure Act (APA) of 1946 (5 U.S.C. §551 *et seq*.). The APA was written to bring regularity and predictability to agency decisionmaking, and provides for both formal and informal rulemaking. Formal rulemaking is used in ratemaking proceedings and in certain other cases when rules are required by statute to be made "on the record" after an opportunity for a trial-type agency hearing. However, few statutes require such on-the-record hearings. Informal rulemaking, also known as "notice and comment" rulemaking, is used much more frequently, and is the focus of this section.

In informal rulemaking, the APA generally requires that agencies (Cabinet departments and independent agencies as well as independent regulatory agencies) publish a notice of proposed rulemaking (NPRM) in the *Federal Register*.[15] The notice must contain (1) a statement of the time, place, and nature of public rulemaking proceedings; (2) reference to the legal authority under which the rule is proposed; and (3) either the terms or substance of the proposed rule or a description of the subjects and issues involved. After giving "interested persons" an opportunity to comment on the proposed rule, and after considering the public comments, the agency may then publish the final rule, incorporating a general statement of its basis and purpose. Although the APA does not specify the length of this public comment period, agencies commonly allow at least 30 days.[16] Public comments as well as other supporting materials (e.g., hearing records or agency regulatory studies but generally not internal memoranda) are placed in a rulemaking "docket"which must be available for public inspection. Finally, the APA states that the final rule cannot become effective until at least 30 days after its publication unless (1) the rule grants or recognizes an exemption or relieves a restriction, (2) the rule is an interpretative rule or a statement of policy, or (3) the agency determines that the rule should take effect sooner for good cause, and publishes that determination with the rule.

The final rule cannot adopt a provision if the NPRM did not clearly provide notice to the public that the agency was considering adopting it. If challenged in court under the APA, an agency rulemaking can be held unlawful or set aside if it is found to be "arbitrary, capricious, an abuse of discretion, or otherwise not in accordance with the law."[17] The court can also "compel agency action unlawfully withheld or unreasonably delayed."

Amendment or revocation of an existing rule generally requires the responsible agency to issue a new rule through the APA process.

Exceptions to the APA Notice Requirement

Although the APA generally requires agencies to publish NPRMs before promulgating a final rule, the act provides exceptions to this requirement. For example, the APA states that the notice and comment procedures generally do not apply when an agency finds, for "good cause," that those procedures are "impracticable, unnecessary, or contrary to the public interest." When agencies use the good cause exception, the act requires that they explicitly say so and provide a rationale for the exception's use when the rule is published in the *Federal Register*. The APA also provides explicit exceptions to the NPRM requirement for certain categories of regulatory actions, such as rules dealing with military or foreign affairs; agency management or personnel; or public property, loans, grants, benefits, or contracts. Further, the APA says that the NPRM requirements do not apply to interpretative rules; general statements of policy; or rules of agency organization, procedure, or practice.[18] However, these rules do have to be published in the *Federal Register*.

The legislative history of the APA makes it clear that Congress did not believe that the act's good cause exception to the notice and comment requirements should be an "escape clause." According to the Senate committee's report accompanying the APA, a "true and supported or supportable finding of necessity or emergency must be made and published" when the agency uses the good cause exception.[19] The legislative history also indicates that Congress envisioned agencies using the notice and comment procedures even in some cases in which the APA's exceptions applied.

A federal agency's invocation of the good cause exception (or other exceptions to notice and comment procedures) is subject to judicial review. After having reviewed the totality of circumstances, the courts can and sometimes do determine that an agency's reliance on the good cause exception was not authorized under the APA.[20] The case law has generally reinforced the view that the good cause exception should be "narrowly construed."[21]

Two procedures for noncontroversial and expedited rulemaking were designed not to involve NPRMs. "Direct final" rulemaking involves agency publication of a rule in the Federal Register with a statement that the rule will be effective on a particular date unless an adverse comment is received within a specified period of time (e.g., 30 days). However, if an adverse comment is filed, the direct final rule is withdrawn and the agency may publish the rule as a proposed rule under normal NPRM procedures. Direct final rulemaking can be viewed as a particular application of the APA's good cause exception in which agencies claim NPRMs are "unnecessary."[22] Both Vice President Gore's National Performance Review and the Administrative Conference of the United States encouraged agencies to use direct final rulemaking for noncontroversial rules.[23]

The Administrative Conference also endorsed the use of what is known as "interim final" rulemaking, in which an agency issues a final rule without an NPRM that is generally effective immediately, but with a post-promulgation opportunity for the public to comment. If the public comments persuade the agency that changes are needed in the interim final rule, the agency may revise the rule by publishing a final rule reflecting those changes. Interim final rulemaking can be viewed as another particular application of the good cause exception in the APA, but with the addition of a comment period after the rule has become effective.[24]

In August 1998, the General Accounting Office reported that about half of the 4,658 final regulatory actions published in the *Federal Register* during 1997 were published without NPRMs.[25] Seven agencies accounted for about 70% of both the final actions and the actions without NPRMs. Most of the actions without NPRMs appeared to involve administrative or technical issues with limited applicability. However, 11 of the 61 final rules published during 1997 that were "major" (e.g., having a $100 million impact on the economy) did not have NPRMs. The agencies most commonly cited the APA's good cause exception as their justification for not publishing NPRMs, frequently noting the time-sensitive nature of the actions being taken. The agencies also frequently used the categorical exceptions permitted in the APA (e.g., actions involving agencies' management or personnel). In some cases GAO concluded that the agencies' explanations for why NPRMs were not used were not clear or understandable, with the agencies sometimes making broad assertions that an NPRM would delay the issuance of rules that were, in some general sense, in the public interest. For example, in one case the agency said that soliciting public comments on the rule was "contrary to the public interest" because the rule authorized a "new and creative method of financing the development of public housing."[26]

National Environmental Policy Act

The National Environmental Policy Act (NEPA) of 1969 (42 U.S.C. §§4321-4347) was the first statute to require an "impact statement" as a way to ensure that federal agencies give special consideration to certain issues during the rulemaking process. NEPA requires all federal agencies to include in every recommendation or report related to "major Federal actions significantly affecting the quality of the human environment" a detailed statement on the environmental impact of the proposed action. Initially, though, agencies make a threshold determination (known as an "environmental assessment") as to whether the rule or other action represents a significant impact on the environment. If not, the agency issues a "finding of no significant impact." If the agency concludes that there is a significant impact, the agency then prepares a full " environmental impact statement" describing the likely effects of the rule.

According to the act and its implementing regulations developed by the Council on Environmental Quality, the environmental impact statement must delineate the direct, indirect, and cumulative effects of the proposed action.[27] Agencies are also required to include in the statement (1) any adverse environmental effects that cannot be avoided should the proposal be implemented, (2) alternatives to the proposed action, (3) the relationship between local short-term uses of the environment and the maintenance and enhancement of long-term productivity, and (4) any irreversible and irretrievable commitments of resources that would be involved if the proposed action should be implemented. Before developing any such environmental impact statement, NEPA requires the responsible federal official to consult with and obtain comments of any federal agency that has jurisdiction by law or special expertise with respect to any environmental impact involved. Agencies must make copies of the statement and the comments and views of appropriate federal, state, and local agencies available to the President, the Council on Environmental Quality, and to the public. The adequacy of an agency's environmental impact statement is subject to judicial review.

In April 2002, the Chairman of the Council on Environmental Quality established a task force composed of federal agency employees to review NEPA implementation practices and procedures. In September 2003, the task force issued a report containing more than 50 recommendations to expedite the NEPA review process.[28] Among other things, the task force recommended that new guidance be developed setting standards for the documentation needed to support a determination that a rule would not have significant environmental effects.

Paperwork Reduction Act

The Paperwork Reduction Act (PRA) (44 U.S.C. §§3501-3520) was originally enacted in 1980, but was subsequently amended in 1986 and again in 1995. One of the purposes of the PRA is to minimize the paperwork burden for individuals, small businesses, and others resulting from the collection of information by or for the federal government. The act generally defines a "collection of information" as the obtaining or disclosure of facts or opinions by or for an agency by 10 or more nonfederal persons. Many information collections, recordkeeping requirements, and third-party disclosures are contained in or are authorized by regulations as monitoring or enforcement tools. In fact, these paperwork requirements are the essence of many agencies' regulatory provisions.[29] The PRA requires agencies to justify any collection of information from the public by establishing the need and intended use of the information, estimating the burden that the collection will impose on respondents, and showing that the collection is the least burdensome way to gather the information.

The original PRA established the Office of Information and Regulatory Affairs (OIRA) within the Office of Management and Budget (OMB) to provide central agency leadership and oversight of government-wide efforts to reduce unnecessary paperwork burden and improve the management of information resources. Agencies must receive OIRA approval (signified by an OMB control number displayed on the information collection) for each collection request before it is implemented, and those approvals must be renewed at least every three years. Failure to obtain OIRA approval for an active collection, or the lapse of that approval, represents a violation of the act, and triggers the PRA's public protection provision. Under that provision, no one can be penalized for failing to comply with a collection of information subject to the act if the collection does not display a valid OMB control number.[30] OIRA can disapprove any collection of information if it believes the collection is inconsistent with the requirements of the PRA.[31]

The PRA clearance process is described in the act and implementing regulations. For new collections, no later than the publication of the NPRM, the issuing agency must submit the proposed rule and any background information to OIRA. At the same time the agency is required to publish a notice in the *Federal Register* stating that OIRA's approval is being sought, thereby providing the public with an opportunity to comment on the proposed collection. For any collection of information that is not contained in a proposed rule, OIRA staff have up to 60 days under the statute to review the proposed collection and ensure, among other things, that the collection is statutorily authorized and necessary, and that the agency's paperwork burden estimate (most commonly measured in terms of "burden hours") is reasonable.[32] At the end of the process the agency is notified of the disposition of the review. OIRA data indicates that the office takes action on between 3,000 and 5,000 information collection requests (new approvals, renewals, or revisions) each year.

The 1995 PRA reaffirmed the principles in the original act and gave significant new responsibilities to OIRA and executive branch agencies. For example, the act currently requires OIRA to "oversee the use of information resources to improve the efficiency and effectiveness of governmental operations to serve agency missions." The PRA also requires federal agencies to establish a process, independent of program responsibility, to evaluate proposed collections of information, manage information resources to reduce information collection burdens on the public, and ensure that the public has timely and equitable access to information products and services.

The coverage of the PRA is extremely broad, including actions by both Cabinet departments and independent agencies as well as independent regulatory agencies, and covering virtually any type of collection of information that these agencies "conduct or sponsor."[33] As a result of the 1995 amendments to the act, the PRA's clearance requirements clearly cover collections of information "requiring the disclosure to third parties or the public,"effectively overturning the Supreme Court's 1990 decision in *Dole v. United Steelworkers of America* (494 U.S. 26).

One of the key features of the PRA of 1995 was the requirement that OIRA, in consultation with the agency heads, set annual government-wide goals for the reduction of information collection burdens by at least 10% in fiscal years 1996 and 1997, and by at least 5% in each of the succeeding four fiscal years. The act also required OIRA to establish agency burden reduction goals each year representing "the maximum practicable opportunity in each agency." At the end of FY1995 (just before the PRA of 1995 took effect) federal agencies estimated that their information collections imposed about 7 billion burden hours on the public. Therefore, if all federal agencies had been able to meet each of the government-wide goals, by September 30, 2001, the burden-hour estimate would have decreased about 35% to about 4.6 billion hours. However, this reduction did not occur. In fact, as of September 30, 2002, the government-wide burden estimate stood at more than 8.2 billion hours — a 17% *increase* since the PRA of 1995 took effect. Nearly half of that increase occurred during FY2002 alone, and about 70% occurred during fiscal years 2001 and 2002.[34] The agencies contend that they are often unable to reduce paperwork requirements without changes in the underlying statutes that require the information to be collected.

Regulatory Flexibility Act

The Regulatory Flexibility Act (RFA) of 1980 (5 U.S.C. §§601-612), requires federal agencies to assess the impact of their forthcoming regulations on "small entities," which the act defines as including small businesses, small governmental jurisdictions, and certain small not-for-profit organizations. Under the RFA, Cabinet departments and independent agencies as well as independent regulatory agencies must prepare a regulatory flexibility analysis at the time proposed and certain final rules are issued. The analysis for a proposed rule is referred to as an "initial regulatory flexibility analysis" (IRFA) and the analysis for a final rule is referred to as a "final regulatory flexibility analysis." The RFA requires the analysis to describe, among other things, (1) the reasons why the regulatory action is being considered; (2) the small entities to which the proposed rule will apply and, where feasible, an estimate of their number; (3) the projected reporting, recordkeeping, and other compliance requirements of the proposed rule; and (4) any significant alternatives to the rule that would accomplish the statutory objectives while minimizing the impact on small entities.

However, these analytical requirements are not triggered if the head of the issuing agency certifies that the proposed rule would not have a "significant economic impact on a substantial number of small entities." The RFA does not define "significant economic impact" or "substantial number of small entities," thereby giving federal agencies substantial discretion regarding when the act's analytical requirements are initiated. Also, the RFA's analytical requirements do not apply to final rules for which the agency does not publish a proposed rule.[35]

The RFA initially did not permit judicial review of agencies' actions under the act. However, amendments to the act in 1996 as part of the Small Business Regulatory Enforcement Fairness Act (SBREFA) (110 Stat. 857, 5 U.S.C. §601 note) permitted judicial review regarding, among other things, agencies' regulatory flexibility analyses for final rules and any certifications that their rules will not have a significant impact on small entities. As a result, a small entity that is adversely affected or aggrieved by an agency's determination that its final rule would not have a significant impact on small entities could seek judicial review of that determination within one year of the date of the final agency action. In granting relief, a court may remand the rule to the agency or defer enforcement against small entities. The addition of judicial review in 1996 is generally viewed as a significant strengthening of the RFA, and is believed to have improved agencies' compliance with the act.[36]

The RFA also contains several other notable provisions. For example, section 602 requires each federal agency to publish a "regulatory flexibility agenda" in the *Federal Register* each October and April listing regulations that the agency expects to propose or promulgate which are likely to have a significant economic impact on a substantial number of small entities.[37] Section 610 of the act requires agencies to review those rules that have or will have a significant impact within 10 years of their promulgation to determine whether they should be continued without change or should be amended or rescinded to minimize their impact on small entities. Section 612 of the RFA requires the Chief Counsel of the Small Business Administration's (SBA) Office of Advocacy to monitor and report at least annually on agencies' compliance with the act. SBA's primary method of monitoring agencies' compliance is to review and comment on proposed regulations when they are published for notice and comment in the *Federal Register*. However, the statute also specifically authorizes the Chief Counsel to appear as *amicus curiae* (i.e., "friend of the court") in any court action to review a rule.

The RFA also requires agencies to ensure that small entities have an opportunity to participate in the rulemaking process, and the 1996 amendments to the act in SBREFA put in place special requirements for proposed rules issued by the Environmental Protection Agency (EPA) and the Occupational Safety and Health Administration (OSHA). EPA and OSHA are required to convene "advocacy review panels" before publishing a regulatory flexibility analysis for a proposed rule. Specifically, the agency issuing the regulation (OSHA or EPA) must notify the SBA Chief Counsel for Advocacy and provide information on the draft rule's potential impacts on small entities and the type of small entities that might be affected. The Chief Counsel then must identify representatives of affected small entities within 15 days of the notification. The review panel must consist of full-time federal employees from the rulemaking agency, the Office of Management and Budget, and SBA's Chief Counsel for Advocacy. During the panel process, the panel must collect the advice and recommendations of representatives of affected small entities about the potential impact of the draft rule. The panel must report on the comments received and on the panel's recommendations no later than 60 days after the panel is convened, and the panel's report must be made public as part of the rulemaking record.[38] An agency may or may not adopt the panel's recommendations.

GAO has examined the implementation of the RFA several times within the past 10 to 15 years, and a recurring theme in GAO's reports is a lack of clarity in the act and a resulting variability in the act's implementation. For example, in 1991 GAO reported that each of the four federal agencies that it reviewed had a different interpretation of key RFA provisions.[39] In 1994 GAO again reported that agencies' compliance with the RFA varied widely from one agency to another and that agencies were interpreting the statute differently.[40] In a 1999 report on the implementation of section 610 of the RFA and in a 2000 report on the implementation of the RFA at the Environmental Protection Agency (EPA), GAO concluded that agencies had broad discretion to determine what the statute required.[41] In all of these reports, GAO suggested that Congress consider clarifying the act's requirements and/or give SBA or some other entity the responsibility to develop criteria for whether and how agencies should conduct RFA analyses. In 2001, GAO testified that the promise of the RFA may never be realized until Congress or some other entity defines what a "significant economic impact" and a "substantial number of small entities" mean in a rulemaking setting.[42] However, other observers have indicated that the definitions of these terms should remain flexible because of significant differences in each agency's operating environment.

Periodically, legislation is introduced to amend the RFA. For example, in the 110th Congress, H.R. 4458, the "Small Business Regulatory Improvement Act," was introduced on December 12, 2007, and was reported by the House Committee on Small Business the next day. Among other things, H.R. 4458 would define "economic impact" as including indirect effects that are "reasonably foreseeable," and would clarify that agencies' reviews of existing rules should not be limited to rules for which a regulatory flexibility analysis had been conducted. The bill would also require agencies to develop a plan for the review of all existing rules within 10 years, require more details in agencies' analyses and notifications, and require annual reports to Congress on certain agency "determinations" as part of their reviews. Although some of these provisions address long-standing issues, some provisions seem unclear and some may add time and costs to the rulemaking process. Most notably, though, H.R. 4458 does not address GAO's long-standing concerns about the lack of clear definitions for key terms in the RFA.[43]

Small Business Regulatory Enforcement Fairness Act

As noted in the previous section of this report, certain provisions in SBREFA amended the RFA to permit judicial review and to permit small entities to participate in EPA and OSHA rulemaking before a proposed rule with a significant impact on small entities is published. Other provisions in SBREFA did not amend the RFA, but imposed new rulemaking-related requirements on federal agencies.

For example, section 212 of SBREFA requires agencies to develop one or more compliance guides for each final rule or group of related final rules for which the agency is required to prepare a regulatory flexibility analysis. Specifically, section 212 requires the guides to (1) be published, (2) be designated as "small entity compliance guides," and (3) explain the actions a small entity is required to take to comply with an associated final rule. However, the discretion inherent in the RFA regarding when a regulatory flexibility analysis is required also applies to whether compliance guides must be developed. Section 212 gives agencies broad discretion in other areas as well. For example, it says agencies "may" prepare separate guides covering groups or classes of similarly affected small entities, and "may" cooperate with associations of small entities to develop and distribute the guides. Agencies are given "sole discretion" in the use of plain language in the guides. The statute does not indicate when the guides must be developed or how they must be "published." In December 2001, GAO reported that section 212 of SBREFA did not appear to have had much of an impact on agencies' rulemaking activities, and its implementation varied across and sometimes within agencies.[44] Using the discretion that the section provided, GAO said "an agency could legally exclude all of its rules from coverage by the statute, designate a previously published document as its small entity compliance guide, or develop and publish a guide with no input from small entities years after the covered rule takes effect." GAO recommended several changes it felt were needed to strengthen and clarify the requirements in section 212.

Section 213 of SBREFA required federal agencies regulating the activities of small entities to establish a program for responding to inquiries concerning compliance with applicable statutes and regulations. The section also says that in any civil or administrative action against a small entity, such guidance "may be considered as evidence of the reasonableness or appropriateness of any proposed fines, penalties or damages sought against such small entity."

Section 222 of SBREFA amended the Small Business Act (15 U.S.C. §631 *et seq.*) to require the SBA Administrator to designate a "Small Business and Agriculture Regulatory Enforcement Ombudsman," who was directed to work with each agency to ensure that small business concerns have an opportunity to comment on agencies' enforcement actions. The ombudsman was directed to annually evaluate and report on each agency's enforcement activities, including a rating of the "responsiveness to small business" of each agency's regional and program offices. Section 222 also required the Administrator to establish a "Small Business Regulatory Fairness Board" in each SBA regional office to report to and advise the ombudsman on "excessive enforcement actions of agencies against small business concerns.

Section 223 of SBREFA requires agencies to provide small entities with some form of relief from civil monetary penalties. Specifically, subsection 223(a) of the act required federal agencies regulating the activities of small entities to establish a policy or program by end of March 1997 for the reduction and, under appropriate circumstances, the waiver of civil penalties by small entities. In February 2001, GAO reported on the implementation of section 223 and concluded that all of the agencies' penalty reduction and waiver policies were within the broad discretion afforded by the statute.[45] However, GAO also reported that some of the policies covered only a portion of the agencies' enforcement actions involving small entities, and some treated small entities no differently than large entities. The agencies' policies also differed in terms of how key terms such as "small entity" and "penalty reduction" were defined, and most were developed before SBREFA took effect. GAO suggested several changes to the statute to strengthen agencies' penalty relief policies and make them more consistent. For example, GAO suggested amending the act to require agencies to maintain data on the number of enforcement actions involving small entities and the amount of penalty relief provided. This recommendation was later implemented with the passage of the Small Business Paperwork Relief Act of 2002 (P.L. 107-198, 116 Stat. 729), which required (among other things) that agencies develop and report such information to selected congressional committees.

Congressional Review Act

The statutory provision commonly known as the Congressional Review Act (CRA) (5 U.S.C. §§801-808) was included as part of SBREFA as enacted in March 1996, and established expedited procedures by which Congress may disapprove agencies' rules by enacting a joint resolution of disapproval.[46] Under the CRA, before any final rule can become effective it must be filed with each House of Congress and GAO. The act also requires federal agencies to submit to GAO and make available to each House of Congress a copy of any cost-benefit analysis prepared for the rule and a report on the agency's actions related to the RFA and any other relevant act or executive order. The definition of a "rule" under the CRA is very broad, and the act applies to rules issued by Cabinet departments and independent agencies as well as independent regulatory agencies.

If OIRA considers the issuing agency's rule to be "major" (e.g., has a \$100 million impact on the economy), the agency must delay the rule's effective date by 60 days after the date of publication in the *Federal Register* or submission to Congress and GAO, whichever is later. Within 15 calendar days of receiving a major rule, GAO is required to provide Congress with a report on the rule assessing the issuing agency's compliance with the procedural steps required by the various acts and executive orders applicable to the rulemaking process. Although the CRA establishes these special requirements for major rules, the CRA procedures for disapproving regulations apply to all rules, whether or not they are declared to be major.

Within 60 days after Congress receives an agency's rule, excluding periods when Congress is in recess or adjournment, a Member of Congress can introduce a resolution of disapproval that, if adopted by both Houses and enacted into law, can nullify the rule, even if it has already gone into effect. Congressional disapproval under the CRA also prevents the agency from proposing to issue a "substantially similar" rule without subsequent statutory authorization, but this provision is not intended to vitiate altogether the agency's power to establish regulations in the area in question.

The CRA provides that Senate action on a disapproval resolution under the act must occur within 60 days of session after the regulation is submitted, and makes available during that period an expedited procedure intended to ensure that the Senate can take up and vote on the measure before the period expires. The act establishes no such expedited procedure for the House. If Congress adjourns less than 60 days of session after a rule is submitted, a new 60 day period for disapproval under the act begins on the 15th legislative day of the next session. If a disapproval resolution is rejected by either House of Congress, the rule can take effect immediately (or as provided by other governing law or rule).

By August 2008, federal agencies had submitted nearly 50,000 rules to GAO (and presumably, Congress) since the CRA took effect in March 1996, including more than 750 major rules. However, only one rule had been overturned through CRA's procedures — OSHA's ergonomics standard in

March 2001 (P.L. 107-5). Many reasons have been suggested for why the CRA has not been used more often,[47] but chief among them may be the fact that, if the President vetoes a resolution of disapproval (which is likely if the underlying rule is developed during his administration), then enactment of the resolution would require approval of a two-thirds majority in both houses of Congress. The rejection of the ergonomics rule was the result of a specific set of circumstances created by a transition in party control of the presidency. The majority party in both houses of Congress was the same as the party of the incoming President (George W. Bush). When the new Congress convened in 2001 and adopted a resolution disapproving the rule published under the outgoing President (William J. Clinton), the incoming President did not veto the resolution. Congress may be most able to use the CRA to disapprove rules in similar, transition-related circumstances.[48]

Congress can also stop agency rulemaking or regulatory enforcement through provisions added to agency appropriations legislation. There appear to be four types of such appropriations provisions: (1) restrictions on the finalization of particular proposed rules, (2) restrictions on regulatory activity within certain areas, (3) implementation or enforcement restrictions, and (4) conditional restrictions (e.g., preventing implementation of a rule until certain actions are taken). Some of these kinds of provisions have been included in appropriations bills for many years in a row. The reasons behind these restrictions vary, with some appearing to be based on economic considerations, some requiring or preventing the implementation of rules issued at the end of a presidential administration, and some included for various other reasons. Such provisions are generally applicable only for the period of time and the agencies covered by the relevant appropriations bill, but (depending on how they are worded) can be more broadly applicable. Also, to the extent that agencies have independent sources of funding (e.g., user fees) or implement their regulations through state or local governments, some of the limitations may not be as restrictive as they seem.[49]

Unfunded Mandates Reform Act

The Unfunded Mandates Reform Act (UMRA) of 1995 was enacted in an effort to reduce the costs associated with federal imposition of responsibilities, duties, and regulations upon state, local, and tribal governments and the private sector without providing the funding appropriate to the costs imposed by those responsibilities. Title I of UMRA established new procedures designed to ensure that Congress fully considers the potential effects of unfunded federal mandates before imposing them in legislation. Among other things, the procedures call for the Congressional Budget Office to provide statements to authorizing committees about whether reported bills contain mandates and, if so, the cost of those mandates.[50]

Title II of UMRA (2 U.S.C. §§1532-1538) contains requirements imposed on covered federal agencies during the rulemaking process. Specifically, the act requires Cabinet departments and independent agencies (but not independent regulatory agencies) to, among other things:

- prepare a written statement containing specific descriptions and estimates for any proposed rule or any final rule for which a proposed rule was published that includes any federal mandate that may result in the expenditure of $100 million or more in any year by state, local, or tribal governments, in the aggregate, or the private sector. One of the items required in the written statement is a qualitative and quantitative assessment of the anticipated costs and benefits of the mandate (Section 202);
- identify and consider a reasonable number of regulatory alternatives and select the least costly, most cost-effective, or least burdensome alternative (or explain why that alternative was not selected) for each rule for which a written statement is prepared (Section 205);
- develop a plan in which agencies provide notice of regulatory requirements to potentially affected small governments (Section 203); and
- develop an effective process to permit elected officers of state, local, and tribal governments (or their designees) to provide input in the development of regulatory proposals containing significant intergovernmental mandates (Section 204).

OIRA has primary responsibility for monitoring agency compliance with title II of UMRA, and issued guidance in March 1995 on the implementation of the title that generally repeated the requirements of the statute. OIRA also publishes an annual report on the implementation of title II.[51]

In February 1998, GAO reported that, because of the way the statute was written, title II of UMRA had little effect on agencies' rulemaking actions during its first two years of implementation.[52] First, many of the act's requirements did not appear to apply to most of the "economically significant" rules (e.g., rules with a $100 million impact on the economy) that were promulgated during this period. For example, if a final rule did not have an associated NPRM or imposed a mandate as a condition of federal financial assistance, the written statement requirement in section 202 of UMRA does not apply. Second, UMRA does not require agencies to take the actions specified if the agencies determine that they are duplicative of other actions or that accurate estimates of the effect of their rules are not feasible. Third, even when UMRA is triggered, it often requires agencies to take actions that are identical or similar to actions that they were already required to take. For example, UMRA's requirements in sections 202 and 205 for the conduct of cost-benefit analysis and identification of regulatory alternatives are similar to the requirements that were already in place under Executive Order 12866, which was issued more than a year before UMRA was enacted. (See below for a discussion of Executive Order 12866.) The consultation requirements in section 204 are traceable to the notice and comment requirements in the APA, and are almost identical to the requirements in Executive Order 12875, which was issued more than a year before UMRA.

In May 2004, GAO again reported that UMRA's written statement requirements did not apply to most major or economically significant final rules issued in 2001 and 2002 (only 9 of 122).[53] However, GAO also said that some of the rules not triggering UMRA's requirements "appeared to have potential financial impacts on affected nonfederal parties similar to those of the actions that were identified as containing mandates at or above the act's thresholds." In March 2005, GAO reported that parties from various sectors (businesses, public interest groups, academia, and others) most commonly cited UMRA's numerous definitions, exclusions, and exceptions as problematic and in need of improvement.[54]

Information Quality Act

Section 515 of the Treasury and General Government Appropriations Act for Fiscal Year 2001, generally known as the "Data Quality Act" or the "Information Quality Act" (IQA) amended the Paperwork Reduction Act and directed OMB to issue government-wide guidelines that "provide policy and procedural guidance to Federal agencies for ensuring and maximizing the quality, objectivity, utility, and integrity of information (including statistical information) disseminated by Federal agencies."[55] The IQA also instructed agencies (both Cabinet departments and independent agencies as well as independent regulatory agencies) to issue their own guidelines not more than one year after the issuance of OMB's government-wide guidelines, and to establish administrative mechanisms allowing affected persons to seek and obtain correction of information maintained and disseminated by the agency. Finally, the act required agencies to report periodically to the Director of OMB on the number and nature of complaints received and how such complaints were handled by the agency. The first agency reports were due by January 1, 2004.

In response to a separate congressional requirement, in April 2004, OMB provided Congress with a report on the implementation of the IQA during FY2003.[56] The report said that agencies received only about 35 substantive correction requests during the year, and said it was "premature to make broad statements about both the impact of the correction request process and the overall responsiveness of the agencies." Many other correction requests listed in the report were on minor issues or involved matters that had been dealt with before the IQA was enacted. OMB indicated that the correction requests came from all segments of society, and said there was no evidence that the IQA had affected the pace of rulemaking. However, OMB Watch (a public interest group) said OMB's report was "seriously flawed" in that it understated the number of correction requests and did not disclose that nearly three-quarters of the requests were from industry.[57]

The IQA builds upon existing agency responsibilities to assure the quality of information collected, used, or disseminated to the public. Proponents of the act contend that the law and the OMB and agency guidelines will improve the quality of agency science and regulation, and force agencies to regulate based on the best science available. Some of these proponents also maintain that the act will help agencies defend their regulations against lawsuits and reduce the number of lawsuits filed. They also point out that in any requests for correction of information, the IQA places the burden of proof on the affected parties making the request; they must demonstrate that a specific dissemination does not meet the standards of either the OMB guidelines or the agency-specific guidelines. However, opponents of the act and the guidelines contend the IQA may have a chilling effect on agency distribution and use of scientific information. These opponents foresee a flood of information quality challenges, correction requests, and court suits on a wide range of scientific issues, which may tie up agency resources and significantly delay health, safety, and environmental regulations. Opponents have also noted that since "quality" is a subjective term and some regulations are based on "best available data," regulations could be arbitrarily rejected under this new law.

A major test of the IQA may be whether agencies' denials of information correction requests are subject to judicial review. In March 2006, the U.S. Court of Appeals for the Fourth Circuit ruled that the act does not permit judicial review.[58] Two district courts had previously reached a similar conclusion,[59] and the Department of Justice had issued a brief stating that the IQA does not permit judicial review.[60]

Peer Review

In a development closely related to the issue of information quality, in September 2003, OMB published a proposed bulletin on "Peer Review and Information Quality" that would have, if made final, provided a standardized process by which all significant regulatory information would be peer reviewed.[61] The authorities that OMB cited for this action were the IQA, the Paperwork Reduction Act, and Executive Order 12866. "Regulatory information" was defined in the bulletin as any scientific or technical study that "might" be used by federal, state, local, or international regulatory bodies.

Specifically, the bulletin proposed requiring each federal agency (each executive agency and independent regulatory agency) to take three actions: (1) have all "significant regulatory information" that it intends to disseminate peer reviewed (with information defined as "significant" if OMB determines that it will have a clear and substantial impact on important public policies or private sector decisions); (2) have "especially significant regulatory information" subject to the above requirements peer reviewed according to even higher standards (with information deemed "especially significant" if, among other things, it supports a regulatory action with a $100 million or more impact on the economy or "is relevant to an Administration policy priority"); and (3) provide OMB at least once each year with information about upcoming significant regulatory disseminations and the agency's plans for conducting peer reviews. The proposed bulletin also said agencies that are likely to disseminate "significant" or "especially significant" regulatory information must supplement or amend their information quality guidelines to incorporate the requirements of the proposed peer review bulletin for "significant" and "especially significant" information. The proposed bulletin indicated that OMB could waive the requirements for peer review if an agency made "a compelling case" that a waiver is necessary (e.g., an imminent health hazard or homeland security threat).

OMB received 187 comments from the public and other agencies on its proposed peer review bulletin, with some supporting its issuance in final and others calling for its withdrawal and reconsideration. On April 15, 2004, OMB published a revised bulletin, and again asked the public for comments.[62] The revisions would, if made final:

- focus the bulletin's coverage on "influential" scientific information, not just "regulatory" information;
- narrow the scope of the section describing the characteristics of peer review for the most important types of information so that it covers only "scientific assessments" (not all influential information) that, among other things, have a $500 million annual impact (rather than a $100 impact on the economy);
- clarify that regulatory impact analyses are not covered by the bulletin, but the models and data underlying them are covered;
- clarify that the bulletin does not cover information products released by government-funded scientists unless it represents an official view of a federal department or agency;
- specify that the responsibility for determining the need for a waiver from the bulletin's peer review requirements in the event of an emergency or otherwise "compelling need" rests with the agencies;
- provide agencies with greater flexibility (e.g., in determining the appropriate intensity of peer review, and when the comments of specific reviewers should be disclosed, and in the use of alternative scientific procedures); and
- clarify that researchers that receive research grants based on "investigator-initiated, peer reviewed competitions" can still serve as peer reviewers.

On December 15, 2004, OMB published a final version of the peer review bulletin on its website.[63] The final bulletin was published in the Federal Register on January 14, 2005.[64] OMB said this version reflects "minor revisions" made in response to more than 50 comments from the public on the revised bulletin. For example, the final bulletin requires agencies to disclose the names of peer reviewers to the public and adds an annual reporting requirement to allow OMB to track how agencies are using the bulletin. However, agencies are still afforded substantial discretion to determine when and what type of peer review is required. OMB also retains substantial discretion in certain areas.

OMB and supporters of the peer review bulletin indicate that peer review standards across the government are currently inconsistent, and that more consistent use of peer review can increase the technical quality and credibility of regulatory science.[65] They also assert that peer review can protect science-based regulations from political criticism and litigation. Opponents view the bulletin as an effort to inject political considerations into the world of science and to use the uncertainty that inevitably surrounds science as an excuse to delay new rules that could cost regulated entities millions or even billions of dollars. They also expressed concerns regarding the need for the bulletin and OMB's authority to issue it.[66]

Other Statutory Provisions Related to Rulemaking

Other statutory provisions have been enacted over the years that, while generally not imposing new rulemaking requirements per se, can affect the rulemaking process.

Federal Advisory Committee Act

Several statutes either require or permit the use of advisory committees in the federal rulemaking process. An advisory committee may be composed of experts in the regulatory field involved, representatives of the interest groups affected by the rule, and related federal or state agencies, and may help set the agency's rulemaking agenda or may simply serve as a sounding board for agency ideas. The enactment of the Federal Advisory Committee Act (FACA) of 1972 (5 U.S.C. App. II) established requirements to ensure that agencies using advisory committees receive impartial and relevant expertise. Specifically, FACA requires that the advice provided by advisory committees be objective and accessible to the public. With certain exceptions, each advisory committee meeting is presumptively open to the public. Adequate advance notice of the meetings must be published in the *Federal Register*, and all papers, records, and minutes of the meetings must generally be made available to the public. FACA also requires that the advisory committees be fairly balanced in regard to the points of view of affected interests and the functions performed. The act defines an advisory committee as any committee or similar group (1) established or used to obtain advice or recommendation for one or more federal agencies or the President and (2) that is not composed wholly of full-time federal officers or employees.

Trade Agreements Act

The Trade Agreements Act of 1979 (19 U.S.C. §§2531-2533) prohibits agencies from setting regulatory standards that create "unnecessary obstacles to foreign commerce" of the United States. The act specifically states that legitimate domestic objectives such as safety or health are not considered unnecessary obstacles. The statute also requires, where appropriate, the use of performance standards rather than design standards and the consideration of international standards as the basis of domestic standards.

Negotiated Rulemaking Act

The Negotiated Rulemaking Act of 1990 (5 U.S.C. §§561-570a), as amended and permanently authorized in 1996 (110 Stat. 3870), seeks to overcome what some observers describe as an adversarial relationship between agencies and affected interest groups that often accompanies agency rulemaking. The concept of negotiated rulemaking (sometimes referred to as regulatory negotiation or "reg-neg") emerged in the 1980s as a supplement to the traditional procedure for developing regulations. Negotiated rulemaking does not replace procedures necessary under the APA. Instead, the act encourages (but does not require) agencies to consider convening a negotiated rulemaking committee before developing and issuing a proposed regulation under the APA. The committee, composed of representatives of the agency and the various interest groups that would be affected by the proposed regulation, addresses areas of concern in the hope that it can reach agreement on the contents of a proposed regulation. The agency can, if it agrees, then issue the agreement as a proposed rule, and eventually a final rule under existing APA requirements. The expectation is that any rule drafted through negotiated rulemaking would be easier to implement and less likely to be the subject of subsequent litigation. However, any proposal agreed to by the negotiated rulemaking committee is not binding on the agency or other parties.

The major provisions of the act require that (1) a negotiated rulemaking committee consist of at least one member of the agency and no more than 25 members, unless the head of the agency determines that more are needed; (2) the agency select an impartial "facilitator" to chair meetings, subject to the approval of the committee by consensus; (3) an agreement on any negotiated rulemaking must be unanimous, unless the negotiated rulemaking committee agrees to other conditions; and (4) the head of an agency, when deciding whether to establish a negotiated rulemaking committee, assure that (a) there are a limited number of identifiable interests that will be significantly affected by the rule; (b) there is a reasonable chance that a committee can be convened with a balanced representation of interested parties willing to negotiate in good faith; and (c) there is a reasonable likelihood that a committee will reach a consensus on the proposed rule within a fixed period of time.

An agency may pay reasonable travel and per diem expenses, and reasonable compensation to negotiating committee members under certain conditions. The agency must comply with FACA in establishing and administering the committee. Agency procedural actions related to establishing, assisting, or terminating the committee are not subject to judicial review, but any judicial review available regarding the rule resulting from negotiated rulemaking is unaffected.[67] Although the use of negotiated rulemaking was expected to improve rulemaking timeliness and reduce litigation, one examination of agencies' efforts in this area indicated that those expectations were not being fulfilled.[68] However, another study indicated that negotiated rulemaking can improve participants' perception of the final rule and of the overall rulemaking process.[69] Although the Negotiated Rulemaking Act gives agencies substantial discretion as to whether the approach should be employed in rulemaking, Congress has sometimes mandated its use by rulemaking agencies and established specific procedures and time frames to follow.[70]

National Technology Transfer and Advancement Act

Section 12(d) of the National Technology Transfer and Advancement Act (15 U.S.C. §272 note), adopted in March 1996, generally requires federal agencies to "use technical standards that are developed or adopted by voluntary consensus standards bodies" to carry out policy objectives unless doing so is "inconsistent with applicable law or otherwise impractical." Agencies are also required to consult with and (if in the public interest and compatible with agency missions, authority, priorities, and resources) participate with voluntary, private sector, consensus bodies. This provision essentially codified policies already in existence in OMB Circular A-119, and also established reporting requirements and authorized the National Institute of Standards and Technology (NIST) within the Department of Commerce to coordinate agencies' conformity assessment activities. According to NIST, federal agencies use consensus standards in hundreds of federal procurement or regulatory programs (e.g., requiring certification from Underwriters Laboratories that a product is safe or requiring individuals in certain professions meet specific educational or competency standards).[71]

Regulatory Right-to-Know Act

Section 624 of the Treasury and General Government Appropriations Act, 2001 (31 U.S.C. §1105 note), sometimes referred to as the "Regulatory Right-to-Know Act," requires OMB to prepare and submit with the budget an "accounting statement and associated report" containing an estimate of the total costs and benefits (including quantifiable and nonquantifiable effects) of federal rules and paperwork, to the extent feasible, (1) in the aggregate, (2) by agency and agency program, and (3) by major rule. The accounting statement is also to contain an analysis of impacts of federal regulation on state, local, and tribal governments, small businesses, wages, and economic growth. The statute requires an accounting statement and report for calendar year 2002 "and each year thereafter."[72] To prepare the report, OMB relies heavily on agencies' estimates of costs and benefits for individual rules published during the previous 10 years. However, if an agency quantified but did not monetize its estimates, OMB monetizes them using "standard" assumptions. In its reports, OMB attempts to capture the agencies' nonquantified benefits and costs in "other information" columns, but OMB's monetized estimates exclude these effects.[73]

Government Paperwork Elimination Act

In 1998, Congress enacted the Government Paperwork Elimination Act (GPEA) (44 U.S.C. §3504 note), which required that by October 21, 2003, federal agencies provide the public, when practicable, with the option of submitting, maintaining, and disclosing information electronically, instead of on paper. GPEA makes OMB responsible for ensuring that federal agencies meet the act's implementation deadline. Although GPEA does not specifically mention rulemaking, both OMB and rulemaking agencies have indicated that its requirements have provided an impetus for developing information technology-based approaches to rulemaking that involves information collection and, more generally, to regulatory management.

E-Government Act

The E-Government Act of 2002 (44 U.S.C.A. §3601 note) was designed to enhance the management and promotion of electronic government services and processes, and contains requirements affecting the rulemaking process. Specifically, section 206 of the act requires agencies, to the extent practicable, to:

- ensure that a publicly accessible website includes all information about that agency that is required to be published in the *Federal Register*,
- accept public comments on proposed rules "by electronic means," and
- ensure that a publicly accessible federal website contains "electronic dockets" for proposed rules containing all comments submitted on the rules as well as "other materials that by agency rule or practice are included in the rulemaking docket under (the APA), whether or not submitted electronically."

The E-Government Act also requires agencies to conduct a "privacy impact assessment" before initiating a new collection of information that uses information technology and contains individually identifying information. In addition, the act established an Office of Electronic Government within OMB, headed by an Administrator appointed by the President. It requires the Administrator of that office to work with the Administrator of OIRA in establishing the strategic direction of the e-government program, and to oversee its implementation.

In January 2003, the Bush Administration launched the "Regulations.gov" website—the first module of its own "e-rulemaking" initiative that would accomplish many of the objectives of the E-Government Act. The website permits the public to identify proposed rules that are open for comment government-wide, and permits the public to comment electronically on those rules.[74] The second module of the e-rulemaking initiative is intended to create one or more electronic dockets for proposed and final rules. The Environmental Protection Agency (EPA) is the lead agency for the e-rulemaking initiative.

E-rulemaking has been described as a way to increase democratic legitimacy, improve regulatory policy decisions, decrease administrative costs, and increase regulatory compliance. However, the implementation of e-rulemaking in the federal government has been controversial. Although the migration of agencies into the government-wide docket was originally planned for 2004, that migration was not completed until 2008. Congress has objected to how e-rulemaking and several other e-government projects have been funded (through appropriations transfers or reimbursements to the projects' "managing partner" agencies), and has voiced other concerns about the overall management and appropriateness of the initiatives. Questions have also been raised regarding the e-rulemaking initiative's centralized structure, its costs (more than $53 million spent through FY2008) and expected financial benefits, the functionality of some of the applications being used, and its effect on public participation in the rulemaking process.

The reasons why the federal e-rulemaking initiative has had such a difficult first five years are many, but one appears to be the lack of direct, consistent funding. From FY2003 through FY2007, Congress appropriated less than $20 million to the E-Government Fund for all e-government projects — much less than the $345 million authorized in the E-Government Act for that period. Congress has also required approval by the Appropriations Committees before any transfers or reimbursements of appropriations are made. Although some have suggested that better communication is needed between Congress and the executive branch, the recent conflicts may reflect basic differences of opinion between the two branches regarding control of federal operations and how the branches should interact. A longterm issue is whether e-rulemaking should continue to be housed in EPA.[75]

Small Business Paperwork Relief Act

In June 2002, Congress enacted and the President signed the Small Business Paperwork Relief Act of 2002 (P.L. 107-198). The act amended the Paperwork Reduction Act to, among other things, require each agency to establish a single point of contact to act as a liaison for small business concerns with regard to information collection and paperwork issues. It also directed agencies to make a special effort to reduce information collection burdens for small businesses with fewer than 25 employees. OMB was directed to publish in the *Federal Register* and make available on the Internet an annual list of the compliance assistance resources available to small businesses.[76] The act also required agencies to report to Congress on the amount of penalty relief provided to small businesses, and established a task force to study the feasibility of streamlining information collection requirements on small businesses.

EXECUTIVE ORDERS AND DIRECTIVES

During the past 20 years, each President has issued executive orders and/or presidential directives designed to guide the federal rulemaking process, often with the goal of reducing regulatory burden. Although independent regulatory agencies are generally not covered by these requirements, they are often encouraged to follow them. By far the most important of the current executive rulemaking requirements is Executive Order 12866,[77] which describes both the principles and the process by which presidential regulatory review currently takes place.

Executive Order 12866

Centralized review of agencies' regulations within the Executive Office of the President has been part of the federal rulemaking process for more than 30 years. Although each of his three predecessors had some type of review process, the most significant development in the evolution of presidential review of rulemaking occurred in 1981, when President Reagan issued Executive Order 12291. The executive order established a set of general requirements for rulemaking, and required federal agencies (other than independent regulatory agencies) to send a copy of each draft proposed and final rule to OMB before publication in the *Federal Register*. It also required covered agencies to prepare a regulatory impact analysis for each "major" rule (e.g., those with a $100 million impact on the economy). As a result of this order, OIRA's responsibilities were greatly expanded from paperwork reviews to examinations of the substance of covered agencies rules — between 2,000 and 3,000 reviews per year. In 1985, President Reagan expanded OIRA's influence further by issuing Executive Order 12498, which required covered agencies (all except independent regulatory agencies) to submit a regulatory plan to OMB for review each year that covered all of their significant regulatory actions underway or planned.

On September 30, 1993, President Clinton issued Executive Order 12866, which revoked Executive Orders 12291 and 12498 and established a new process for OIRA review of rules.[78] Like its predecessors, the new executive order limited OIRA's reviews to proposed and final rules published by agencies other than independent regulatory agencies. However, it also limited OIRA reviews to actions identified by the rulemaking agency or OIRA as "significant" regulatory actions, defined as those that were "economically significant" (e.g., those with a $100 million impact on the economy) or that (1) were inconsistent or interfered with an action taken or planned by another agency; (2) materially altered the budgetary impact of entitlements, grants, user fees, or loan programs; or (3) raised novel legal or policy issues. As a result, the number of rules that OIRA reviewed dropped from between 2,000 and 3,000 per year to between 500 and 700 per year.

Executive Order 12866 also differs from its predecessors in other respects. For example, the order requires that OIRA generally complete its reviews of proposed and final rules within 90 calendar days. It also requires both rulemaking agencies and OIRA to disclose certain information about how the regulatory reviews were conducted. For example, agencies are to identify for the public (1) the substantive changes made to rules between the draft submitted to OIRA for review and the action subsequently announced, and (2) changes made at the suggestion or recommendation of OIRA. OIRA is required to, among other things, provide agencies with a copy of all communications between OIRA personnel and parties outside of the executive branch, and to maintain a public log of all regulatory actions under review and of all of the documents provided to the agencies.[79]

For each significant draft rule, the executive order requires the issuing agency to provide to OIRA the text of the draft rule, a description of why the rule is needed, and a general assessment of the rule's costs and benefits. For draft rules that are "economically significant," the executive order requires a detailed cost-benefit analysis, including an assessment of the costs and benefits of "potentially effective and reasonably feasible alternatives to the planned regulation." One of the "principles of regulation" in the order is that agencies shall "propose or adopt a regulation only upon a reasoned determination that the benefits of the intended regulation justify its costs." The order also says that when setting regulatory priorities, "each agency shall consider, to the extent reasonable, the degree and nature of the risks posed by various substances or activities within its jurisdiction." The executive order's "regulatory philosophy" states that unless a statute requires another regulatory approach, "in choosing among alternative regulatory approaches, agencies should select those approaches that maximize net benefits."[80]

During the formal Executive Order 12866 review process, OIRA analyzes the draft rule in light of the principles of the executive order and discusses the rule with staff and officials at the rulemaking agency. OIRA may also discuss the draft rule with other agencies with whom interagency coordination will be necessary, and may meet or otherwise communicate with interested stakeholders outside of the federal government.[81] At the end of the review OIRA either concludes that the draft rule is consistent with the principles of the executive order (the majority of the cases) or returns the rule to the agency "for further consideration." In some cases agencies withdraw their draft rules during OIRA's review. If the draft is a proposed rule, the agency may then publish an NPRM. If the draft is a final rule, the agency may then publish a final rule and allow the rule to take effect. OIRA staff also sometimes review draft rules informally before their formal submission under the executive order — particularly when there is a statutory or legal deadline or when a rule has a large impact on society.

OIRA's formal review process has not changed substantially since Executive Order 12866 was issued in 1993.[82] However, GAO reported in September 2003 that there had been several changes in OIRA policies and practices since the current OIRA Administrator (Dr. John Graham) took office in July 2001, including (1) increased use of public letters explaining why OIRA returned rules to agencies for their consideration and suggesting regulatory action, (2) increased emphasis on cost- benefit analysis and peer review of agencies' rules, (3) stricter adherence to the 90- day time limit for OIRA review, (4) improvements in the transparency of the OIRA review process, and (5) an increase in the size and skills of OIRA's staff.[83] Underlying many of these changes is a shift in how recent OIRA administrators view the office's role in the rulemaking process — from "counselor" to the agencies to regulatory "gatekeeper." GAO also concluded that, recent changes notwithstanding, the OIRA review process was still not very transparent to the public, and recommended several changes in OIRA's disclosure policies.

GAO and others have also examined agencies' analyses of economically significant rules under the executive order.[84] For example, in 1998 GAO reported that some of the 20 economic analyses that it examined from five agencies did not incorporate all of the best practices set forth in OMB's guidance.[85] Five of the analyses did not discuss alternatives to the proposed regulatory action and, in many cases, it was not clear why the agencies used certain assumptions. Also, five of the analyses did not discuss uncertainty associated with the agencies' estimates of benefits and/or costs or document the agencies' reasons for not doing so.

Executive Order 12866 also includes several other notable requirements. For example, section 5 of the order requires agencies to periodically review their existing significant regulations to determine whether they should be modified or eliminated. In March 1995, President Clinton reemphasized this requirement by directing each agency to conduct a page-by-page review of all existing regulations. In June 1995, the President announced that 16,000 pages had been eliminated from the *Code of Federal Regulations*. GAO reported on this review effort in October 1997, noting that the page elimination totals that four agencies reported did not take into account pages that had been added while the eliminations took place.[86] GAO also reported that about half of the actions taken appeared to have no effect on the burden felt by regulated entities, would have little effect, or could increase regulatory burden.

Executive Order 13422

On January 18, 2007, President George W. Bush issued Executive Order 13422, making the most significant amendments to Executive Order 12866 since it was published. The changes made by this new executive order are controversial, characterized by some as a "power grab" by the White House that undermines public protections and lessens congressional authority and by others as "a paragon of common sense and good government." The most important changes made by Executive Order 13422 fall into five general categories: (1) a requirement that agencies identify in writing the specific market failure or problem that warrants a new regulation, (2) a requirement that each agency head designate a presidential appointee within the agency as a "regulatory policy officer" who can control upcoming rulemaking activity in that agency, (3) a requirement that agencies provide their best estimates of the cumulative regulatory costs and benefits of rules they expect to publish in the coming year, (4) an expansion of OIRA review to include significant guidance documents,[87] and (5) a provision permitting agencies to consider whether to use more formal rulemaking procedures in certain cases.

The changes made by the executive order were controversial, and in the first half of 2007, two House subcommittees held three oversight hearings on the order. A provision was added to the appropriations measure funding OMB for FY2008 that would have prevented the implementation of the executive order, but the measure was eliminated from the final version of the legislation. The significance of the changes made to the review process by Executive rder 13422 may become clear only through their implementation, but those changes represent a clear expansion of presidential authority over rulemaking agencies. In that regard, Executive Order 13422 can be viewed as part of a broader statement of presidential authority presented throughout the Bush Administration.[88]

Other Executive Orders and Directives

Agencies other than independent regulatory agencies must also be aware of an array of other rulemaking requirements contained in executive orders and presidential directives. For example:

- Executive Order 13132 on "Federalism" requires covered federal agencies to "have an accountable process to ensure meaningful and timely input by State and local officials in the development of regulatory policies that have federalism implications."[89] The order defines "federalism implications" as "substantial direct effects on the States, on the relationship between the national government and the States, or on the distribution of power and responsibilities among the various levels of government." Federal agencies are prohibited from promulgating any regulation with unfunded federalism implications unless they have (1) consulted with state and local officials early in the development of the proposed rule, and (2) prepared a "federalism summary impact statement" consisting of a description of the prior consultation with state and local officials, a summary of their concerns and the agency's position regarding the need to issue the rule, and a statement of the extent to which the officials' concerns have been met. The order gives agencies substantial discretion regarding its implementation. For example, it does not define what type of regulatory action constitutes "substantial direct effects," and says the consultation and impact statement requirements apply "to the extent practicable."[90]
- Executive Order 12630 on constitutionally protected property rights says each agency "shall be guided by" certain principles when formulating or implementing policies that have "takings" implications.[91] For example, the order says that private property should be taken only for "real and substantial threats," and "be no greater than is necessary."[92]
- Executive Order 12889 on the North American Free Trade Agreement generally requires agencies subject to the APA to provide at least a 75-day comment period for any "proposed Federal technical regulation or any Federal sanitary or phytosanitary measure of general application."[93]
- Executive Order 12898 on environmental justice says (among other things) that each agency must develop a strategy that identifies and

addresses disproportionately high and adverse human health or environmental effects of its programs, policies, and activities on minority populations and low income populations.[94] It also says that environmental human health research should include diverse segments of the population in epidemiological and clinical studies, and that agencies should identify rules that should be revised to meet the objectives of the order.

- Executive Order 12988 on civil justice reform generally requires agencies reviewing existing and new regulations to ensure that they comply with specific requirements (e.g., "eliminate drafting errors and ambiguity" and "provide a clear legal standard for affected conduct") to improve regulatory drafting in order to minimize litigation.[95] Agencies formulating proposed regulations are directed to "make every reasonable effort" to ensure that they, among other things, specify in clear language any preemptive or retroactive effects, and the effect on existing law.
- Executive Order 13045 on protection of children from environmental health risks and safety risks says that for any substantive rulemaking action that is likely to result in an economically significant rule that concerns an environmental health risk or safety risk that may disproportionately affect children, the agency must provide OIRA with (1) an evaluation of the environmental or safety effects on children and (2) an explanation of why the planned regulation is preferable to other potentially effective and reasonably feasible alternatives.[96]
- Executive Order 13175 on consultation and coordination with Indian tribal governments generally prohibits agencies from promulgating any regulation not required by law that has tribal implications and imposes substantial direct costs on tribal governments unless the necessary funds are provided or the agency consults with tribal officials and provides a "tribal summary impact statement" describing those consultations.[97] Similar consultation and impact statement requirements apply to rules that preempt tribal laws.
- Executive Order 13211 on energy impacts requires agencies (to the extent permitted by law) to prepare and submit to OMB a "statement of energy effects" for significant energy actions.[98] The statement, published in the NPRM and the final rule, is to include a detailed statement of "any adverse effects on energy supply, distribution, or use" for the action and reasonable alternatives and their effects.

- Executive Order 13272 on small entities generally requires federal agencies to issue (by February 2003) written procedures and policies to ensure proper consideration during the rulemaking process of the impacts of their draft rules on small entities.[99] The order also requires agencies to notify the SBA Chief Counsel for Advocacy of any draft rules that may have a significant economic impact on a substantial number of small entities, and to give "every appropriate consideration" to any comments the Chief Counsel provides.

In addition to executive orders, presidential memoranda or directives can also affect the rulemaking process. For example:

- a March 4, 1995, presidential memorandum directed federal agencies to (among other things) focus their regulatory programs on results, not process, and expand their use of negotiated rulemaking.
- an April 21, 1995, memorandum directed agencies to waive or reduce penalties in certain circumstances, and to reduce the frequency of reports the public is required to provide to the government.
- a June 1, 1998, presidential directive required agencies to use plain language in proposed and final rulemaking documents.

CONCLUSION

During the past 60 to 65 years, Congress and various Presidents have made numerous attempts to add structure, economy, efficiency, accountability, and greater public access and transparency to the regulatory process. In this regard, Congress has enacted laws such as the Administrative Procedure Act, the Regulatory Flexibility Act, the Paperwork Reduction Act, and the Unfunded Mandates Reform Act that require some type of procedure, review, and/or analysis of draft rules by the rulemaking agencies themselves or by outside parties. Presidential rulemaking requirements have often focused on coordination of agencies' regulatory efforts with the President's priorities and attempts to improve the quality of regulations through cost-benefit analysis, risk assessment analysis, and the consideration of specific factors in the rulemaking process (e.g., environmental justice, children, and property rights). Underlying many of these congressional and presidential requirements is an attempt to ensure that certain interests or issues are considered during the rulemaking process and/or to minimize the burden associated with federal regulations.

However, these rulemaking requirements impose burdens of their own on rulemaking agencies, and clearly are a factor (although it is unclear whether they are the most important factor) in the length of time it takes agencies to issue rules. Federal agencies must be aware of the cross-cutting and the program-specific statutory and executive requirements underlying their regulations and must craft rules that are consistent with those requirements — or run the risk of having their rules returned to them by OIRA or rejected by Congress or the courts. Several of these statutes and orders indicate that their requirements may be integrated with or satisfied by the requirements in other statutes or orders. For example, the Regulatory Flexibility Act states that federal agencies can develop their regulatory agendas and perform their regulatory flexibility analyses "in conjunction with or as a part of any other agenda or analysis required by any other law." Some observers believe that integration and consolidation of all these requirements could improve the rulemaking process. In 1993 the Administrative Conference of the United States noted that the simple requirements in the Administrative Procedure Act for informal rulemaking had been "overlain with an increasing number of constraints," including those imposed by Congress, Presidents, and the courts. The Administrative Conference recommended a "coordinated framework of proposals aimed at promoting efficient and effective rulemaking." Since then, the number of rulemaking requirements has increased.

On the other hand, many of these statutory and executive order provisions provide the agencies substantial discretion regarding when and how the rulemaking requirements are to be applied. For example, because the Regulatory Flexibility Act does not define the term "significant impact on a substantial number of small entities," agencies have a great deal of latitude to determine when a regulatory flexibility analysis is required. Similarly, Executive Order 13132 does not define the term "significant federalism implications," so agencies have substantial discretion in deciding whether the analytical requirements of the order have been triggered. Other rulemaking requirements are written in such a way that they actually apply to only a small number of rules. For example, title II of the Unfunded Mandates Reform Act does not apply to any rules published by independent regulatory agencies or any rules for which an agency determines there is "good cause" not to publish a notice of proposed rulemaking. Other rules are exempt from UMRA if they are conditions of federal financial assistance or enforce constitutional rights.

The discretion and exceptions built into these rulemaking statutes and orders diminish their impact, and allow agencies knowledgeable of their provisions to avoid many of the analyses and procedures they seem to require. For example, on hundreds of occasions, agencies have stated in the preambles to their rules that because they believed there was "good cause" not to issue a notice of proposed rulemaking, the requirements of the RFA and/or UMRA do not apply. Agencies also have standard language that they insert into preambles certifying that their rules do not require regulatory flexibility analyses or UMRA written statements. And if agencies are not required to prepare regulatory flexibility analyses for their proposed rules, they are also exempt from the SBREFA requirements to prepare small entity compliance guides and (in the case of OSHA and EPA) to convene advocacy review panels.

Because of the inevitability of regulation and its associated burden, efforts to either tighten existing requirements or impose new ones are likely to continue. A clear understanding of the existing requirements and how they have been implemented may inform any such future efforts.

End Notes

[1] Colin Diver, "Regulatory Precision," in Keith Hawkins and John Thomas, eds., *Making Regulatory Policy* (Pittsburgh: University of Pittsburgh Press, 1989), p. 199.

[2] Cornelius M. Kerwin, *Rulemaking: How Government Agencies Write Law and Make Public Policy*, 2nd ed., (Washington: CQ Press, 1999), p. ix.

[3] 5 U.S.C. §551 (4).

[4] As used in this report, the term "independent regulatory agencies" refers to the boards and commissions identified as such in the Paperwork Reduction Act (44 U.S.C. §3502(5)), including the Federal Communications Commission, the Federal Energy Regulatory Commission, the Nuclear Regulatory Commission, and the Securities and Exchange Commission. The term "independent agencies" refers to other agencies that answer directly to the President, but are not part of Cabinet departments.

[5] See, for example, Thomas O. McGarity, "Some Thoughts on 'Deossifying' the Rulemaking Process, *Duke Law Journal*, vol. 41 (June 1992), pp. 1385-1462; Richard J. Pierce, Jr., "Seven Ways to Deossify Agency Rulemaking," 47 *Administrative Law Review*, vol. 47, winter 1995, pp. 59-93; Paul R. Verkuil, "Rulemaking Ossification — A Modest Proposal," *Administrative Law Review*, vol. 47 (summer 1995), pp. 453-459.

[6] National Advisory Committee on Occupational Safety and Health, *Report and Recommendations Related to OSHA 's Standards Development Process* (Washington: June 6, 2000).

[7] For example, 29 U.S.C. § 1306(a)(3)(A) states that the annual premium rate payable in the case of a single-employer plan for basic benefits is "an amount equal to the sum of $19 plus the additional premium (if any) determined under subparagraph (E) for each individual who is a participant in such plan during the plan year."

[8] DOT's 1998 appropriations act stated that "(n)one of the funds in this Act shall be available to prepare, propose, or promulgate any regulations ... in any model year that differs from the standards promulgated for such automobiles prior to the enactment of this section."

[9] For an examination of the amount of regulatory discretion afforded in specific statutes, see U.S. General Accounting Office, *Regulatory Burden: Some Agencies' Claims Regarding Lack of Rulemaking Discretion Have Merit*, GAO/GGD-99-20, Jan. 8, 1999.

[10] *Industrial Union Department v. American Petroleum Institute*, 448 U.S. 607 (1980).

[11] See, for example, *American Textile Mfrs. Inst., Inc. v. Donovan,* 452 U.S. 490 (1981) and *United Steelworkers v. Marshall*, 647 F.2d 1189 (D.C. Cir. 1980), cert. denied, 453 U.S. 913 (1981).

[12] See, for example, *Motor Vehicle Manufacturers Association v State Farm Mutual Automobile Insurance Co.*, 463 U.S. 29 (1983). The Supreme Court said the agency "must examine the relevant data and articulate a satisfactory explanation of its action, including a 'rational connection between the facts found and the choice made.'"

[13] 1 C.F.R. ch. I, pts. 1-22.

[14] Electronic access to the *Federal Register* is provided through a Government Printing Office website at [http://www.gpoaccess.gov/fr/index.html].

[15] Some agencies begin the rulemaking process by publishing an "advance notice of proposed rulemaking in which the agency notifies the public that it is considering an area for rulemaking and often requests comments on the appropriate scope or topics of the rule. The APA does not require the use of advance notices, but some other statutes require it for particular types of rules. Similarly, agencies may issue a "supplemental notice of proposed rulemaking" after an NPRM is issued if they wish to obtain public comment on new factual proposals before issuing a final rule.

[16] Executive Order 12866, discussed in detail later in this report, suggests that agencies allow the public at least 60 days to comment for "significant" rules.

[17] The APA judicial review provisions are codified at 5 U.S.C 701-706.

[18] In addition to the APA exceptions, Congress sometimes includes specific exemptions from notice and comment procedures in other statutes. For example, section 161(d) under title I of the Federal Agriculture Improvement and Reform Act of 1996 (P.L. 104-127, 110 Stat. 934-935) instructed the Secretary of Agriculture and the Commodity Credit Corporation to issue regulations not later than 90 days after the date of enactment of the title, without regard to the notice and comment provisions of the APA.

[19] Senate Committee on the Judiciary, "Administrative Procedure Act: Legislative History," Senate Document 248, 79th Congress, 2nd Session (1946).

[20] For discussions of these court cases, see Ellen R. Jordan, "The Administrative Procedure Act's 'Good Cause' Exemption," *Administrative Law Review*, 36, spring 1984, pp. 113-178; and Catherine J. Lanctot, "The Good Cause Exception: Danger to Notice and Comment Requirements Under the Administrative Procedure Act," *Georgetown Law Journal*, 68 (Feb. 1980), pp. 765-782.

[21] See *American Federation of Government Employees, AFL-CIO v. Block*, 655 F.2d 1153, 1156 (D.C. Cir 1981); and *Mobay Chemical Corp. v. Gorsuch*, (682 F.2d 419, 426 (3rd Cir.), cert. denied, 459 U.S. 988 (1982). In another case (*Action on Smoking and Health v. CAB*, 713 F.2d 795, 800 [D.C. Cir 1983]), the court said that allowing broad use of the good cause exception would "carve the heart out of the statute."

[22] For more, see Ronald M. Levin, "More on Direct Final Rulemaking: Streamlining, Not Corner Cutting," *Administrative Law Review*, 51 (summer 1999), pp. 757-766.

[23] See Office of the Vice President, *Improving Regulatory Systems: Accompanying Report of the National Performance Review* (Washington: Sept. 1993). The Administrative Conference was established by statute as an independent agency in 1964 to promote improvements in the efficiency, adequacy, and fairness of procedures by which federal agencies conduct

regulatory programs, administer grants and benefits, and perform related governmental functions. It was abolished in 1995.

[24] For more, see Michael Asimow, "Interim Final Rules: Making Haste Slowly," *Administrative Law Review*, 51 (summer 1999), pp. 703-755.

[25] U.S. General Accounting Office, *Federal Rulemaking: Agencies Often Published Final Actions Without Proposed Rules*, GAO/GGD-98-126, Aug. 31, 1998.

[26] See Juan J. Lavilla, "The Good Cause Exemption to Notice and Comment Rulemaking Requirements Under the Administrative Procedure Act," *The Administrative Law Journal*, 3 (fall 1989), pp. 3 17-423 for another study on the use of the good cause exception.

[27] NEPA regulations are codified at 40 CFR Parts 1500-1508.

[28] NEPA Task Force, Report to the Council on Environmental Quality, *Modernizing NEPA Implementation* (Washington: Sept. 2003).

[29] For example, EPA's Toxics Release Inventory (TRI) program is essentially a database created through collections of information imposed on businesses to inform the public about chemical hazards in their communities. TRI reports require businesses in certain industries to report the quantity of any of more than 600 chemicals entering each environmental medium on site, transfers of the chemical in wastes to off-site locations, on-site treatment methods and efficiency, and source reduction and recycling activities.

[30] For an up-to-date inventory of OMB-approved information collections, see [http://www.whitehouse.gov/omb/library/OMBINV.LIST.OF.AGENCIES.html].

[31] Independent regulatory agencies can, by majority vote, void any OIRA disapproval of a proposed collection of information.

[32] An agency's annual paperwork burden-hour estimate is a function of (1) the frequency of the information collection, (2) the estimated number of respondents, and (3) amount of time that the agency estimates it takes each respondent to complete the collection. For example, if an agency estimates that an information collection conducted twice each year will take each of the estimated 10,000 respondents 10 hours to complete each time, the total annual burden hour estimate for the collection is 200,000 burden hours (2 times 10,000 times 10).

[33] The act's definition of an agency excludes only the General Accounting Office, the Federal Election Commission, the governments of the District of Columbia, U.S. territories and possessions, and government-owned contractor-operated facilities.

[34] OMB is required to report to Congress on the implementation of the PRA, and does so through an annual "information collection budget." For paperwork estimates as of Sept. 30, 2002, see Office of Management and Budget, Office of Information and Regulatory Affairs, *Managing Information Collection and Dissemination: Fiscal Year 2003* (Washington: Apr. 2003). For an analysis of those data, see U.S. General Accounting Office, *Paperwork Reduction Act: Record Increase in Agencies' Burden Estimates*, GAO-03-691T, Apr. 11, 2003.

[35] Many agencies are apparently aware of this limitation; GAO estimated that in more than 500 final rules published in 1997 the agencies specifically stated that the RFA was not applicable or that a regulatory flexibility analysis was not required because the action was not preceded by an NPRM. See GAO/GGD-98-126, p. 31.

[36] U.S. Small Business Administration, *20 Years of the Regulatory Flexibility Act: Rulemaking in a Dynamic Economy* (Washington: 2000).

[37] This requirement, as well as a similar requirement in Executive Order 12866, is generally met via entries in the *Unified Agenda of Federal Regulatory and Deregulatory Actions*. The *Unified Agenda* is published twice each year in the *Federal Register* by the Regulatory Information Service Center, and provides uniform reporting of data on regulatory activities under development throughout the federal government.

[38] For an examination of the first five advocacy review panels were implemented, see U.S. General Accounting Office, *Regulatory Reform: Implementation of the Small Business Advocacy Review Panel Requirements*, GAO/GGD-98-36, March 18, 1996.

[39] U.S. General Accounting Office, *Regulatory Flexibility Act: Inherent Weaknesses May Limit Its Usefulness for Small Governments*, GAO/HRD-9 1-16, Jan. 11, 1991.

[40] U.S. General Accounting Office, *Regulatory Flexibility Act: Status of Agencies' Compliance*, GAO/GGD-94-105, Apr. 27, 1994.

[41] U.S. General Accounting Office, *Regulatory Flexibility Act: Agencies' Interpretations of Review Requirements Vary*, GAO/GGD-99-55, Apr. 2, 1999; U.S. General Accounting Office, *Regulatory Flexibility Act: Implementation in EPA Program Offices and Proposed Lead Rule*, GAO/GGD-00-193. Sept. 20, 2000.

[42] U.S. General Accounting Office, *Regulatory Flexibility Act: Key Terms Still Need to Be Clarified*, GAO-01-669T, Apr. 24, 2001.

[43] For more information about the RFA, see CRS Report RL34355, *The Regulatory Flexibility Act: Implementation Issues and Proposed Reforms*, by Curtis W. Copeland.

[44] U.S. General Accounting Office, *Regulatory Reform: Compliance Guide Requirement Has Had Little Effect on Agency Practices*, GAO-02-1 72, Dec. 28, 2001.

[45] U.S. General Accounting Office, *Regulatory Reform: Implementation of Selected Agencies' Civil Penalty Relief Policies for Small Entities*, GAO-01-280, Feb. 20, 2001.

[46] For a detailed discussion of CRA procedures, see CRS Report RL3 1160, *Disapproval of Regulations by Congress: Procedure Under the Congressional Review Act*, by Richard S. Beth.

[47] A related CRS analysis of the implementation of the CRA describes several possible impediments to the law's use. See CRS Report RL301 16, *Congressional Review of Agency Rulemaking: An Assessment After Nullification of OSHA's Ergonomics Standard*, by Morton Rosenberg. See also Morton Rosenberg, "Whatever Happened to Congressional Review of Agency Rulemaking?: A Brief Overview, Assessment, and Proposal for Reform," *Administrative Law Review*, vol. 51, fall 1999, pp. 1051-1092.

[48] See, for example, Susan E. Dudley, "Reversing Midnight Regulations," *Regulation*, vol. 24 (Spring 2001), p. 9, who noted that the "veto threat is diminished [after a transition], since the president whose administration issued the regulations is no longer in office." For a discussion of which rules may be carried over and disapproved after a transition, see CRS Report RL34633, *Congressional Review Act: Disapproval of Rules in a Subsequent Session of Congress*, by Curtis W. Copeland and Richard S. Beth.

[49] For more information, see CRS Report RL34354, *Congressional Influence on Rulemaking and Regulation Through Appropriations Restrictions*, by Curtis W. Copeland.

[50] For an overview of UMRA, see CRS Report RS20058, *Unfunded Mandates Reform Act Summarized*, by Keith Bea and Richard S. Beth. For a report on the implementation of Title I of UMRA, see U.S. Congressional Budget Office, *A Review of CBO 's Activities in 2002 Under the Unfunded Mandates Reform Act* (Washington: May 2003).

[51] In recent years, OIRA's annual report on UMRA has been combined with its report on the costs and benefits of federal regulations. See, for example, Office of Management and Budget, Office of Information and Regulatory Affairs, *2007 Report to Congress on the Benefits and Costs of Federal Regulations and Unfunded Mandates on State, Local, and Tribal Entities* (Washington: June 2008).

[52] U.S. General Accounting Office, *Unfunded Mandates: Reform Act Has Had Little Effect on Agencies' Rulemaking Actions*, GAO/GGD-98-30, Feb. 4, 1998.

[53] U.S. General Accounting Office, *Unfunded Mandates: Analysis of Reform Act Coverage*, GAO-04-637, May 12, 2004.

[54] U.S. Government Accountability Office, *Unfunded Mandates: Views Vary About Reform Act's Strengths, Weaknesses, and Options for Improvement*, GAO-05-454, March 31, 2005.

[55] OMB published those government-wide guidelines in interim form on September 28, 2001, and in updated final form on February 22, 2002. See Office of Management and Budget, "Guidelines for Ensuring and Maximizing the Quality, Objectivity, Utility, and Integrity of Information Disseminated by Federal Agencies; Republication," *Federal Register*, vol. 67, no. 36, Feb. 22, 2002, p. 8452.

[56] For a copy of this report, see [http://www.whitehouse.gov/omb/inforeg/fy03_info_quality_rpt.pdf].
5[7] For a copy of this report, see [http://www.ombwatch.org/infor/dataqualityreport.pdr].
[58] *Salt Institute; Chamber of Commerce of the United States of America v. Michael O. Leavitt, Secretary of Health and Human Services*, No. 05-1097, Mar. 6, 2006.
[59] *In re: Operation of the Missouri River Sys. Litig.*, No. 03-MD-1555 at 49 (D. Minn. June 21, 2004) (order granting motions for summary judgment); and *Salt Institute and the Chamber of Commerce of the United States of America v. Tommy G. Thompson, Secretary, U.S. Department of Health and Human Services*, Civil Action No. 04-359, Nov. 15, 2004. In the *Salt Institute* case, the court ruled that there is no private right of action under the IQA, saying that the "language in the IQA reflects Congress's intent that any challenges to the quality of information disseminated by federal agencies should take place in administrative proceedings before federal agencies and not the courts." The court also said that judicial review under the APA was not available because the agency's actions did not constitute a "final agency action," and because the agency decisions were within the discretion provided to the agency by law.
[60] For more information on the IQA, see CRS Report RL32532, *The Information Quality Act: OMB's Guidance and Initial Implementation*, by Curtis W. Copeland.
[61] Office of Management and Budget, Executive Office of the President, "Proposed Bulletin on Peer Review and Information Quality," *Federal Register*, vol. 68, no. 178, Sept. 15, 2003, p. 54023.
[62] For a copy of the revised peer review bulletin, see [http://www.whitehouse.gov/omb/inforeg/peer_review041404.pdf]. For a summary of the public and agency comments provided regarding the first bulletin, see [http://www.whitehouse.gov/omb/inforeg/peer_review_comment.pdf]. Copies of the comments can be viewed at [http://www.whitehouse.gov/omb/inforeg/2003iq/iq_list.html].
[63] Office of Management and Budget, *Final Information Quality Bulletin for Peer Review*, Dec. 15, 2004, available at [http://www.whitehouse.gov/omb/inforeg/peer2004/peer_bulletin.pdf].
[64] Office of Management and Budget, *Final Information Quality Bulletin for Peer Review*, 70 *Federal Register* 2664 (Jan. 14, 2005).
[65] In a Sept. 20, 2001, memorandum to the President's Management Council, the OIRA Administrator previously indicated that, during its reviews of agencies' draft rules under Executive Order 12866, it would give a "measure of deference" to regulatory analyses that had been peer reviewed.
[66] For more information, see CRS Report RL32680, *Peer Review: OMB's Proposed, Revised, and Final Bulletins*, by Curtis W. Copeland and Eric A. Fischer.
[67] For a complete discussion of negotiated rulemaking, see Administrative Conference of the United States, *Negotiated Rulemaking Sourcebook* (Sept. 1995).
[68] Cary Coglianese, "Assessing Consensus: The Promise and Performance of Negotiated Rulemaking," *Duke University Law Journal*, vol. 46 (1997), pp. 1255-1349.
[69] Laura I. Langbein and Cornelius M. Kerwin, "Regulatory Negotiation versus Conventional Rulemaking: Claims, Counterclaims, and Empirical Evidence," *Journal of Public Administration Research and Theory*, vol. 10 (2000), pp. 599-632.
[70] For more information, see CRS Report RL3 2452, *Negotiated Rulemaking*, by Curtis W. Copeland.
[71] For a discussion of federal policies relating to certification and consensus standards, see U.S. General Accounting Office, *Certification Requirements: New Guidance Should Encourage Transparency in Agency Decisionmaking*, GAO/GGD-99-170, Sept. 24, 1999.
[72] The accounting statement requirement had been included in appropriations bills for several previous years on a year-to-year basis.
[73] See [http://www.whitehouse.gov/omb/inforeg/regpol-reports_congress for copies of OMB's reports to Congress on this issue.

[74] For a comparison of the Regulations.gov website with individual agency systems, see U.S. General Accounting Office, *Electronic Rulemaking: Efforts to Facilitate Public Participation Can Be Improved*, GAO-03-90, Sept. 17, 2003.

[75] For more information, see CRS Report RL342 10, *Electronic Rulemaking in the Federal Government*, by Curtis W. Copeland.

[76] These lists of compliance assistance resources are available on the OMB website at [http://www.whitehouse.gov/omb/inforeg/infocoll.html#sbpra] and on the SBA website at [http://www.sba.gov/ombudsman/compliance/complianceassist.html].

[77] Executive Order 12866, "Regulatory Planning and Review," 58 *Federal Register* 51735, Oct. 4, 1993.

[78] Although issued on September 30, 1993, the executive order was not printed in the *Federal Register* until several days later. See The President, "Executive Order 12866 — Regulatory Planning and Review," *Federal Register*, vol. 58, no. 190 (Oct. 4, 1993).

[79] For a current list of regulations under OIRA review or reviews completed within the past 30 days, see [http://www.whitehouse.gov/omb/inforeg/regpol-regs _underl 2866.html].

[80] In January 1996, OIRA published a document that described "best practices" for preparing the economic analyses called for by the executive order. This document was revised and issued as guidance in 2000. In September 2003, OMB and the Council of Economic Advisors finalized new guidance for agencies on regulatory analysis, refining and replacing the 1996 "best practices" document. For a copy of this guidance, see [http://www. whitehouse.gov/omb/circulars/a004/a-4.pdf].

[81] OIRA has indicated that it will try and accommodate any request for a meeting with parties outside of the federal government. OIRA discloses these contacts on its website at [http://www.whitehouse.gov/omb/oira/meetings.html]. A representative from the agency issuing the rule must be invited to any such meeting.

[82] Executive Order 13258 reassigned certain responsibilities from the Vice President to the President's chief of staff, but otherwise did not change the OIRA review process. See The President, "Executive Order 13258 — Amending Executive Order 12866 on Regulatory Planning and Review," *Federal Register*, vol. 67, no. 40, Feb. 28, 2002, p. 9385.

[83] U.S. General Accounting Office, *Rulemaking: OMB's Role in Reviews of Agencies' DraftRules and the Transparency of Those Reviews*, GAO-03-929, Sept. 22, 2003.

[84] See, for example, Richard D. Morgenstern, ed., *Economic Analyses at EPA: Assessing Regulatory Impact* (Washington: Resources for the Future, 1997); and Robert W. Hahn, ed., *Risks, Costs, and Lives Saved: Getting Better Results from Regulation* (Washington: AEI Press, 1996).

[85] U.S. General Accounting Office, *Regulatory Reform: Agencies Could Improve Development, Documentation, and Clarity of Regulatory Economic Analyses,* GAO/RCED98-142, May 26, 1998.

[86] U.S. General Accounting Office, *Regulatory Reform: Agencies' Efforts to Eliminate and Revise Rules Yield Mixed Results*, GAO/GGD-98-3, Oct. 2, 1997.

[87] On the same day that E.O. 13422 was issued, OMB also issued a "Final Bulletin for Agency Good Guidance Practices" that mirrored, in many respects, the provisions in this section of the executive order. Unlike the order, however, the bulletin requires agencies to include certain standard elements in their significant guidance documents, to list those documents on the agencies' websites, and to publish a notice in the *Federal Register* soliciting public comments on economically significant documents. To view a copy of this bulletin, see [http://www.whitehouse.gov/omb/memoranda/fy2007/m07-07.pdf]; and Office of Management and Budget, "Final Bulletin for Agency Good Guidance Practices," 72 *Federal Register* 3432, January 25, 2007.

[88] For more information, see CRS Report RL33862, *Changes to the OMB Regulatory Review Process by Executive Order 13422*, by Curtis W. Copeland.

[89] Executive Order 13132, "Federalism," 64 *Federal Register* 43255, Aug. 10, 1999.

[90] Executive Order 12612, the previous executive order on federalism, also gave federal agencies broad discretion to determine the applicability of its requirements. GAO examined the implementation of this order and concluded that its analytical requirements were rarely implemented. See U.S. General Accounting Office, *Federalism: Previous Initiatives Have Had Little Effect on Agency Rulemaking*, GAO/T-GGD-99-3, June 30, 1999.

[91] Executive Order 12630, "Governmental Actions and Interference with Constitutionally Protected Property Rights," 53 *Federal Register* 8859, Mar. 18, 1988.

[92] For an analysis of how this executive order has been implemented, see U.S. General Accounting Office, *Regulatory Takings: Implementation of Executive Order on Government Actions Affecting Private Property Use*, GAO-03-1 015, Sept. 19, 2003.

[93] Executive Order 12889, "Implementation of the North American Free Trade Agreement," 58 *Federal Register* 69681, Dec. 30, 1993.

[94] Executive Order 12898, "Federal Actions to Address Environmental Justice in Minority Populations and Low-Income Populations," 59 *Federal Register* 7629, Feb. 16, 1994.

[95] Executive Order 12988, "Civil Justice Reform," 61 *Federal Register* 4729, Feb. 7, 1996.

[96] Executive Order 13045, "Protection of Children from Environmental Health Risks and Safety Risks," 62 *Federal Register* 19885, Apr. 23, 1997.

[97] Executive Order 13175, "Consultation and Coordination with Indian Tribal Governments," 65 *Federal Register* 67249, Nov. 9, 2000.

[98] Executive Order 13211, "Actions Concerning Regulations That Significantly Affect Energy Supply, Distribution, or Use," 66 *Federal Register* 28355, May 22, 2001.

[99] Executive Order 13272, "Proper Consideration of Small Entities in Agency Rulemaking," 67 *Federal Register* 53461, Aug. 16, 2002.

In: Federal Rulemaking and Regulations
Editors: Paul Lee
ISBN: 978-1-60876-069-5
© 2010 Nova Science Publishers, Inc.

Chapter 5

FEDERAL RULEMAKING: THE ROLE OF THE OFFICE OF INFORMATION AND REGULATORY AFFAIRS

Curtis W. Copeland

ABSTRACT

This chapter describes how OIRA reviews covered agencies draft rules, OIRAs effects on the rules, and changes in OIRAs procedures and policies in recent years. Much of that discussion is drawn from a September 2003 report on OIRA by the General Accounting Office (GAO). First, though, this chapter provides a history of presidential regulatory review and describe how OIRAs review process was established. Finally, the chapter describes several potential legislative issues regarding OIRAs regulatory review authority.

SUMMARY

The Paperwork Reduction Act of 1980 created the Office of Information and Regulatory Affairs (OIRA) within the Office of Management and Budget (OMB). Executive Order 12291, issued by President Reagan in 1981, gave

OIRA the responsibility to review the substance of agencies' regulatory actions before publication in the *Federal Register*. The office's regulatory review role was initially highly controversial, and it has been criticized at different times as being both too active and too passive regarding agencies' rules. Although OIRA has a number of specific statutory responsibilities (e.g., paperwork review and regulatory accounting), as a component of OMB it is part of the Executive Office of the President, and helps ensure that covered agencies' rules reflect the President's policies and priorities.

OIRA's current regulatory review responsibilities are detailed in Executive Order 12866, which was issued by President Clinton in 1993. The office reviews significant draft rules from agencies (other than independent regulatory agencies) at both the proposed and final rulemaking stages, and also informally reviews certain rules before they are formally submitted. For rules that are "economically significant" (most commonly defined as those having a $100 million impact on the economy), OIRA also reviews the economic analyses. Since 1994, OIRA has reviewed between 500 and 700 significant proposed and final rules each year, and can clear the rules with or without changes, return the rules to the agencies for reconsideration, or encourage the agencies to withdraw them. The executive order also requires OIRA or the rulemaking agencies to disclose certain elements of the review process to the public, including the changes made at OIRA's recommendation. A September 2003 report by the General Accounting Office indicated that OIRA had a significant effect on more than a third of the 85 rules in the study, but OIRA's most common effect was to suggest changes to explanatory language in the preambles to the rules. At the start of the George W. Bush Administration, OIRA made a number of changes to its review process, including increased use of return letters, added emphasis on economic analysis to support the rules, and improvements in the transparency of the office's review process. Overall, in contrast to the "counselor" role it played during the Clinton Administration, OIRA appeared to have returned to the "gatekeeper" role that it had during its first 12 years of existence. Possible legislative issues involving OIRA include codification of the office's review function and principles, increasing or decreasing the office's funding and staffing, adding review of rules from independent regulatory agencies, and improvements in the transparency of OIRA's review process.

The Office of Information and Regulatory Affairs (OIRA) is one of several statutory offices within the Office of Management and Budget (OMB),[1] and can play a significant—if not determinative—role in the rulemaking process for most federal agencies. In addition to its many other responsibilities, OIRA currently reviews the substance of between 500 and 700 significant proposed and final rules each year before agencies publish them in the *Federal Register*,[2] and can clear the rules with or without change, return them to the agencies for reconsideration, or encourage the agencies to withdraw the rules. Between 70 and 100 of the rules that OIRA reviews each year are each considered "economically significant" or "major" (e.g., have a $100 million impact on the economy). The office was created by Congress and has a number of specific statutory responsibilities, but also helps ensure that agencies' rules reflect the President's policies and priorities.

OIRA's role in the federal rulemaking process has been highly controversial in all four of the presidential administrations in which it has been in existence, but some of the criticisms directed at the office have varied over time. In some administrations, OIRA has been accused of controlling the agenda of the rulemaking agencies too much, directing them to change substantive provisions in draft rules or even stopping proposed regulatory actions that it believes are poorly crafted or unnecessary. At other times, though, OIRA has been accused of not exerting enough authority over the agencies' rules. Other, more persistent criticisms have focused on the lack of transparency of OIRA's regulatory reviews to the public and the sometimes unseen influence that regulated entities and other nongovernmental organizations can have on agencies' rules through those reviews.

This report describes how OIRA reviews covered agencies' draft rules, OIRA's effects on the rules, and changes in OIRA's procedures and policies in recent years. Much of that discussion is drawn from a September 2003 report on OIRA by the General Accounting Office (GAO, now the Government Accountability Office).[3] First, though, this report will provide a brief history of presidential regulatory review and describe how OIRA's review process was established. Finally, the report describes several potential legislative issues regarding OIRA's regulatory review authority.

THE ESTABLISHMENT OF REGULATORY REVIEW IN OIRA

OIRA was created within OMB by Section 3503 of the Paperwork Reduction Act (PRA) of 1980 (44 U.S.C. Chapter 35).[4] The PRA provided that OIRA would be headed by an administrator, and designated the OIRA administrator as the "principal advisor to the Director on Federal information policy." The act also said that the Director of OMB "shall delegate to the

(OIRA) Administrator the authority to administer all functions under this chapter." Specific areas of responsibility in the PRA that were assigned to the Director (and later delegated to OIRA) included information policy, information collection request clearance and paperwork control, statistical policy and coordination, records management, privacy, and automatic data processing and telecommunications.[5] With regard to paperwork reduction, the act generally prohibited agencies from conducting or sponsoring a collection of information until they had submitted their proposed information collection requests to OIRA and the office had approved those requests. The PRA's requirements cover rules issued by virtually all agencies, including Cabinet departments, independent agencies, and independent regulatory agencies and commissions.[6]

Although the PRA gave OIRA substantive responsibilities in many areas, the bulk of the office's day-to-day activities under the act were initially focused on reviewing and approving agencies' proposed information collection requests. OIRA had 77 staff members when the PRA took effect in 1981, of which about half were involved in reviewing agencies' information collection requests. That year, OIRA took nearly 5,000 paperwork review actions—approving new and revised collections, extending existing collections, and reinstating expired collections. The office's paperwork clearance workload since then has generally been between 4,000 and 6,000 actions each year, although the number of OIRA staff overall and those reviewing proposed collections has declined substantially.[7] Many federal regulations have an information collection component, but the PRA did not authorize OIRA to review or comment on the non-paperwork elements of those regulations, or on regulations without an information collection component.[8]

OIRA and Reagan Executive Orders on Regulatory Review

In 1980, President Reagan was elected on a platform critical of government's role in society in general and of federal regulations in particular. Shortly after taking office, he established a "Presidential Task Force on Regulatory Relief," headed by Vice President George H. W. Bush and composed of Cabinet officers (although the bulk of the task force's work was reportedly performed by OMB staff). The task force's responsibilities included (1) monitoring the establishment of OMB's responsibility to coordinate and review new rules, (2) the development of legislative changes to regulatory statutes, and (3) the revision of existing regulations. In relation to this last responsibility, the task force ultimately identified a total of 119 rules for alteration or cancellation by the issuing agencies, nearly half of which had been issued by the Department of Transportation or the Environmental Protection Agency. Although the task force said that implementation of the changes it recommended would save more than $150 billion over the next 10 years, critics charged that this estimate ignored the benefits associated with the rules on what they referred to as the administration's regulatory "hit list." The task force's legislative efforts were less successful, failing to get Congress to enact revisions to clean air and water laws or to enact broad regulatory reform legislation that would have limited agencies' rulemaking powers.[9]

In February 1981—less than one month after taking office—President Reagan issued Executive Order 12291[10] on "Federal Regulation," which greatly increased both the scope and importance of OIRA's responsibilities.[11] Specifically, the executive order generally required covered agencies (Cabinet departments and independent agencies, but not independent regulatory agencies) to:

- refrain from taking regulatory action "unless the potential benefits to society for the regulation outweigh the potential costs to society," select regulatory objectives to maximize net benefits to society, and select the regulatory alternative that involves the least net cost to society;
- prepare a "regulatory impact analysis" for each "major" rule, which was defined as any regulation likely to result in (among other things) an annual effect on the economy of $100 million. Those analyses were required to contain a description of the potential benefits and costs of the rule, a description of alternative approaches that could achieve the regulatory goal at lower cost (and why they weren't selected), and a determination of the net benefits of the rule. The issuing agency was to make the initial determination of whether a rule was "major," but the executive order gave OMB the authority to require a rule to be considered major; and
- send a copy of each draft proposed and final rule to OMB before publication in the *Federal Register*. The order authorized OMB to review "any preliminary or final regulatory impact analysis, notice of proposed rulemaking, or final rule based on the requirements of this Order." Non-major rules were required to be submitted to OMB at

least 10 days before publication, but major rules had to be submitted as much as 60 days in advance.

Executive Order 12291 authorized the director of OMB to review any draft proposed or final rule or regulatory impact analysis "based on the requirements of this Order." The executive order indicated that the review should be completed within 60 days, but allowed the director to extend that period whenever necessary. It also authorized the director to exempt classes of regulations from any or all of the order's requirements,[12] and generally required agencies to "refrain" from publishing any final rules until they had responded to OMB's comments. The executive order made OMB's authority to review agencies' draft rules subject to the overall direction of the presidential task force on regulatory relief.[13]

Although the executive order did not specifically mention OIRA, shortly after its issuance the Reagan Administration decided to integrate OMB's regulatory review responsibilities under the executive order with the responsibilities given to OMB (and ultimately to OIRA) by the PRA. As a result, OIRA's responsibilities for substantive review of rules under the executive order were added to the office's substantial responsibilities under the PRA. In 1981, OIRA reviewed the substance of nearly 2,800 rules under Executive Order 12291—in addition to the nearly 5,000 paperwork review actions it took that year.

In 1985, President Reagan extended OIRA's influence over rulemaking even further by issuing Executive Order 12498, which required Cabinet department and independent agencies (but not independent regulatory agencies) to submit a "regulatory program" to OMB for review each year that covered all of their significant regulatory actions underway or planned.[14] Previously, Executive Order 12291 required each of those agencies to publish semiannual "regulatory agendas" of proposed regulations that the agency "has issued or expects to issue," and any existing rule that was under review.[15] These agendas were required to contain a schedule for completing action on any major rule for which the agency had published a notice of proposed rulemaking. The new executive order went further, saying that, except in "unusual circumstances," OMB could return any rule submitted for review under Executive Order 12291 to the issuing agency for "reconsideration" if it was not in the agency's regulatory program for that year, or was "materially different" from what was described in the program.

In other words, OIRA could return a draft rule to an issuing agency if the office did not have advance notice of the rule's submission, even if the rule was otherwise consistent with the requirements in Executive Order 12291.[16] The regulatory agenda and program requirements in these executive orders also permitted OIRA to become aware of forthcoming agency actions well in advance of the submission of a draft proposed rule, thereby permitting the office to stop or alter an objectionable rule before the rulemaking process developed momentum. Although Reagan Administration officials compared this planning process to the process used to develop the President's budget, critics noted that the budget process has a final step that the regulatory process lacks—review and approval by Congress.

Comparison to Previous Regulatory Review Efforts

The establishment of this regulatory review function within OIRA was a significant development both in the office's history and in the overall movement to reform the federal regulatory process. In another sense, though, Executive Orders 12291 and 12498 represented the continuation of presidential review of rules, not the start of such reviews. Some form of centralized review of agencies' regulations within the Executive Office of the President has been part of the rulemaking process since the early 1970's. For example:

- In 1971, President Nixon established a "Quality of Life Review" program in which executive departments and independent agencies submitted all "significant" draft proposed and final rules pertaining to "environmental quality, consumer protection, and occupational and public health and safety" to OMB, which then circulated them to other agencies for comment.[17] In their submissions, agencies were to provide a summary of their proposals, including their principal objectives, the alternatives that they considered, and a comparison of the expected benefits and cost of those alternatives. Agencies were also required to submit a schedule showing estimated dates of proposed and final significant rules.
- In 1974, President Ford issued Executive Order 11821, which required agencies to prepare an "inflation impact statement" for each "major" proposed rule.[18] The statement was a certification that the inflationary impact of the rule had been evaluated in accordance with criteria and procedures developed by OMB. The executive order directed OMB to develop criteria for the identification of major rules

that may have a significant impact on inflation, but specified that the office must consider costs, effects on productivity, effects on competition, and effects on supplies of important products and services. Before a major rule was published in the *Federal Register*, the issuing agency was required to submit the associated impact statement to the Council on Wage and Price Stability (CWPS). CWPS would then either provide comments directly to the agency or participate in the regular rulemaking comment process.

- In 1978, President Carter issued Executive Order 12044, which (among other things) required agencies to publish semiannual agendas of any significant rules under development or review, and to prepare a regulatory analysis for at least all rules with a $100 million impact on the economy.[19] The analysis was to contain a succinct statement of the problem, a description of the alternative approaches considered, and the "economic consequences" of those alternatives. OMB was instructed to "assure the effective implementation of this Order," but was not given specific review responsibilities. President Carter also established (1) a "Regulatory Analysis Review Group" (RARG) to review the analyses prepared for certain major rules and to submit comments during the comment period, and (2) a "Regulatory Council" to coordinate agencies' actions to avoid conflicting requirements and duplication of effort.

In several ways, though, the analytical and review requirements in Executive Order 12291 were significantly different from these previous efforts. For example, the requirement in the new executive order that agencies choose the least costly approach to a particular regulatory objective went further than the requirement in President Carter's Executive Order 12044, which simply required agencies to analyze and consider alternative regulatory approaches. Also, whereas the regulatory oversight functions were divided among many offices (OMB, CWPS, RARG, and the regulatory council) during the Carter Administration, Executive Order 12291 consolidated these functions within OIRA.[20] Another major difference was the amount of influence that OIRA had compared to its predecessors. Under previous executive orders, CWPS and RARG had primarily an advisory role. In contrast, under Executive Order 12291, OIRA could overrule agency determinations regarding whether the rule was "major" (and therefore required a regulatory impact analysis), and could delay the regulation until the agency had adequately responded to its concerns (e.g., if it believed the agency had not considered all reasonable alternatives, that its analysis was not sound, or that it was contrary to administration policy). OIRA's significant influence on rulemaking was underscored by its organizational position within OMB—the agency that reviews and approves the rulemaking agencies' budget requests. Finally, and perhaps most importantly, the nature and transparency of the review process was significantly different under Executive Order 12291. Under the Carter Administration's approach, RARG and CWPS prepared and filed comments on agencies' regulatory proposals during the formal public comment period, *after* they were published in the *Federal Register*. In the case of RARG filings, a draft of the comments was circulated to all RARG members, and the comments and any dissents were placed on the public record at the close of the comment period. In contrast, OIRA's reviews occurred *before* the rules were published for comment, and Executive Order 12291 did not require that OIRA's comments on the draft rule be disclosed. This pre-publication review process made OIRA's regulatory reviews under Executive Order 12291 qualitatively different than its predecessors.

Early Views Regarding OIRA Reviews

The expansion of OIRA's authority in the rulemaking process via Executive Orders 12291 and 12498 was highly controversial. Although some believed that the authority did not go far enough (e.g., did not cover independent regulatory agencies), most of the concerns were that the expansion had gone too far. For example, a number of the concerns raised by Members of Congress, public interest groups, and others focused on whether OIRA's role violated the constitutional separation of powers and the effect that OIRA's review had on public participation and the timeliness of agencies' rules.[21] Some believed that OIRA's new authority displaced the discretionary authority of agency decision makers in violation of congressional delegations of rulemaking authority, and that the President exceeded his authority in issuing the executive orders. Others indicated that OIRA did not have the technical expertise needed to instruct agencies about the content of their rules. Still other concerns focused on OIRA's ability to carry out its many responsibilities. In 1983, GAO concluded that the expansion of OIRA's responsibilities under Executive Order 12291 had adversely affected the office's ability to carry out its PRA responsibilities, and recommended that Congress consider amending the act to prohibit OIRA from carrying out other responsibilities like regulatory review.[22]

Many of the early concerns about OIRA focused on the lack of transparency of the regulatory reviews, and specifically questioned whether OIRA had become a clandestine conduit for outside influence in the rulemaking process. Critics pointed out that in the first few months after the executive order was issued, OIRA met with representatives from dozens of businesses and associations seeking regulatory relief and returned dozens of rules to the agencies for reconsideration.[23] In response to these concerns, the OMB Director issued a memorandum in June 1981 stating that any factual material provided to OIRA regarding proposed rules should also be sent to the relevant rulemaking agency. The memorandum did not, however, apply to information provided to OIRA orally, and did not require that OIRA's meetings with outside parties be disclosed to the public.

OIRA's role in the rulemaking process remained controversial for the next several years. In 1983, Congress was so dissatisfied with OIRA's performance in the areas of regulatory and paperwork review that it permitted the office's appropriation authority to expire (although the office's statutory authority under the PRA was not affected and it continued to receive an appropriation via OMB).[24] In 1985, five House committee chairmen filed a friend-of-the-court brief in a lawsuit brought against the Department of Labor regarding the department's decision (reportedly at the behest of OMB) not to pursue a proposed standard concerning exposure to ethylene oxide, a sterilizing chemical widely used in hospitals and suspected of causing cancer. The chairmen claimed that OMB's actions represented a usurpation of congressional authority.

Congress reauthorized OIRA in 1986, but only after making the administrator subject to Senate confirmation. By 1986, Congress began considering legislation to restrict OIRA's regulatory review role and to block OIRA's budget request. In an attempt to head off that legislation, in June 1986 the OIRA administrator issued a memorandum for the heads of departments and agencies subject to Executive Order 12291 describing new OIRA procedures to improve the transparency of the review process. For example, the memorandum said that only the administrator or the deputy administrator could communicate with outside parties regarding rules submitted for review, and that OIRA would make available to the public all written materials received from outside parties. OIRA also said that it would, upon written request after a rule had been published, make available all written correspondence between OIRA and the agency head regarding the draft submitted for review.[25]

In 1987 the National Academy of Public Administration published a report on presidential management of agency rulemaking that summarized the criticisms of the OIRA review process as well as the positions of its proponents.[26] The report also described a number of issues in regulatory review and offered recommendations for improvement. For example, the report recommended that "regulatory management be accepted as an essential element of presidential management." It also recommended that regulatory agencies "log, summarize, and include in the rulemaking record all communications from outside parties, OMB, or other executive or legislative branch officials concerning the merits of proposed regulations."

In 1988, the Administrative Conference of the United States also examined the issue of presidential review of agency rulemaking and concluded that the reviews could improve coordination and resolve conflicts among agencies.[27] The Administrative Conference also said, though, that presidential review "does not displace responsibilities placed in the agency by law nor authorize the use of factors not otherwise permitted by law." The Conference recommended public disclosure of proposed and final agency rules submitted to OIRA under the executive order, communications from OMB relating to the substance of rules, and communications with outside parties, and also recommended that the reviews be completed in a "timely fashion."[28]

OIRA and the George H. W. Bush Administration

President George H. W. Bush continued the implementation of Executive Orders 12291 and 12498 during his administration, but external events significantly affected OIRA's operation and, more generally, the federal rulemaking process. In 1989, President Bush's nominee to head OIRA was not confirmed. Later, in response to published accounts that the burden of regulation was once again increasing, President Bush established the President's "Council on Competitiveness" (also known as the Competitiveness Council) to review regulations issued by agencies. Chaired by Vice President Quayle, the council oversaw and was supported by OIRA, and reviewed particular rules that it believed would have a significant impact on the economy or particular industries. According to OIRA representatives, the council signified continued White House-level interest in the regulatory arena, and also represented a continuation of the type of role played by the Presidential Task Force on Regulatory Relief during the Reagan Administration.

Many of the Competitiveness Council's actions were highly controversial, with critics assailing both the effects of those actions (e.g., rolling back environmental or other requirements) and the secrecy in which the council acted.[29] The council attempted to maintain strict secrecy regarding both its deliberations and those in the private sector with whom it communicated or consulted.[30] Critics decried what they believed to be "backdoor rulemaking" by the Competitiveness Council, but the council continued its operations until the end of the Bush Administration in 1993.

Meanwhile, OIRA continued its operations under Executive Order 12291, reviewing between 2,100 and 2,500 rules each year from 1989 through 1992.

REGULATORY REVIEW UNDER EXECUTIVE ORDER 12866

In September 1993, President Clinton issued Executive Order 12866 on "Regulatory Planning and Review," which revoked Executive Orders 12291 and 12498 and abolished the Council on Competitiveness.[31] Although different from its predecessors in many respects, Executive Order 12866 (which is still in effect) continued the general framework of presidential review of rulemaking. For example, it requires covered agencies (again, Cabinet departments and independent agencies but not independent regulatory agencies) to submit their proposed and final rules to OMB before publishing them in the *Federal Register*. The order also requires agencies to prepare cost-benefit analyses for their "economically significant" rules (essentially the same as "major" rules under Executive Order 12291). As discussed in detail below, however, Executive Order 12866 established a somewhat new regulatory philosophy and a new set of rulemaking principles, limited OIRA's reviews to certain types of rules, and established transparency requirements that included but went beyond those that had been put in place by the administrator's June 1986 memorandum. Section 2(b) of the order assigns responsibility for review of agency rulemaking to OMB, and specifically names OIRA as "the repository of expertise concerning regulatory issues." The order also named the Vice President as principal advisor to the President on regulatory policy, planning, and review.[32]

Specific Provisions in the Executive Order

In its statement of regulatory philosophy, Executive Order 12866 says, among other things, that agencies should assess all costs and benefits of available regulatory alternatives, including both quantitative and qualitative measures. It also provides that agencies should select regulatory approaches that maximize net benefits (unless a statute requires another approach). Where permissible and applicable, the order states that agencies should adhere to a set of principles when developing rules, including (1) consideration of the degree and nature of risk posed when setting regulatory priorities, (2) adoption of regulations only upon a "reasoned determination that the benefits of the intended regulation justify its costs," and (3) tailoring regulations to impose the least burden on society needed to achieve the regulatory objectives. Some of the stated objectives of the order are "to reaffirm the primacy of Federal agencies in the regulatory decision-making process; to restore the integrity and legitimacy of regulatory review and oversight; and to make the process more accessible and open to the public." According to OIRA representatives, the "primacy" of the agencies provision signaled a significant change in regulatory philosophy, vesting greater control of the rulemaking process with regulatory agencies and taking away authority from OIRA. Also, the requirement that the benefits of a regulation "justify" its costs was a noticeably lower threshold than the requirement in Executive Order 12291 that the benefits "outweigh" the costs.

Section 6 of Executive Order 12866 established agency and OIRA responsibilities in the centralized review of regulations. In contrast to the broad scope of review under Executive Order 12291, the new order limited OIRA reviews to actions identified by the rulemaking agency or OIRA as "significant" regulatory actions, which are defined in section 2(f) of the order as the following:

> "Any regulatory action that is likely to result in a rule that may (1) have an annual effect on the economy of $100 million or more or adversely affect in a material way the economy, a sector of the economy, productivity, competition, jobs, the environment, public health or safety, or State, local, or tribal governments or communities; (2) create a serious inconsistency or otherwise interfere with an action taken or planned by another agency; (3) materially alter the budgetary impact of entitlements, grants, user fees, or loan programs or the rights and obligations of recipients thereof; or (4) raise novel legal or policy issues arising out of legal mandates, the President's priorities, or the principles set forth in the Executive order."

As **Figure 1** shows, by focusing OIRA's reviews on significant rules, the number of draft proposed and final rules that OIRA examined fell from between 2,000 and 3,000 per year under the Executive Order 12291 to between 500 and about 700 rules per year under Executive Order 12866.

Executive Order 12866 also differs from its predecessors in other respects. For example, the order generally requires that OIRA complete its review of proposed and final rules within 90 calendar days,33 and requires both the agencies and OIRA to disclose certain information about how the regulatory reviews were conducted. Specifically, agencies are required to identify for the public (1) the substantive changes made to rules between the draft submitted to OIRA for review and the action subsequently announced and (2) changes made at the suggestion or recommendation of OIRA. OIRA is required to provide agencies with a copy of all written communications between OIRA personnel and parties outside of the executive branch, and a list of the dates and names of individuals involved in substantive oral communications. The order also instructs OIRA to maintain a public log of all regulatory actions under review and of all of the above-mentioned documents provided to the agencies.[34]

OIRA's Formal Review Process

As **Figure 2** shows, OIRA reviews agencies' draft rules at both the proposed and final stages of rulemaking.[35] In each phase, the review process starts when the rulemaking agency formally submits a regulatory review package to OIRA consisting of the rule, any supporting materials, and a transmittal form. The OIRA docket librarian then logs the receipt of the review package and forwards it to the appropriate desk officer. In some cases, agencies withdraw their rules from OIRA during the review period and the rules may or may not be subsequently resubmitted. At the end of the review period, OIRA either returns the draft rule to the agency "for reconsideration" or OIRA concludes that the rule is consistent with the executive order. OIRA codes the rule in its database as "consistent with change" if there had been any changes to the rule, regardless of the source or extent of the change. OIRA codes rules in its database as "consistent with no change" only if they are exactly the same at the end of the review period as the original submission. If the draft rule is a proposed rule and is judged by OIRA to be consistent with the executive order, the agency may then publish a notice of proposed rulemaking in the *Federal Register*, obtain comments during the specified comment period, review the comments received, and make any changes to the rule that it believes are necessary to respond to those comments. (Executive

Order 12866 says that this comment period should, in most cases, be at least 60 days for significant rules reviewed by OIRA.) If the draft is a final rule, the agency may publish the rule after OIRA concludes its review and the rule will generally take effect either at that point or at some later date specified by the agency.

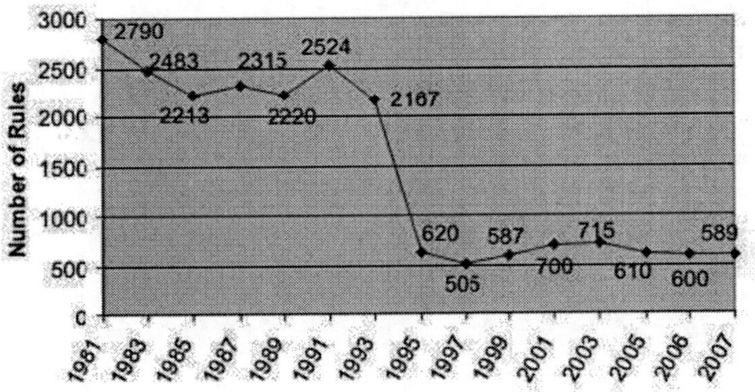

Source: http://www.reginfo.gov/public/do/eoCountsSearchInit?action=init

Figure 1. The Number of Rules That OIRA Reviewed Dropped Under Executive Order 12866, Issued in 1993

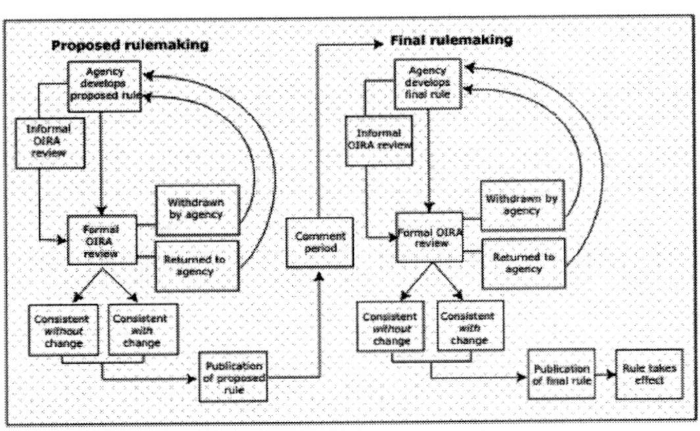

Source: GAO

Figure 2. OIRA Reviews Draft Proposed and Final Rules

Table 1. Most Rules That OIRA Reviewed Were Coded in Database as Changed or Not Changed

	Percentage of rules OIRA reviewed that were coded:				
Year	Consistent with change	Consistent without change	Withdrawn	Returned	Other
1994	37.3	53.4	4.3	0.2	4.9
1995	39.0	53.1	5.2	0.5	2.3
1996	51.5	41.4	5.1	0.0	2.0
1997	56.0	37.4	5.1	0.8	0.6
1998	59.3	36.1	3.1	0.0	1.4
1999	62.2	31.5	3.1	0.0	3.2
2000	60.4	34.3	3.9	0.0	1.4
2001	45.6	28.1	22.0	2.6	1.7
2002	54.3	31.7	7.6	0.7	5.6
2003	60.3	30.1	6.9	0.3	2.2
2004	62.7	29.8	6.5	0.2	0.8
2005	65.4	27.0	6.6	0.2	1.0
2006	69.2	26.5	3.7	0.0	0.7
2007	72.3	21.1	6.3	0.2	0.2

Source: OIRA.

Note: "Other" includes rules that were sent improperly, emergency rules, and rules with a statutory or judicial deadline. Numbers do not total to 100.0 due to rounding.

In most of the years since Executive Order 12866 was issued, more than 90% of the rules that OIRA reviewed were coded in the database as either "consistent with change" or "consistent without change." (See **Table 1**.) Only a small percentage of rules were withdrawn, and even fewer were returned to the agencies. The proportion of rules coded as "changed" has varied somewhat over time, but the last several years of the Clinton Administration (1997 through 2000) were fairly similar to the most recent non-transition years of the George W. Bush Administration (2002 through 2005). The data indicate that there were a relatively large number of rules that were withdrawn and returned in 2001 compared to other years. The withdrawn rules reflect actions taken at the start of the George W. Bush Administration pursuant to a memorandum issued by Assistant to the President and Chief of Staff Andrew H. Card, which generally directed Cabinet departments and independent agencies to (1) not send proposed or final rules to the Office of the Federal Register, (2) withdraw from the Office rules that had not yet been published in the *Federal Register*, and (3) postpone for 60 days the effective date of rules that had been published but had not yet taken effect.[36] As discussed in greater detail later in this chapter OIRA returned a number of rules to the agencies for reconsideration shortly after a new administrator was appointed in 2001.

The type of review that OIRA conducts under Executive Order 12866 sometimes depends on the type of draft rule submitted. For example, if the draft rule contains a collection of information covered by the PRA, the desk officer would also review it for compliance with that act. If the draft rule is "economically significant" (e.g., has an annual impact on the economy of at least $100 million), the executive order requires agencies to prepare an economic analysis describing, among other things, the alternatives that the agency considered and the costs and benefits of those alternatives.[37] For those economically significant rules, OIRA desk officers are to review the economic analyses using the office's guidance on how to prepare regulatory analyses under the executive order.[38]

An attachment to a September 20, 2001, memorandum to the President's Management Council described the general principles and procedures that OIRA reportedly uses in the implementation of Executive Order 1 2866.[39] For example, the attachment indicated that the office would, where appropriate, (1) include an evaluation of whether the agency has conducted an adequate risk assessment, (2) give "a measure of deference" to regulatory impact analyses and other supporting technical documents that have been peer reviewed in accordance with specified procedures, (3) ensure that regulatory clearance packages satisfy the requirements in other executive orders (e.g., include the certifications required by Executive Order 13132 on "Federalism" and Executive Order 13175 on "Consultation and Coordination with Indian and Tribal Governments"), (4) consult with the Small Business Administration (SBA) and the SBA Chief Counsel for Advocacy, and (5) ensure that agencies evaluate the possible impact of the draft rule on the programs of other federal agencies.

There is usually some type of communication during the review process (often via e-mail or telephone) between the OIRA desk officer and the rulemaking agency regarding specific issues in the draft rule. Briefings and meetings are sometimes held between OIRA and the agency during the review process, with OIRA branch chiefs, the deputy administrator, or the administrator involved in some of these meetings. According to OIRA representatives, the desk officers always consult with the resource management officers on the budget side of OMB as part of their reviews, and reviews of draft rules are not completed until those resource management officers sign off. If the draft rule is economically significant, the desk officer would also consult with a government economist to help review the required economic analysis. For other rules the desk officer might consult with other OIRA staff on issues involving statistics and surveys, information technology and systems, or privacy issues. In certain cases, OIRA may circulate a draft rule to other parts of the Executive Office of the President (e.g., the Office of Science and Technology Policy or the Council on Environmental Quality) or other agencies (e.g. the Departments of Energy, the Interior, or Transportation for certain Environmental Protection Agency rules).

Executive Order 12866 requires OIRA to complete its regulatory reviews within certain time frames—(1) within 10 working days of submission for any preliminary actions prior to a notice of proposed rulemaking (e.g., a notice of inquiry or an advance notice of proposed rulemaking) or (2) within 90 calendar days of submission for all other regulatory actions (or 45 days if OIRA had previously reviewed the material). In some instances, however, agency officials said OIRA will ask the rulemaking agency to withdraw the rule and resubmit it, restarting the review period. The executive order does not permit OIRA to "approve" or "disapprove" a draft rule; it is up to the agency to decide whether to proceed with publication of a rule after it had been returned, or to accept OIRA's suggested changes. OIRA representatives said it is often an iterative process in which the agencies and OIRA negotiate issues and clarify terms. Nevertheless, agencies very rarely publish rules that OIRA returns or ignore substantive OIRA "suggestions." In some instances, agency officials will formally or informally appeal OIRA determinations to the White House.

OIRA's Informal Reviews

Figure 2 also shows that, for some rules, there is an additional phase of "informal review" before the rule is officially submitted to OIRA. In its December 2001 report on the costs and benefits of federal regulations, OIRA stated that the office's original review process "was designed as an end-of-the-pipeline check against poorly conceived regulations."[40] OIRA also said, however, that by the time an agency formally submits a rule to OIRA for review there may be "strong institutional momentum" behind the proposal and, as a result, the agency may be reluctant to address certain issues that OIRA analysts might raise. Therefore, OIRA indicated "there is value in promoting a role for OIRA's analytic perspective earlier in the process, before the agency becomes too entrenched." OIRA went on to state the following:

> "A common yet informal practice is for agencies to share preliminary drafts of rules and/or analyses with OIRA desk officers prior to formal decision making at the agency. This practice is useful for agencies since they have the opportunity to educate OIRA desk officers in a more patient way, before the formal 90-day review clock at OMB begins to tick. The practice is also useful for OIRA analysts because they have the opportunity to flag serious problems early enough to facilitate correction before the agency's position is irreversible."

OIRA cannot informally review each of the hundreds of significant proposed and final rules that are submitted to the office each year. Informal reviews are most common when there is a statutory or legal deadline for a rule or when the rule is extremely large and requires discussion with not only OMB but also other federal agencies. The Environmental Protection Agency (EPA) and the Departments of Agriculture, Health and Human Services, and Transportation often issue those types of rules, and therefore are more likely to have their rules reviewed informally before formal submission.

OIRA has informally reviewed agencies' draft rules since its review function was established in 1981, but informal reviews reportedly became more common when Executive Order 12866 was adopted in 1993 and OIRA's reviews were focused on "significant" rules. There have been some indications, though, that OIRA has increased its use of informal reviews even further in recent years. For example, in its March 2002 draft report to Congress on the costs and benefits of federal regulation, OIRA said "agencies are beginning to invite OIRA staff into earlier phases of regulatory development in order to prevent returns late in the rulemaking process. It is at these early stages where OIRA's analytic approach can most improve on the quality of regulatory analyses and the substance of rules." Separately, in 2002, the OIRA administrator said "an increasing number of agencies are becoming more receptive to early discussions with OMB, at least on highly significant rulemakings."[41]

The administrator also indicated that agencies' "receptivity" to informal reviews may be enhanced by the possibility of a returned rule. For example, in early 2002 he said that OIRA was trying "to create an incentive for agencies to come to us when they know they have something that in the final analysis is going to be something we're going to be looking at carefully. And I think that agencies that wait until the last minute and then come to us—well, in a sense, they're rolling the dice."[42]

EFFECTS OF OIRA'S REVIEWS

Although a great deal has been written about OIRA's reviews of agencies' draft rules, few studies have systematically tried to determine the extent to which those reviews result in substantive changes to the rules. One such study (using data prior to the advent of Executive Order 12988) concluded that OIRA's reviews resulted in the rejection of some regulations that would have been economically inefficient, but did not appear to have improved the cost-effectiveness (e.g., costsper-life saved) of many of the rules.[43] Other studies have used OIRA's database showing the number of rules that were coded as "consistent with change" and "consistent without change" in an attempt to determine the significance of OIRA's effects on agencies' rules and whether those effects have changed over time.[44] As mentioned previously, however, the "consistent with change" code includes changes made at the initiation of the agencies as well as changes suggested by OIRA. Also, the code does not differentiate between minor editorial changes and changes that radically alter the effect of the rule. "Returns" and "withdrawals" in OIRA's database also need careful interpretation. A return may be for purely administrative reasons, not for substantive OIRA objections. Conversely, a withdrawal of a rule by an agency may have been initiated by OIRA. In order to use these data effectively, researchers should examine the associated documentation in the agencies' and OIRA's rulemaking dockets.

GAO's Analysis of OIRA's Effects

GAO published such an analysis in September 2003, supplementing information from OMB's database with information in the dockets and interviews with agency officials.[45] GAO reported that from July 1, 2001, through June 30, 2002, OIRA completed 642 reviews of agencies' draft proposed and final rules. Of these,

- About 33% (214) were coded in the database as "consistent with no change," indicating that OIRA considered the rules consistent with the executive order as submitted.
- About 50% (322) were coded as "consistent with change," indicating that the rules had changed after being submitted to OIRA, and that

OIRA subsequently concluded that the rule was consistent with the executive order's requirements.

- About 8% (50) were coded as "withdrawn" by the agency.
- About 3% (21) were coded as "returned" to the agency by OIRA.
- About 5% (35) had some other disposition (e.g., "sent improperly," "emergency," or "statutory or judicial deadline").

In order to make its review manageable, GAO focused on 85 of those rules that were coded as changed, withdrawn, or returned and that were submitted to OIRA by nine selected health, safety, or environmental agencies or offices: the Animal and Plant Health Inspection Service within the Department of Agriculture; the Food and Drug Administration within the Department of Health and Human Services; the Occupational Health and Safety Administration within the Department of Labor; the Federal Aviation Administration (FAA), the Federal Motor Carrier Safety Administration, and the National Highway Traffic Safety Administration (NHTSA) with the Department of Transportation (DOT); and the offices of air and radiation, water, and solid waste and emergency response within EPA. Seventy-one of the 85 rules had been coded "consistent with change," nine were coded as "returned," and five were coded as "withdrawn."

OIRA's Impact on Rules

GAO's analysis of the underlying documents indicated that OIRA had a significant effect on at least 25 of the 85 draft rules. Specifically:

- Of the 71 "changed" rules, GAO concluded that OIRA had suggested significant changes to 17 of them—changes that affected the scope, impact, or estimated costs or benefits of the rules as originally submitted. In general, the focus of OIRA's suggested changes appeared to be on reducing regulatory burden (and, in some cases, the expected benefits as well). Fourteen of the 17 significantly changed rules were from EPA's office of air and radiation or its office of water. For example, at OIRA's recommendation, EPA removed manganese from a list of hazardous wastes, deleted certain types of engines from coverage of a rule setting emissions standards, and delayed the compliance dates for two other types of emissions. Of the remaining 54 "changed" rules, the most significant changes made at OIRA's suggestion involved adding explanatory language to the preambles of the rules and asking for comment on particular provisions. In 20 of the 54 rules, OIRA suggested only minor editorial changes (e.g., correcting spelling errors or citations) or made no suggestions at all.

- Of the nine rules that had been returned to the agencies by OIRA, two were returned because they had been improperly submitted, not because of substantive defect. OIRA returned the remaining seven rules because of concerns about the agencies' regulatory analyses or a perceived lack of coordination between rulemaking agencies. For example, OIRA returned one EPA rule because the agency did not provide a quantitative analysis of costs and benefits, and returned a NHTSA rule because OIRA did not believe that the agency had demonstrated that it had selected the best available alternative. Five of the seven rules returned for substantive reasons had been submitted by the FAA.
- Of the five rules that were withdrawn, GAO determined that only one had been withdrawn at OIRA's suggestion. The other four rules were withdrawn solely at the agencies' initiative or as a result of a mutual decision by the agencies and OIRA.

If anything, GAO's analysis understates the influence that OIRA has on agencies' rules because its findings were often limited to the documentation that was available. If OIRA suggested a change to a rule before it was formally submitted to OIRA (e.g., during informal review), GAO's analysis would not reflect those changes. In fact, the rule might not have even been in the universe of rules that GAO examined (i.e., those coded as changed, returned, or withdrawn during OIRA's formal review). Other forms of OIRA influence may be even more indirect and harder to document. For example, some agencies have indicated that they do not even propose certain regulatory provisions because they believe that OIRA would find them objectionable.

Regulated Entities' Contacts with OIRA

GAO also reported that regulated entities directly contacted OIRA either before or during its review process regarding 11 of the 25 rules that OIRA significantly affected.[46] Eight of those 11 cases involved EPA rules, and the nature of the contacts ranged from meetings with OIRA representatives to letters sent to OIRA. In 7 of the 11 cases, GAO concluded that what OIRA ultimately recommended to the rulemaking agencies was similar to what these regulated parties recommended to OIRA—in some cases, using similar language to that used by the regulated entities. For example, during OIRA's review of an EPA rule on identification and listing of hazardous waste, industry representatives met with and sent letters to OIRA opposing the listing of manganese as a hazardous waste constituent. (The industry representatives had made essentially the same argument to EPA during the public comment phase, but EPA did not agree.) The main focus of OIRA's comments to EPA at the conclusion of its review was that final action on listing manganese as a hazardous contaminant should be deferred. Notwithstanding the congruence between the comments of the regulated entities and OIRA's comments, GAO said it was impossible to determine the extent to which this or other suggestions made by the regulated entities might have influenced OIRA's actions, if at all.

CHANGES IN OIRA'S POLICIES AND PRACTICES DURING THE GEORGE W. BUSH ADMINISTRATION

The formal process by which OIRA reviews agencies' draft rules has changed little since Executive Order 12866 was issued in 1993.[47] There have, however, been several subtle yet notable changes in OIRA policies and practices in recent years—particularly after Dr. John D. Graham became OIRA administrator in July 2001. In October 2002, Administrator Graham said "the changes we are making at OMB in pursuit of smarter regulation are not headline grabbers: No far-reaching legislative initiatives, no rhetoric-laden executive orders, and no campaigns of regulatory relief. Yet we are making some changes that we believe will have a long-lasting impact on the regulatory state."[48]

Return of the "Gatekeeper" Role

As noted previously, during the Reagan Administration, OIRA was often criticized for acting as a regulatory gatekeeper, actively overseeing and recommending changes to agencies' rules. During the Clinton Administration, however, the opposite concerns were expressed. A number of observers criticized OIRA for not overseeing the actions of the rulemaking agencies more aggressively. In September 1996, the then-administrator of OIRA testified that "we have consciously changed the way we relate to the agencies," and described OIRA's relationship with the rulemaking agencies as "collegial" and "constructive."[49] She also said she agreed with an article that said OIRA functioned during that period "more as a counselor during the review process than as an enforcer of the executive order."[50]

OIRA during the George W. Bush Administration has returned to the role it had during the Reagan Administration, even describing itself in an annual report as the "gatekeeper for new rulemakings."[51] OIRA Administrator Graham said one of the office's functions is "to protect people from poorly designed rules," and said OIRA review is a way to "combat the tunnel vision that plagues the thinking of single-mission regulators." He has also compared OIRA's review of agencies' rules to OMB's role in reviewing agencies' budget requests. This return to the gatekeeper perspective of OIRA's role has implications for an array of OIRA's functions, and underlays many of the other changes described below.

Increased (and Decreased) Use of Return Letters

As noted previously in **Table 1**, during the Clinton Administration, OIRA only rarely returned rules to the agencies for reconsideration. Specifically, according to OIRA's database, of the more than 4,000 rules that OIRA reviewed from 1994 through 2000, OIRA returned only seven rules to the agencies—three in 1995 and four in 1997. OIRA administrators during that period said they viewed the use of return letters as evidence of the failure of the collaborative review process, since OIRA and the agencies were part of the same presidential Administration.

In contrast, OIRA Administrator Graham referred to return letters as the office's "ultimate weapon," and viewed them as a way to make clear that the office is serious about the review process. In the first eight months after he took office in July 2001, OIRA returned 21 draft rules to the agencies for reconsideration. DOT had the most rules returned during 2001 and 2002 (eight), followed by the Social Security Administration (five) and the Department of Veterans Affairs (four).[52] The letters commonly indicated that OIRA returned the rules because of concerns about the agencies' analyses (e.g., whether the agencies had considered all reasonable alternatives or had selected the alternative that would yield the greatest net benefits).

Subsequently, however, the pace of OIRA's return letters slowed. Although the average number of rules that OIRA reviewed each month stayed about the same, in the period from March 2002 until January 2008, OIRA returned a total of seven draft rules to the agencies—a dramatic decline from the 21 returns during Administrator Graham's first eight months in office.[53] OIRA officials attributed the decline in return letters to the improved quality of agencies' regulatory submissions after the initial flurry of returns.

Advent (and Decline) of Prompt Letters

OIRA has traditionally been a reactive force in the rulemaking process, commenting on draft proposed and final rules that are generated by the agencies. Although OIRA occasionally suggested regulatory topics to the agencies during previous administrations, the practice was relatively uncommon and the discussions were not made public. In contrast, OIRA Administrator Graham was more publicly proactive, sending several agencies "prompt letters" (and posting them on the OIRA website) suggesting that they develop regulations in a particular area or encouraging the agencies' ongoing efforts.[54] For example, one such letter encouraged NHTSA to give greater priority to modifying its frontal occupant protection standard, and another letter suggested that OSHA make the promotion of automatic external heart defibrillators a higher priority. Other prompt letters recommended that the agencies better focus certain research or programs. Between September 2001 and December 2003, OIRA sent a total of 13 prompt letters to regulatory agencies, and several of the agencies took action in response to the letters. Since then, however, the number of prompt letters diminished substantially. Only two prompt letters were issued in 2004, none in 2005, one in 2006, and none in 2007.

Increased Emphasis on Economic Analysis

Although OIRA has always encouraged agencies to provide well-developed economic analyses for their draft rules, Administrator Graham expressed greater interest in this issue than his predecessors. Also, according to agency officials, there has been a perceptible "stepping up the bar" in the amount of support required for their rules, with OIRA reportedly more often looking for regulatory benefits to be quantified and a cost-benefit analysis for every regulatory option that the agency considered, not just the option selected.

In September 2003, OIRA published revised guidelines for economic analysis under the executive order—updating "best practices" guidance issued in January 1996.[55] The new guidelines were generally similar to the earlier guidance, but differed in several key areas—e.g., encouraging agencies to (1) perform both cost-effectiveness and cost-benefit analyses in support of their major rules,[56] (2) use multiple discount rates when the benefits and costs of rules are expected to occur in different time periods,[57] and (3) use a formal probability analysis of benefits and costs when a rule is expected to have more than a $1 billion impact on the economy (unless the effects of the rule are clear).

Although OIRA has said that regulations based on economic analysis are more likely to be better than those that are not, it has also signaled that these analyses are sometimes difficult or impossible for certain types of rules. In November 2005, OIRA Administrator Graham said "[h]omeland security regulations account for about half of our major-rule costs in 2004 but we do not yet have a feasible way to fully quantify benefits."[58] He also said that cost-benefit analysis may not be appropriate for homeland security rules, and that a more practical "soft" test was being used for them.[59] Some have questioned why assessments of homeland security rules should be treated differently than health, safety, and environmental rules.[60]

Increased Transparency

As noted previously, many of the longstanding concerns about OIRA's role in the rulemaking process have centered on the perceived lack of transparency of its reviews. Executive Order 12866 attempted to address some of those concerns, requiring (among other things) that agencies disclose after the publication of a rule the changes made to the rule during OIRA's review and the changes made at the suggestion or recommendation of OIRA. The executive order requires OIRA to maintain a publicly available log disclosing the status of all regulatory actions under review and the names and dates of those involved in substantive oral communications (e.g., meetings, telephone calls) between OIRA staff and parties outside of the executive branch. These requirements notwithstanding, concerns about the lack of transparency continued. For example, even after issuance of the executive order, OIRA disclosed contacts with outside parties only if they occurred during the office's formal review period, not if they occurred during its informal reviews.

In October 2001, the OIRA administrator published a memorandum to OIRA staff on the office's website that extended the executive order's disclosure requirements in several areas. For example, the memorandum said that OIRA would disclose substantive meetings and other contacts with outside parties about a rule under review even if OIRA was only informally reviewing the rule. OIRA also said it would disclose substantive telephone calls with outside parties that were initiated by the administrator, not just calls initiated by outside parties. OIRA has also posted on its website lists of regulations currently under review,[61] reviews concluded in the previous 30 days,[62] and its contacts with outside parties.[63] Although these changes have improved the transparency of OIRA's reviews, as discussed later in this chapter, the effects of OIRA's reviews (particularly informal reviews) are not always apparent.

Changes in OIRA Staffing

When OIRA was created in FY1981, the office had a "full-time equivalent" (FTE) ceiling of 90 staff members. By 1997, OIRA's FTE allocation had declined to 47—a nearly 50% reduction. Although Executive Order 12866 (issued in late 1993) permitted OIRA to focus its resources on "significant" rules, this decline in OIRA staffing also occurred during a period in which regulatory agencies' staffing and budgetary levels were increasing and OIRA was given a number of new statutory responsibilities. Specifically, as discussed later in this chapter, OIRA was expected to perform various duties under the Unfunded Mandates Reform Act of 1995, the Small Business Regulatory Enforcement Fairness Act of 1996, and the Regulatory Right-to-Know Act of 2001.

Starting in 2001, OIRA's staffing authorization began to increase; by 2002, it stood at 55 FTEs. Between 2001 and 2003, OIRA hired five new staff members in such fields as epidemiology, risk assessment, engineering, and health economics. OIRA indicated that these new hires reflected the increasing importance of science-based regulation in federal agencies, and would enable OIRA to ask penetrating technical questions about agency proposals.

Changes to OIRA Review by Executive Order 13422

On January 18, 2007, President George W. Bush issued Executive Order 13422, making the most significant amendments to Executive Order 12866 since it was published in 1993. The changes made by this new executive order are controversial, characterized by some as a "power grab" by the White House that undermines public protections and lessens congressional authority,[64] and by others as "a paragon of common sense and good government."[65]

The most important changes made to Executive Order 12866 by Executive Order 13422 fall into five general categories: (1) a requirement that agencies identify in writing the specific market failure or problem that warrants a new regulation, (2) a requirement that each agency head designate a presidential appointee within the agency as a "regulatory policy officer" who can control upcoming rulemaking activity in that agency, (3) a requirement that agencies provide their best estimates of the cumulative regulatory costs and benefits of rules they expect to publish in the coming year, (4) an expansion of OIRA review to include significant guidance documents, and (5) a provision permitting agencies to consider whether to use more formal rulemaking procedures in certain cases.

A separate CRS report discusses each of these changes, noting areas that are unclear and the potential implications of the changes; provides background information on presidential review of rules; discusses three congressional hearings on the executive order in 2007; and notes congressional efforts to block the implementation of the order.[66] It concludes by pointing out that the significance of the changes made to the review process by Executive Order 13422 may become clear only through their implementation. The changes made by this executive order represent a clear expansion of presidential authority over rulemaking agencies. In that regard, Executive Order 13422 can be viewed as part of a broader statement of presidential authority presented throughout the Bush Administration.

OIRA's Other Responsibilities

In addition to its regulatory review responsibilities under Executive Order 12866 and its multiple responsibilities under the Paperwork Reduction Act (paperwork review, information resources management, statistical policy and coordination, records management, privacy and security, and information technology), Congress has assigned OIRA a number of other specific functions related to the rulemaking and regulatory process. For example:

- The Unfunded Mandates Reform Act of 1995 (2 U.S.C. 1532-1538) generally requires agencies to prepare written statements describing the effects of their rules that are subject to the act's requirements. The act requires the director of OMB to collect those written statements and provide them to the Congressional Budget Office, to establish pilot programs to test innovative regulatory approaches, and to prepare an annual report on the implementation of the act. The OMB director has delegated these responsibilities to OIRA.[67]
- The Small Business Regulatory Enforcement Fairness Act of 1996 (SBREFA) (5 U.S.C. 601 note) required EPA and OSHA to convene "advocacy review panels" before publishing proposed rules expected to have a significant economic impact on a substantial number of small entities.[68] The act specifically requires the review panel to include full-time employees from OIRA as well as other agencies.
- SBREFA also contains provisions commonly referred to as the "Congressional Review Act," which (among other things) requires agencies to delay the effective date of "major" rules, and requires GAO to submit a report on those rules within 15 days of their issuance. SBREFA defines a major rule as one that the OIRA administrator concludes has resulted or is likely to result in (among other things) a $100 million annual effect on the economy.[69]
- Section 515 of the Treasury and General Government Appropriations Act for Fiscal Year 2001 (44 U.S.C. 3504 (d)(1) and 3516), generally known as the "Data Quality Act" or the "Information Quality Act," directed OMB to take several actions (all of which were delegated to OIRA). Specifically, the act required OMB to issue governmentwide guidelines that "provide policy and procedural guidance to Federal agencies for ensuring and maximizing the quality, objectivity, utility, and integrity of information (including statistical information) disseminated by Federal agencies." OMB published those guidelines in final form on February 22, 2002.[70] The act also required agencies to develop their own guidelines (which were reviewed by OMB), and to report to OMB on the number and nature of complaints received and how such complaints were handled by the agency.

- Section 624 of the Treasury and General Government Appropriations Act, 2001, (31 U.S.C. 1105 note), sometimes known as the "Regulatory Right-to-Know Act," requires OMB to prepare and submit with the budget an annual "accounting statement and associated report" containing an estimate of the costs and benefits (including quantifiable and nonquantifiable effects) of federal rules and paperwork, to the extent feasible, (1) in the aggregate, (2) by agency and agency program, and (3) by major rule. The accounting statement is also required to contain an analysis of impacts of federal regulation on state, local, and tribal governments, small businesses, wages, and economic growth. Similar one-year requirements were in previous appropriations acts.
- The same legislation requires OMB to include "recommendations for reform" in its cost-benefit reports. Rather than rely on its own expertise, OIRA decided to solicit suggestions from the public. For example, in March 2002, OIRA asked the public for recommendations to eliminate or modify existing rules as well as to expand or extend existing programs. In response, OIRA received more than 300 suggestions, which OIRA turned over to the appropriate agencies for prioritization. In February 2004, OIRA asked the public for suggested reforms of rules affecting the manufacturing sector. OIRA said it was focusing on manufacturing because of the relatively large impact that regulations have on that sector.[71]
- The Small Business Paperwork Relief Act of 2002 (P.L. 107-198) requires OMB to annually publish, in the *Federal Register* and on the Internet, a list of compliance assistance resources available to small businesses. The act also requires OMB to convene and chair a task force to study the feasibility of streamlining paperwork requirements on small businesses. The task force was required to file an initial report by the end of June 2003, and is required to file a second report by the end of June 2004.
- The E-Government Act of 2002 (P.L. 107-347) requires the OIRA administrator to work with the administrator of the Office of Electronic Government to establish the strategic direction of the governmentwide e-government program and to oversee its implementation. OIRA has been particularly active in the Administration's e-rulemaking initiative.
- In the Treasury and General Government Appropriations Act, 2002 (P.L. 107-67), Congress stated that about $6.3 million of OMB's

$70.7 million appropriation was for OIRA, but stipulated that nearly $1.6 million of that amount should not be obligated until OMB "submits a report to the Committees on Appropriations that provides an assessment of the total costs and benefits of implementing Executive Order No. 13 166."[72]

- The conference report for OMB's appropriation for FY2004 (to accompany H.R. 2673) directed OIRA to submit a report to the House and Senate Committees on Appropriations by June 1, 2004, on "whether agencies have been properly responsive to public requests for correction of information pursuant to the (Data Quality Act)."[73]

Congress also sometimes limits OIRA's actions through riders on OMB's appropriation. For example, since 1983, language has been included in OMB's appropriation stating that none of the funds appropriated to OMB could be used for the purpose of reviewing any agricultural marketing orders issued by the Department of Agriculture. Marketing orders, which cover dozens of commodities from lemons to milk, basically keep prices up by regulating supplies, and had been targeted for elimination or amendment by President Reagan's task force on regulatory relief in the early 1 980s. In response, Members of Congress have inserted this restriction in each subsequent appropriation bill, asserting that the Department of Agriculture, not OMB, has statutory authority in this area.

In other cases, OIRA has taken on additional responsibilities, sometimes basing its actions on previous statutory or executive order authorities. For example:

- In December 2004, OIRA published a final bulletin establishing government-wide guidance aimed at enhancing the practice of peer review of government science documents.[74] The bulletin applied to all "influential scientific information" and "highly influential scientific assessments." The final version of the bulletin gave agencies significantly greater discretion to decide when information required peer review than the September 2003 proposed bulletin, but OIRA retained significant authority in certain areas (e.g., when information is "highly influential" and requires more stringent peer review).
- In November 2005, OMB published a proposed bulletin "Good Guidance Practices," saying that it was concerned that agency guidance documents "may not receive the benefit of careful consideration accorded under the procedures for regulatory

development and review.[75] OMB did not cite any specific statutes or executive orders as authorizing the issuance of the bulletin, but did indicate that it was "responsible both for promoting good management practices and for overseeing and coordinating the Administration's regulatory policy." The bulletin would require agencies to develop written procedures for the approval of significant guidance documents, and to publish "economically significant" documents in the *Federal Register* and invite comments.

- In January 2006, OIRA published a proposed bulletin on agency risk assessment practices for public comment and peer review by the National Academy of Sciences.[76] The legal authorities cited for the bulletin included the Information Quality Act and "OMB's general authorities to oversee the quality of agency analyses, information and regulatory actions." The bulletin described a series of general risk assessment and reporting standards, and also laid out a set of "special standards for influential risk assessments." It requires agencies to certify that each covered risk assessment has complied with the bulletin's requirements, but allows agency heads to waiver or defer some or all of its requirements.

OIRA and the Future of Presidential Regulatory Review

For more than 25 years, OIRA has played a central role in the federal rulemaking process. Although some argued early in OIRA's history that the office's regulatory review role was unconstitutional, few observers continue to hold that view. No court has directly addressed the constitutionality of the OIRA regulatory review process, but in 1981 (the year that OIRA was created) the D.C. Circuit said the following:

> The court recognizes the basic need of the President and his White House staff to monitor the consistency of agency regulations with Administration policy. He and his advisors surely must be briefed fully and frequently about rules in the making, and their contributions to policymaking considered. The executive power under our Constitution, after all, is not shared—it rests exclusively with the President.[77]

OIRA is located within the Executive Office of the President and is the President's direct representative in the governmentwide rulemaking process. As Executive Order 12866 states, OIRA is the "repository of expertise on regulatory issues" within the Executive Branch, and is uniquely positioned both within OMB (with its budgetary influence) and within the federal rulemaking process (reviewing and commenting on rules just before they are published in the *Federal Register*) to enable it to exert maximum influence.

Variations in how OIRA operates—as a gatekeeper or a counselor—are largely a function of the wishes of the President that the office serves. For example, in a June 2001 article in *Harvard Law Review*, Elena Kagan posited that, while it is generally acknowledged that President Reagan used OIRA's review function as a tool to control the policy and political agenda in an anti-regulatory manner, President Clinton did much the same thing to accomplish pro-regulatory objectives.[78]

She said he did so by exercising directive authority and asserting personal ownership over a range of agency actions, thereby making them "presidential" in nature. She also characterized this emergence of enhanced methods of presidential control over the regulatory state—what she termed the "presidentialization of administration"—as "the most important development in the last two decades in administrative process."

Other observers, however, view OIRA (like other executive branch agencies) as having more of a shared allegiance between the President and the Congress. They point out that OIRA was created by Congress, and has been given a number of statutory responsibilities through the PRA and other laws. Nevertheless, even supporters of a strong legislative perspective recognize that OIRA is part of the Executive Office of the President, and that Congress gave OIRA its responsibilities because of its strategic position within that office.[79] With both statutory and executive order responsibilities, OIRA embodies a broader tension between Congress and the President for control of administrative agencies.

Although major differences of opinion exist among observers of the federal rulemaking process regarding the appropriateness of OIRA's regulatory review role, the broad reach and influence of the office's is undebatable. Rulemaking agencies formally challenge OIRA's returns and "suggestions" for change only rarely, and sometimes refrain from even submitting draft rules for review if they believe they will be opposed by OIRA. Regulated entities also recognize OIRA's influence, and seem to view the office as a "court of second resort" if they are unable to influence regulatory agencies to their position directly.

Possible Legislative Issues

Congress also recognizes the importance that OIRA plays in the rulemaking process, and usually holds several hearings each year examining OIRA's implementation of its responsibilities pursuant to various statutes and executive orders. Proposals for changes to OIRA's authority and responsibilities have focused on such issues as (1) providing a statutory underpinning for regulatory reviews, (2) increasing or decreasing the office's funding and staffing, (3) including independent agencies' rules under the office's regulatory review function, and (4) improving the transparency of OIRA's regulatory review processes.

Statutory Authority for Regulatory Review

As noted previously, Congress has enacted legislation expanding OIRA's statutory responsibilities, and has considered (but not enacted) legislation that would provide a statutory basis for OIRA's regulatory review function. For example, in the 106th Congress, section 632 of S. 746 (the "Regulatory Improvement Act of 1999") would have required the President (via OMB and OIRA) to "establish a process for the review and coordination of Federal agency regulatory actions." The proposed legislation also would have placed in statute many of the transparency requirements in Executive Order 12866.

Congress has also considered legislation that would affect OIRA as part of broader OMB changes. For example, during the 107th Congress, proposed legislation was introduced (H.R. 616) that would have established an Office of Management within the Executive Office of the President and redesignated OMB as the Office of the Federal Budget. As part of that process, OIRA and other offices within OMB would have been abolished and their functions and authorities transferred to the new Office of Management. Neither of these bills was enacted.

Funding and Staffing

OIRA does not have a specific line item in the budget, so its funding is part of OMB's appropriation. Similarly, OIRA's staffing levels are allocated from OMB's totals. Although OIRA staffing has increased in recent years, as of May 2004, OIRA had fewer staff than it had when its regulatory review function was first established in 1981. Currently, about 30 OIRA desk officers and branch chiefs review about 3,000 agency information collection requests each year and between 500 and 700 significant rules each year. At various times in its history, certain Members of Congress have attempted to reduce funding for OIRA in order to signal congressional displeasure with the office's actions.[80] Other observers, however, believe that OIRA's funding should be increased, not reduced, arguing that a relatively small amount of additional resources for OIRA could yield substantial benefits.[81]

At other times, proposed legislation has been introduced designating how OIRA staff should be used. For example, in the 108th Congress, a provision in H.R. 2432 as originally introduced would have required the OMB Director to "assign, at a minimum, the equivalent of at least 2 full time staffers to review the Federal information collection burden on the public imposed by the Internal Revenue Service." The Internal Revenue Service accounts for more than 80% of the estimated paperwork burden, but OIRA indicated that it devoted less than one FTE to reviewing the agency's paperwork requests (because much of the burden is mandated by statute). The Bush Administration objected to this specific direction of OIRA staff, so the sponsors of the bill agreed to delete this requirement before it was approved by the House of Representatives in May 2004.

Addition of Independent Agencies' Rules

Although several of the statutes that OIRA helps to administer include rules issued by independent regulatory agencies (e.g., the PRA, the Regulatory Flexibility Act, the Congressional Review Act, and the Data Quality Act), the executive orders that have established regulatory review within OIRA have explicitly excluded rules issued by those agencies.[82] Some observers have suggested that this limitation be lifted, arguing that independent regulatory agencies issue regulations that have a significant impact on the economy (about $230 billion per year according to OIRA) but their rules often contain little quantitative information on regulatory costs and benefits.[83] Those opposed to this expansion in OIRA's duties point out that independent regulatory agencies were established to be relatively independent of the President, and inclusion of their rules under OIRA's would be counter to this purpose. In response, proponents argue that independent regulatory agencies' rules are already reviewed for purposes such as paperwork clearance and ensuring that data quality requirements are met, so examining the substance of the rules is just an extension of those reviews.

Transparency of Reviews

One consistent area of concern to some observers has been the lack of transparency of the OIRA review process to the public. Notwithstanding recent improvements, they argue that it is difficult for the public to know with any degree of certainty what changes OIRA has suggested to agencies' draft rules, what contacts OIRA has made with regulated entities and other outside parties regarding those rules, or whether documents were exchanged between OIRA and the agencies. In its September 2003 report, GAO said that the documentation that agencies are required to provide showing the changes made at OIRA's suggestion or recommendation were not always available and, when done, were not always clear or consistent. GAO also said that the transparency requirements incumbent on OIRA were not always clear, and recommended several improvements. For example:

- Although OIRA indicated that it can have its greatest impact on agencies' rules during *informal* reviews before review packages are formally submitted, OIRA indicated that agencies only had to disclose the changes made at OIRA's suggestion during *formal* review (some of which were as short as one day). GAO recommended that OIRA define this requirement in the executive order to include informal reviews, just as it did with regard to the requirements involving the office's communications with outside parties.
- As noted previously, the "consistent with change" code in OIRA's database does not differentiate between OIRA- or agency-initiated changes, or changes that were major or minor in nature. GAO recommended that the database be changed to more clearly indicate which rules were substantively changed at OIRA's suggestion.
- GAO also recommended refinements to the executive order's requirements applicable to OIRA (e.g., more clearly indicating on its website the regulatory actions being discussed at meetings with outside parties and the affiliations of the participants) and the requirements applicable to the agencies (e.g., defining the types of "substantive" changes that agencies should disclose).

In commenting on GAO's report, the administrator of OIRA said that the office planned to review its implementation of the executive order's transparency requirements and would work to improve the clarity of its meeting log. The administrator did not, however, believe that changes made during informal OIRA reviews should be disclosed—even though he said that OIRA can have its greatest influence during informal reviews. Disclosure of these informal review changes could be required through an administrative directive issued by the OIRA administrator or, alternatively, through legislation.

Reversal of Executive Order 13422

On June 27, 2007, during House floor consideration of H.R. 2829, the Financial Services and General Government (FSGG) Appropriations Act, 2008 (which funds OMB, among other agencies), Representative Brad Miller and Representative Linda Sanchez offered a "general provision" amendment stating that "None of the funds made available by this Act may be used to implement Executive Order 13422." The amendment was agreed to as Section 901 of H.R. 2829 as passed by the House.

In the wake of this action, on July 12, 2007, the Director of OMB sent a letter to the chairmen and ranking members of the House and Senate Appropriations Committees stating that "If the President were presented with a bill that contained a restriction on the implementation of Executive Order 13422, the President's Senior Advisors would recommend that he veto the bill." The Director urged the rejection of any provision that would interfere in any way with the implementation of the executive order "because it involves a matter that directly affects the operation of [OMB] and involves the President's authority to manage the Executive Branch."

As reported by the Senate Subcommittee on Financial Services, the FSGG appropriations bill contained a provision stating that no funds in the measure could be used to implement either Executive Order 13422 or an OMB bulletin on guidance documents. However, one of the "manager's package" amendments to the legislation that was adopted when the bill was reported by the full Senate Appropriations Committee on July 12, 2007, deleted this provision from the legislation. The FSGG appropriations bill was later folded into the Consolidated Appropriations Act for FY2008 (H.R. 2764), and President Bush signed the bill into law on December 26, 2007 (P.L. 110-161). The legislation did not contain any language regarding Executive Order 13422. It is possible that some Members of Congress may again try to limit the implementation of the executive order in funding legislation for FY2009.

End Notes

[1] The other statutory offices, which are collectively referred to as the "management" side of OMB, are the Office of Federal Financial Management, the Office of Federal Procurement Policy, and the Office of Electronic Government and Information Technology. OMB's resource management offices, which review agencies' budget submissions, are sometimes collectively referred to as OMB's "budget" side.

[2] The Administrative Procedure Act of 1946 (5 U.S.C. 551 et seq.). generally requires agencies to publish a notice of proposed rulemaking in the *Federal Register*, permit the public to comment on the proposed rule, and then publish a final rule addressing the comments

provided. For an overview of many of the statutes and executive orders governing federal rulemaking, see CRS Report RL32240, *The Federal Rulemaking Process: An Overview*, by Curtis W. Copeland.

[3] U.S. General Accounting Office, *Rulemaking: OMB's Role in Reviews ofAgencies' Draft Rules and the Transparency of Those Reviews*, GAO-03-929, Sept. 22, 2003.

[4] For a discussion of the PRA, see CRS Report RL30590, *Paperwork Reduction Act Reauthorization and Government Information Management Issues*, by Harold C. Relyea.

[5] The PRA was later amended in 1986 and again in 1995, and the list of OIRA's duties changed somewhat. For example, the 1986 amendments sharpened the management focus of the act and changed "information policy" to "information resources management." As discussed later in this report, the 1986 amendment also required the administrator of OIRA to be appointed by the President, subject to advice and consent of the Senate.

[6] As used in this report, the term "independent regulatory agencies" refers to agencies established to be independent of the President, including the Federal Communications Commission, the Securities and Exchange Commission, and the Consumer Product Safety Commission. The term "independent agencies" refers to agencies that are independent of Cabinet departments but not independent regulatory agencies (e.g., the Environmental Protection Agency and the Office of Personnel Management).

[7] For example, by 1989, OIRA's overall staffing had declined to fewer than 60 employees, of whom OIRA estimated 35 were reviewing information collection requests. By 1997, OIRA staffing declined 48 employees, of whom 22 were reviewing paperwork requests. See U.S. General Accounting Office, *Regulatory Management: Implementation of Selected OMB Responsibilities Under the Paperwork Reduction Act*, GAO/GGD-98-120, July 9, 1998.

[8] In some cases, though, the paperwork requirement may be the essence of the regulation. For example, EPA's Toxics Release Inventory (TRI) program is essentially a database created through collections of information imposed on businesses in order to inform the public about chemical hazards in their communities.

[9] The task force was disbanded in August 1983 after issuing a final report.

[10] Executive Order 12291, "Federal Regulation," 46 *Federal Register* 13193, Feb. 19, 1981.

[11] For a description of the effects of this order, see Erik D. Olson, "The Quiet Shift of Power: Office of Management & Budget Supervision of Environmental Protection Agency Rulemaking Under Executive Order 12291," *Virginia Journal of Natural Resources Law*, vol. 4 (Fall 1984), pp. 1-80.

[12] The exemptions that OMB granted fell into four broad categories: (1) rules that were essentially nonregulatory in nature, (2) rules that delegated regulatory authority to the States, (3) rules that generally affected individual entities and that did not involve broader policy issues, and (4) rules for which a delay of even a few days could have imposed substantial costs and that were unlikely to involve significant policy issues. OMB granted about 30 exemptions, most of which were established in 1981 or 1982.

[13] Although the task force was chaired by Vice President Bush, the executive director was the administrator of OIRA. Other members included the Director of OMB, the Attorney General, and the Secretaries of Commerce, Labor, and the Treasury.

[14] Executive Order 12498, "Regulatory Planning Process," 50 *Federal Register* 1036, Jan. 8, 1985.

[15] As discussed later in this report, President Carter first required the use of these agendas in 1978.

[16] An OIRA representative said that although the office had this authority it never used it, noting that would have been difficult to defend the return of an agency's rule for purely procedural reasons.

[17] This requirement was formally established through an October 1971 memorandum from then-OMB Director George Schultz. According to some observers, the requirements were routinely imposed only on the Environmental Protection Agency.

[18] Executive Order 11821, "Inflation Impact Statements," 39 *Federal Register* 41501, Nov. 29, 1974. The order also required such statements for agency-proposed major legislation.

[19] Executive Order 12044, "Improving Government Regulations," 43 *Federal Register* 12661, Mar. 24, 1978.

[20] George Eads, "Harnessing Regulation: The Evolving Role of White House Oversight," *Regulation*, vol. 5 (May/June 1981), pp. 19-26.

[21] U.S. Congress, House Committee on Energy and Commerce, Subcommittee on Oversight and Investigations, *Role of OMB in Regulation*, 97th Cong., 1st sess., June 18, 1981 (Washington: GPO, 1981). See also Morton Rosenberg, "Beyond the Limits of Executive Power: Presidential Control of Agency Rulemaking Under Executive Order 12291," *Michigan Law Review*, vol. 80 (Dec. 1981), pp. 193-247.

[22] U.S. General Accounting Office, *Implementing the Paperwork Reduction Act: Some Progress, But Many Problems Remain*, GAO/GGD-83-35, April 20, 1983.

[23] Letter from James C. Miller III, administrator of OIRA, to the Honorable John D. Dingell, Chairman, Subcommittee on Oversight and Investigations, House Committee on Energy and Commerce, April 28, 1981.

[24] OIRA's authorization for appropriation also expired in 2001, and (as of the date of this report) has not been reestablished.

[25] For further information on this policy, see Judith Havemann, "No 'Shade-Drawn' Dealings for OMB; Congress Gets Disclosure of Regulation-Review Procedures," *Washington Post*, June 17, 1986, p. A-21.

[26] National Academy of Public Administration, *Presidential Management of Rulemaking in Regulatory Agencies* (Jan. 1987).

[27] Administrative Conference of the United States, *Presidential Review of Agency Rulemaking*, Conference Recommendation 88-9 (1988). The Administrative Conference was established in 1968 to provide advice regarding procedural improvements in federal programs, and was eliminated by Congress in 1995.

[28] The National Academy of Public Administration and the American Bar Association have also recognized the potential value of presidential regulatory review. They also recommended reforms such as improved transparency and better communication between OIRA and agency staff.

[29] Christine Triano and Nancy Watzman, *All the Vice President's Men: How the Quayle Council on Competitiveness Secretly Undermines Health, Safety, and Environmental Programs* (Washington: OMB Watch/Public Citizen, 1991).

[30] See Bob Woodward and David Broder, "Quayle's Quest: Curb Rules, Leave 'No Fingerprints," *Washington Post*, Jan. 9, 1992, p. A1.

[31] Executive Order 12866, "Regulatory Planning and Review," 58 *Federal Register* 51735, Oct. 4, 1993. For an electronic copy of this executive order, see http://www.whitehouse.gov/omb/inforeg/eo12866.pdf.

[32] Executive Order 13258, issued in February 2002, amended Executive Order 12866 and reassigned all roles originally assigned to the Vice President to the President's chief of staff. For a copy of this executive order, see http://www.whitehouse.gov/omb/inforeg/eo13258.pdf.

[33] Section 6(b)(2) of the executive order states that OIRA "shall waive review or notify the agency in writing of the results of its review," generally within 90 calendar days after a draft rule has been submitted. Nevertheless, in some cases, OIRA does not complete its review within 90 days. For example, as of January 8, 2008, one Department of Commerce rule (on "Right Whale Ship Strike Reduction") had been under review at OIRA for 322 days.

[34] For a discussion of the differences between the transparency requirements under Executive Order 12291 and Executive Order 12866, see William D. Araiza, "Judicial and Legislative Checks on Ex Parte OMB Influence Over Rulemaking," *Administrative Law Review*, 54 (Spring 2002), 611-630, and Peter M. Shane, "Political Accountability in a System of

Checks and Balances: The Case of Presidential Review of Rulemaking," *Arkansas Law Review*, 48 (1995), 161-214.

[35] OIRA may also formally or informally review other rulemaking documents before proposed rules (e.g., advance notices of proposed rulemaking).

[36] Executive Office of the President, White House Office, "Regulatory Review Plan," 66 *Federal Register* 7702, Jan. 24, 2001. To view a copy of this memorandum, see http://www.whitehouse.gov/omb/inforeg/regreview_plan.pdf. For a discussion of the rules whose effective dates were postponed, see U.S. General Accounting Office, *Regulatory Review: Delay of Effective Dates of Final Rules Subject to the Administration's Jan. 20, 2001, Memorandum,* GAO-02-370R, Feb. 2002.

[37] Section 3(f) of the executive order also defines an economically significant rule as adversely affecting "in a material way, the economy, a sector of the economy, productivity, competition, jobs, the environment, public health or safety, or State, local, or tribal governments or communities."

[38] This guidance was issued as OMB Circular A-4 in September 2003. For a copy of this guidance, see http://www.whitehouse.gov/omb/circulars/a004/a-4.pdf.

[39] For a copy of this September 20, 2001 memorandum and the attachment, see http://www.whitehouse.gov/omb/ inforeg/oira_review-process.html.

[40] Office of Management and Budget, *Making Sense of Regulation: 2001 Report to Congress on the Cost and Benefits of Regulations and Unfunded Mandates on State, Local and Tribal Entities,* Dec. 2001, available at http://www.whitehouse.gov/omb/inforeg/costbenefitreport.pdf.

[41] Dr. John D. Graham, remarks prepared for the American Hospital Association, July 17, 2002. For a copy of this speech, see http://www.whitehouse.gov/omb/inforeg/graham_ama071702.html.

[42] Rebecca Adams, "Regulating the Rulemakers: John Graham at OIRA," *CQ Weekly*, Feb. 23, 2002, pp. 520-526.

[43] Scott Farrow, *Improving Regulatory Performance: Does Executive Office Oversight Matter*? (Pittsburgh: Carnegie Mellon University, July 26, 2000).

[44] See, for example, Steven Croley, "White House Review of Agency Rulemaking: An Empirical Investigation," *University of Chicago Law Review*, vol. 70 (Summer 2003), pp. 821-885.

[45] U. S. General Accounting Office, *Rulemaking: OMB's Role in Reviews of Agencies' Draft Rules and the Transparency of Those Reviews*, GAO-03-929, Sept. 22, 2003.

[46] Environmental and public interest groups also contacted OIRA regarding three of the rules.

[47] There has been only one amendment to Executive Order 12866 since it was issued. As mentioned earlier in this report, Executive Order 13258 reassigned all roles originally assigned to the Vice President in Executive Order 12866 (e.g., to be principal advisor to the President on regulatory policy, planning, and review) to the President's chief of staff.

[48] John D. Graham, "Presidential Oversight of the Regulatory State: Can It Work?," speech at the Heinz School, Carnegie Mellon University, Oct. 4, 2002.

[49] U.S. Congress, Senate Committee on Governmental Affairs, Subcommittee on Financial Management and Accountability, *Oversight of Regulatory Review Activities of the Office of Information and Regulatory Affairs,* 104th Cong., 2nd sess., Sept. 25, 1996 (Washington: GPO, 1997).

[50] William Niskanen, "Clinton's Regulatory Record: Policies, Process, and Outcomes," *Regulation*, vol. 19 (1996), pp. 27-28.

[51] Office of Management and Budget, *Stimulating Smarter Regulation: 2002 Report to Congress on the Costs and Benefits of Federal Regulations and Unfunded Mandates on State, Local, and Tribal Entities*, Dec. 2002, available at http://www.whitehouse.gov/omb/inforeg/2002_report_to_congress

[52] Copies of OIRA's return letters are available on OMB's website at http://www.whitehouse.gov/omb/inforeg/ return_letter.html.

[53] Two of the five returns during this period involved the same DOT rule.

[54] Copies of these prompt letters are available on OMB's website at http://www.whitehouse.gov/omb/inforeg/ prompt_letter.html.

[55] As noted earlier in this report, this guidance (OMB Circular A-4) is available at http://www.whitehouse.gov/omb/ circulars/a004/a-4.pdf.

[56] Cost-benefit analysis involves the systematic identification of all costs and benefits associated with a forthcoming regulation. Cost-effectiveness analysis seeks to determine how a given goal can be achieved at the least cost. In contrast to cost-benefit analysis, the concern in cost-effectiveness analysis is not with weighing the merits of the goal, but with identifying and analyzing the costs of alternatives to reach that goal (e.g., dollars per life saved).

[57] Discounting can have a significant effect on the present value of future health benefits. For example, in a February 2003 speech the OIRA administrator noted that the present value of 1,000 lives saved 50 years in the future is only 34 lives in present value when evaluated at a 7 % discount rate.

[58] John Graham, "The Smart-Regulation Agenda: Progress and Challenges," speech before the AEI-Brookings Joint Center for Regulatory Studies, Nov. 7, 2005.

[59] Nancy Ognanovich, "Head of OMB Regulatory Office Says Analyzing Homeland Security Rules Difficult," *BNA Daily Report for Executives*, Nov. 8, 2005, p. A39.

[60] For example, former OIRA administrator Sally Katzen said "when it matters to them to get rules out quickly, they wink and blink. But in the areas of public health and safety, where they have longstanding relations with the business communities involved, they're insistent on satisfying these standards," in Rebecca Adams, "Graham Leaves OIRA With a Full Job Jar," *CQ Weekly*, Jan 23, 2006, p. 226.

[61] See http://www.whitehouse.gov/omb/library/OMBREGSP.html.

[62] See http://www.whitehouse.gov/omb/library/OMBREGSC.html.

[63] A list of OIRA's meetings with outside parties can be found at http://www.whitehouse.gov/omb/oira/meetings.html. A list of its oral communications can be found at http://www.whitehouse.gov/omb/oira/oral_communications.html.

[64] Public Citizen, "New Executive Order Is Latest White House Power Grab," available at http://www.citizen.org/ pressroom/release.cfm?ID=2361. See also Margaret Kriz, "Thumbing His Nose," *National Journal*, July 28, 2007, pp. 32-34.

[65] Attributed to William Kovacs, Vice President of Environment, Energy, and Regulatory Affairs, U.S. Chamber of Commerce, in John Sullivan, "White House Sets Out New Requirements for Agencies Developing Rules, Guidance," *Daily Report for Executives*, Jan. 19, 2007, p. A-31.

[66] CRS Report RL33862, *Changes to the OMB Regulatory Review Process by Executive Order* 13422, by Curtis W. Copeland.

[67] For a more complete discussion of UMRA, see CRS Report RS20058, *Unfunded Mandates Reform Act Summarized*, by Keith Bea and Richard S. Beth.

[68] This requirement is codified at 5 U.S.C. 609.

[69] For a more complete discussion of the Congressional Review Act, see CRS Report RL30116, *Congressional Review of Agency Rulemaking: An Update and Assessment of The Congressional Review Act after a Decade*, by Morton Rosenberg.

[70] Office of Management and Budget, "Guidelines for Ensuring and Maximizing the Quality, Objectivity, Utility, and Integrity of Information Disseminated by *Federal Agencies*; Notice; Republication," 67 Federal Register 8451, Feb. 22, 2002.

[71] A similar requirement for "recommendations for reform" was included in section 628(a)(3) of the FY2000 Treasury and General Government Appropriations Act. OIRA received 71 suggestions from the public in response to its call for "suggestions on specific regulations that could be rescinded or changed that would increase net benefits to the public," most of which came from the Mercatus Center at George Mason University. OIRA reviewed these suggestions and identified 23 as a "high priority" for review. Eight of the 23 high priority recommendations involved EPA rules, and five involved rules from the Department of Labor. Although business groups generally applauded this effort, environmentalists and

public interest groups characterized it as the development of a "hit list" of rules that the Bush Administration wanted to eliminate.

[72] Executive Order 13166, "Improving Access to Services for Persons With Limited English Proficiency," *65 Federal Register* 50121, Aug. 16, 2000. For a copy of the report, see http://www.whitehouse.gov/omb/inforeg/lepfinal3-14.pdf.

[73] OIRA submitted this report in April 2004. For a copy of the report, see http://www.whitehouse.gov/omb/inforeg/ fy03_info_quality_rpt.pdf.

[74] To view a copy of this bulletin, see http://www.whitehouse.gov/omb/memoranda/fy2005/m05-03.pdf.

[75] To view a copy of this document, see http://www.whitehouse.gov/omb/inforeg/good_guid/ good_guidance_preamble.pdf.

[76] To view a copy of this bulletin, see http://www.whitehouse.gov/omb/inforeg/ proposed_ risk_assessment_bulletin_010906.pdf.

[77] *Sierra Club v. Costle*, 657 F.2d 298 (D.C. Cir. 1981).

[78] Elana Kagan, "Presidential Administration," *Harvard Law Review*, vol. 18 (June 2001), pp. 2245-2385.

[79] For example, David H. Rosenbloom, in *Building a Legislative-Centered Public Administration* (Tuscaloosa, AL: The University of Alabama Press, 2001) states that "where coordinated government-wide clearance is required to achieve Congress' policy objectives, there may be few or no alternatives (to paperwork and regulatory review within OMB)."

[80] For example, as noted previously, in OMB's appropriation for 2002, Congress stipulated that nearly $1.6 million should not be obligated until OMB submitted a report assessing the total costs and benefits of implementing Executive Order No. 13166. Also, in the conference report for OMB's FY2004 appropriation (under the heading "Office of Information and Regulatory Affairs"), the conferees directed that $1 million "be withheld from obligation until resolution of existing programmatic concerns by House conferees are addressed and the House and Senate Committee on Appropriations approve of such obligations."

[81] See, for example, Robert W. Hahn and Robert E. Litan, *Why Congress Should Increase Funding for OMB Review of Regulations*, AEI-Brookings Joint Center for Regulatory Studies, Policy Matter 03-33, Oct. 2003.

[82] For purposes of regulatory review, both Executive Order 12291 and Executive Order 12866 defined a covered "agency" as excluding those agencies specified in 44 U.S.C. 3502(10).

[83] See, for example, the Center for Regulatory Effectiveness, *A Blueprint for OMB Review of Independent Agency Regulations*, Mar. 2002. The previously mentioned bill (S. 746) that proposed to establish in law presidential review of rules would have included rules issued by independent regulatory agencies.

In: Federal Rulemaking and Regulations
Editors: Paul Lee
ISBN: 978-1-60876-069-5
© 2010 Nova Science Publishers, Inc.

Chapter 6

NEGOTIATED RULEMAKING

Curtis W. Copeland

SUMMARY

Negotiated rulemaking, which is a supplement to traditional rulemaking, is a process in which representatives of federal agencies and affected parties work together in a committee to reach consensus on what can ultimately become a proposed rule. Although negotiated rulemaking is not appropriate for all regulations, advocates believe that the approach can speed rule development, reduce litigation, and generate more creative and effective regulatory solutions.

The Negotiated Rulemaking Act of 1990 established the basic statutory authority for the approach while giving agencies wide latitude in its implementation, and the Clinton Administration advocated a broader application of the approach. Agencies are permitted to use "conveners" to determine whether negotiated rulemaking is appropriate and to select participants, and to use "facilitators" to chair the negotiated rulemaking committee meetings. At the end of the process, agencies must still publish proposed and final regulations for public comment, but any proposal agreed to by the negotiating committee is not binding on the agency or other parties.

Although the Negotiated Rulemaking Act gives agencies substantial discretion as to whether the approach should be employed in rulemaking, Congress has sometimes mandated its use by rulemaking agencies and established specific procedures and time frames to follow. Studies examining the implementation of negotiated rulemaking have reached different conclusions regarding the approach's effect on rulemaking timeliness, litigation, as well as other issues. Researchers also disagree regarding how the effectiveness of negotiated rulemaking should be measured.

The Administrative Procedure Act (APA) of 1946 (5 U.S.C. §551 *et seq.*) generally requires federal agencies to publish their proposed rules (also called regulations) in the *Federal Register,* to provide the public with an opportunity to comment on those proposed rules, and to publish a final rule at least 30 days before its effective date. The APA does not, however, specify how agencies are to develop their proposed rules or who should participate in that process. Consequently, agencies sometimes develop rules without discussing relevant issues with all affected interests, and there may be little or no opportunity for an informal exchange of views among affected parties or between those parties and the rulemaking agency either before or after the proposed rule is published.

Negotiated rulemaking (sometimes referred to as regulatory negotiation or "reg-neg") is a supplement to the traditional APA rulemaking process in which agency representatives and representatives of affected parties work together to develop what can ultimately become the text of a proposed rule.[1] In this approach, negotiators try to reach consensus by evaluating their priorities and making tradeoffs, with the end result being a draft rule that is mutually acceptable. Negotiated rulemaking has been encouraged (although not usually required) by both congressional and executive branch actions, and has received bipartisan support as a way to involve affected parties in rulemaking before agencies have developed their proposals. Some questions have been raised, however, regarding whether the approach actually speeds rulemaking or reduces litigation.

Development of Negotiated Rulemaking

The development of negotiated rulemaking is traceable to dissatisfaction with what some viewed as the formal, complex, and adversarial nature of traditional rulemaking procedures. For example, in 1982, administrative law expert Philip J. Harter — an early advocate of negotiated rulemaking — said a "malaise" had settled over the federal rulemaking process because of the defensive and arms-length manner in which agencies and affected parties interacted.[2] He suggested a different approach in which differences were acknowledged and resolved through face-to-face negotiations, and laid out a series of principles that could make those negotiations successful.

Also in 1982, the Administrative Conference of the United States (ACUS) recommended that agencies consider using negotiated rulemaking as a way to develop proposed rules, published criteria for determining when negotiated rulemaking was likely to be successful, and suggested specific procedures to be followed when implementing the approach.[3] For example, ACUS said agencies should use "conveners" to determine whether negotiated rulemaking is appropriate and to identify affected interests. ACUS also recommended that Congress pass legislation explicitly authorizing agencies to use negotiated rulemaking, but giving them substantial flexibility to adapt negotiation methods.

In 1983, the Federal Aviation Administration became the first federal agency to try negotiated rulemaking (regarding flight and rest time requirements for domestic airline pilots), followed by the Environmental Protection Agency (EPA) and the Occupational Health and Safety Administration. In 1985, ACUS recommended refinements to the procedures based on these agencies' experience with the approach.[4] For example, ACUS said that agencies sponsoring the effort should take part in the negotiations, and pointed out that negotiated rulemaking could be used at several stages of the rulemaking process.

Congressional Action

The Negotiated Rulemaking Act of 1990 (5 U.S.C. §§561-570), as amended and permanently authorized in 1996 by the Administrative Dispute Resolution Act of 1996 (110 Stat. 2870, 3873), essentially enacted the ACUS recommendations, establishing basic statutory authority and requirements for the use of the approach while giving agencies wide latitude in its implementation. The act supplements (but does not supplant) APA rulemaking procedures, and establishes a framework by which agencies are encouraged (but not required) to use negotiated rulemaking to develop proposed rules. The act established public notice requirements and procedures by which affected parties can petition for inclusion in the process, and clarified that agencies must generally comply with the Federal Advisory Committee Act in establishing and administering the negotiating committee.[5] The negotiated rulemaking committee, composed of representatives of the agency and from the various non-federal interests that would be affected by the proposed regulation, addresses areas of concern in the hope that it can reach agreement on the contents of a proposed regulation. The agency can, if it agrees, then issue the agreement as a proposed rule, and eventually as a final rule, under existing APA procedures. The expectation is that any rule drafted through negotiated rulemaking would be easier to implement and less likely to be the subject of subsequent litigation.[6]

Executive Branch Actions

In September 1993, the Clinton Administration's National Performance Review (NPR) recommended (among other things) that federal agencies increase their use of negotiated rulemaking.[7] That same month, President Clinton issued Executive Order 12866, which, in part, directed federal agencies to "explore and, where appropriate, use consensual mechanisms for developing regulations, including negotiated rulemaking."[8] President Clinton also issued a separate memorandum in September 1993 directing each agency to identify at least one rulemaking for which the agency would use negotiated rulemaking during 1994, or to explain why the use of the approach was not feasible.[9]

In May 1998, President Clinton issued another memorandum to the heads of executive branch departments and agencies intended to promote greater use of negotiated rulemaking.[10] Specifically, he designated the Regulatory Working Group (which had been established by Executive Order 12866 and was composed of the heads of agencies with significant domestic regulatory responsibilities) as an interagency committee to "facilitate and encourage agency use of negotiated rulemaking."

The Negotiated Rulemaking Process

The Negotiated Rulemaking Act permits agencies to establish a negotiated rulemaking committee if the head of the agency determines that doing so is "in the public interest." In making that determination, the act says the head of the agency must consider whether (1) a rule is needed, (2) there are a limited number of identifiable interests that will be significantly affected by the rule, (3) there is a "reasonable likelihood" that a balanced committee can be convened that will adequately represent those identifiable interests and is willing to negotiate in good faith to reach consensus on a proposed rule, (4) there is a "reasonable likelihood" that the committee will reach a consensus on the proposed rule within a fixed period of time, (5) the negotiated rulemaking process will not delay the issuance of the proposed or final rule, (6) the agency has adequate resources that it is willing to commit to the committee, and (7) the agency will use the committee's consensus as the basis of the proposed rule "to the maximum extent possible consistent with the legal obligations of the agency." The act also specifically permits the use of conveners to help the agency identify affected parties and to determine whether a committee should be established.

If the agency decides to establish a negotiated rulemaking committee, the act requires the agency to publish a notice in the *Federal Register* (and, as appropriate, relevant trade or other specialized publications) containing (among other things) a description of the subject and scope of the rule, a list of affected interests, a list of those proposed to represent those interests and the agency, and a solicitation for comments.[11] The comment period must be for at least 30 calendar days. Membership on the committee is limited to 25 members (including at least one from the sponsoring agency), unless the agency head determines that more members are needed. The agency can select (subject to the approval of the committee by consensus) an impartial "facilitator" to chair meetings and oversee the administration of the committee. The facilitator does not have to be a federal employee, but agencies are required to determine whether a person under consideration to be a convener or a facilitator has any financial or other conflict of interest.

Any agreement on a negotiated rule must be unanimous, unless the negotiated rulemaking committee agrees to other conditions. If the committee reaches consensus, it must submit a report to the sponsoring agency containing the proposed rule and any other information it deems appropriate. However, any proposal agreed to by the committee is not binding on the agency or other parties; the agency may decide not to issue a proposed rule at all or not as designed by the committee, and interest groups represented on the committee may oppose the rule that they helped craft.[12]

The committee terminates no later than promulgation of the final rule. An agency may pay reasonable travel and *per diem* expenses, and reasonable compensation to negotiating committee members under certain conditions. Agency procedural actions related to establishing, assisting, or terminating the committee are not subject to judicial review, but any judicial review available regarding the rule resulting from negotiated rulemaking is unaffected.

Congressional Mandates to Negotiate

Although the Negotiated Rulemaking Act gives agencies substantial discretion as to whether the approach should be employed in rulemaking, Congress has sometimes mandated its use by rulemaking agencies and established specific procedures and time frames to follow. For example:

- Section 7212 of the Intelligence Reform and Terrorism Prevention Act of 2004 (P.L. 108-458) required the Secretary of Transportation to use negotiated rulemaking in developing regulations establishing minimum standards for drivers licenses or personal identification cards.
- Section 222 of the "Consolidated Appropriations Act, 2004" (P.L. 108-199) required the Secretary of Housing and Urban Development to "conduct negotiated rulemaking with representatives from interested parties for purposes of any changes to the formula governing the Public Housing Operating Fund."
- Section 1901(b)(3)(A) of the No Child Left Behind Act (P.L. 107-110) required the Secretary of Education to "establish a negotiated rulemaking process on, at a minimum, standards and assessments." The section went on the stipulate that those involved in the process should be selected from among those that provided advice and recommendations on how the title should be carried out, and said that the process should follow the process outlined in the Negotiated Rulemaking Act (except that it should not be subject to the Federal Advisory Committee Act).
- Section 1125(a)(5) of the No Child Left Behind Act required the Secretary of Education to establish a negotiated rulemaking committee to prepare, for schools funded by the Bureau of Indian Affairs, a catalog of the condition of school facilities, a school replacement and new construction report, and a renovation repairs report. The act specified the contents of each report and required that it be submitted to particular congressional committees within 24 months.
- Section 106(b)(2) of the Native American Housing Assistance and Self-Determination Act of 1996 (P.L. 104-330) required that all regulations under the act must be issued according to negotiated rulemaking procedures, and required that the negotiating committee be composed only of representatives of the federal government and

"geographically diverse small, medium, and large Indian tribes." Section 6 of the Native American Housing Assistance and Self-Determination Reauthorization Act of 2002 (P.L. 107-292) required negotiated rulemaking for any rules issued pursuant to amendments to the original act.

- Section 490D(b)(3) of the Higher Education Amendments of 1998 (P.L. 105-244) required that negotiated rulemaking must be used for all subsequent regulations pertaining to the act's title on student assistance "unless the Secretary determines that applying such a requirement with respect to given regulations is impracticable, unnecessary, or contrary to the public interest." The Secretary is required to publish such a determination in the *Federal Register* at the same time as the proposed rule.

Several bills that have been introduced in the 110th Congress would, if enacted, also require the use of negotiated rulemaking. For example, the Indian Health Care Improvement Act Amendments of 2007 and 2008 (H.R. 1328 and S. 1200) would (among other things) revise the Indian Catastrophic Health Emergency Fund (CHEF) requirements and require the Secretary of HHS to use negotiated rulemaking for the promulgation of CHEF regulations.

Evaluations of Negotiated Rulemaking

According to ACUS and other advocates of the approach, negotiated rulemaking can have a number of beneficial effects, including the following:

- reduced time, money and effort expended on developing and enforcing rules,
- earlier implementation of associated rules,
- better agency understanding of regulated parties' concerns,
- greater understanding by regulated parties of their responsibilities and higher compliance rates,
- more creative and effective regulatory solutions,
- less litigation associated with the rule, and
- more cooperative relationships between the agency and other parties.

ACUS and others have also identified a number of disadvantages of negotiated rulemaking.

- ACUS noted that the approach can be more resource-intensive than traditional rulemaking, at least in the short term, and does not work when the number of affected interests is too large (e.g., more than 25 negotiators).
- One author said that the approach has been used only rarely (reportedly for less than one-tenth of 1% of all rules), and he said only a few of those rules were considered "major" or "significant."[13] The author noted that the Negotiated Rulemaking Act instructs agencies to select rules based on their likelihood of consensus, not their importance.
- Another author said that negotiated rulemaking has been used sparingly "for the good reason that it represents a corporatist abdication of public authority to private interests," and that even when used it only results in a proposed rule that is subject to the same procedural requirements as rules developed conventionally.[14]
- Another commenter asserted that negotiated rulemaking does not work when developing regulations based on broad statutes, and may "inadvertently perpetuate the problem (of statutory vagueness) by facilitating efforts to shift blame for controversial public policies from legislators to bureaucrats."[15]
- Yet another study concluded that "the principles, theory, and practice of negotiated rulemaking subtly subvert the basic, underlying concepts of American administrative law — an agency's pursuit of the public interest through law and reasoned decisionmaking. In its place, negotiated rulemaking would establish privately bargained interests as the source of putative public law."[16]

Nevertheless, a number of observers continue to view negotiated rulemaking favorably, with one regulatory expert describing it as offering the public "the most direct and influential role in rulemaking of any reform of the process ever devised."[17]

Empirical Studies

Studies of how negotiated rulemaking works in practice have reached substantially different conclusions about its effects and prospects.

- In 1990, eight agencies that had convened negotiation committees reportedly told ACUS that even though full consensus was not always possible, the information developed through the process contributed substantially to the rule that was produced.[18]
- A 1992 study of four EPA negotiated rulemaking efforts indicated that the approach reduced the time needed to develop rules (particularly during the period between proposed and final rulemaking).[19] However, another study five years later examining more EPA negotiations reached the opposite conclusion, finding that conventional rules and negotiated rules took about the same amount of time and that negotiated rules were more likely to be challenged in court.[20] Similarly, a 1999 study also concluded that negotiated rulemaking had "no discernible effect" on the amount of time between proposed and final rulemaking.[21]
- Another study indicated that negotiated rulemaking can improve participants' perception of the final rule and of the overall rulemaking process.[22] Participants in negotiated rulemaking were reportedly more pleased with the quality of the information the process generated than those who filed comments on conventional rules, and more likely to view their participation as having an effect on the final rule. The study also indicated, however, that negotiated rulemaking imposes substantial costs on participants, who are required to attend multiple meetings and interact with other stakeholders for long periods of time.

Substantial disagreements exist regarding how the effectiveness of negotiated rulemaking should be measured (e.g., timeliness and the amount of litigation).[23] Most researchers agree, however, that the approach is not appropriate for all rules, and that more research is needed to determine its effects on rules, the rulemaking process, and participants in that process.

End Notes

[1] For a more complete discussion of negotiated rulemaking and relevant agency documents, see David M. Pritzker and Deborah S. Dalton, eds., *Negotiated Rulemaking Sourcebook* (Washington: Administrative Conference of the United States, 1995).

[2] Philip J. Harter, "Negotiating Regulations: A Cure for Malaise," *Georgetown Law Journal* 71 (1982), pp. 1-118.

[3] Administrative Conference of the United States, Recommendation 82-4, 1 CFR 305.82.4. The Administrative Conference was established in 1968 to provide advice regarding procedural improvements in federal programs, and was eliminated by Congress in 1995.

[4] Administrative Conference of the United States, Recommendation 85-5, 1 CFR 305.85-5.

[5] The Federal Advisory Committee Act (codified at 5 U.S.C. App. 2) regulates the formation and operation of advisory committees used by federal agencies that are not entirely composed of full-time federal employees.

[6] Another process for early stakeholder involvement in rulemaking was established by the Small Business Regulatory Enforcement Fairness Act of 1996 (P.L. 104-121, codified at 5 U.S.C. §609). The act required the Environmental Protection Agency and the Occupational Safety and Health Administration to convene a small business advocacy review panel before publishing any proposed rule that they determine may have a significant economic impact on a substantial number of small entities. Although the panels are required to be composed of federal employees, the panel must collect the advice and recommendations of representatives of affected small entities.

[7] Vice President Al Gore, *From Red Tape to Results: Creating a Government That Works Better and Costs Less* (Sept. 1993), recommendation REG03.

[8] Executive Order 12866, "Regulatory Planning and Review," 58 *Federal Register* 51735, Oct. 4, 1993. The order was issued on Sept. 30, 1993.

[9] U.S. President (Clinton), "Negotiated Rulemaking," Sept. 30, 1993.

[10] U.S. President (Clinton), "Designation of Interagency Committees to Facilitate and Encourage Agency Use of Alternate Means of Dispute Resolution and Negotiated Rulemaking," May 1, 1998.

[11] If the agency subsequently decides not to establish a negotiated rulemaking committee, the agency is required to publish another notice in the *Federal Register* explaining why it decided not to go forward. A copy of the notice must be sent to each person who applied for or nominated another person for membership on the committee.

[12] See *USA Group Loan Services, Inc. v. Riley*, 82 F.3d 708 (7th Cir. 1996).

[13] Cary Coglianese, "Is Consensus an Appropriate Basis for Regulatory Policy?," in Eric Orts and Kurt Deketelaere, eds., *Environmental Contracts: Comparative Approaches to Regulatory Innovation in the United States and Europe* (Kluwer Law International, 2001), pp. 93-113.

[14] William F. West, "Formal Procedures, Informal Processes, Accountability, and Responsiveness in Bureaucratic Policy Making: An Institutional Policy Analysis," *Public Administration Review* 64 (Jan/Feb 2004), pp. 66-80.

[15] Juliet A. Williams, "The Delegation Dilemma: Negotiated Rulemaking in Perspective," *Policy Studies Review* 17 (spring 2000), pp. 125-146.

[16] William Funk, "Bargaining Toward the New Millennium: Regulatory Negotiation and the Subversion of the Public Interest," *Duke Law Journal* 46 (1997), pp. 1351-1388.

[17] Cornelius M. Kerwin, *Rulemaking: How Government Agencies Write Law and Make Policy*, 2nd ed. (Washington: CQ Press, 1999), p. 179.

[18] David Pritzer and Deborah Dalton, eds., "Agency Experience with Negotiated Rulemaking," in *Negotiated Rulemaking Sourcebook* (Washington: Administrative Conference of the United States, 1990), pp. 327-344.

[19] Cornelius Kerwin and Scott Furlong, "Time and Rulemaking: An Empirical Test of Theory," *Journal of Public Administration Research and Theory* 2 (1992), pp.1 13-138.

[20] Cary Coglianese, "Assessing Consensus: The Promise and Performance of Negotiated Rulemaking," *Duke Law Journal* 46 (1997), pp. 1255-1349.

[21] Steven J. Balla and John R. Wright, "Consensual Rulemaking and the Time it Takes to Develop Rules," presented at the Fifth National Public Management Research Conference, College Station, TX, Dec. 3-4, 1999.

[22] Laura I. Langbein and Cornelius M. Kerwin, "Regulatory Negotiation versus Conventional Rulemaking: Claims, Counterclaims, and Empirical Evidence," *Journal of Public Administration Research and Theory* 10 (2000), pp. 599-632. See also Jody Freeman and Laura I. Langbein, "Regulatory Negotiation and the Legitimacy Benefit," *New York University Environmental Law Journal* 9 (2000), pp. 60-151.

[23] Philip J. Harter, "Assessing the Assessors: The Actual Performance of Negotiated Rulemaking," *New York University Environmental Law Journal* 9 (2000), pp. 32-59; and Cary Coglianese, "Assessing the Advocacy of Negotiated Rulemaking: A Response to Philip Harter," *New York University Environmental Law Journal* 9 (2001), pp. 386-447.

In: Federal Rulemaking and Regulations
Editors: Paul Lee
ISBN: 978-1-60876-069-5
© 2010 Nova Science Publishers, Inc.

Chapter 7

THE REGULATORY FLEXIBILITY ACT: IMPLEMENTATION ISSUES AND PROPOSED REFORMS

Curtis W. Copeland

SUMMARY

The Regulatory Flexibility Act (RFA) of 1980 (5 U.S.C. §§601-612) requires federal agencies to assess the impact of their forthcoming regulations on "small entities" (i.e., small businesses, small governments, and small not-for-profit organizations). For example, the act requires the analysis to describe why a regulatory action is being considered; the small entities to which the rule will apply and, where feasible, an estimate of their number; the projected reporting, recordkeeping, and other compliance requirements of the rule; and any significant alternatives to the rule that would accomplish the statutory objectives while minimizing the impact on small entities. This analysis is not required, however, if the head of the agency certifies that the rule will not have a "significant economic impact on a substantial number of small entities." The RFA does not define "significant economic impact" or "substantial number of small entities," thereby giving federal agencies substantial discretion regarding when the act's requirements are triggered. Other requirements in the RFA and elsewhere (e.g., that agencies reexamine their existing rules, develop compliance guides, and convene advocacy review panels) also depend on the whether the agencies determine that their rules have a "significant" impact on a "substantial" number of small entities.

GAO has examined the implementation of the RFA many times during the past 20 years, and has consistently concluded that the lack of clear definitions for key terms like "significant economic impact" and "substantial number of small entities" have hindered the act's effectiveness. Therefore, GAO has repeatedly recommended that Congress define those terms, or give the Small Business Administration or some other federal agency the authority and responsibility to do so.

H.R. 4458, the "Small Business Regulatory Improvement Act," was introduced on December 12, 2007, and was reported bythe House Committee on Small Business the next day. Among other things, H.R. 4458 would define "economic impact" as including indirect effects that are "reasonably foreseeable," and would clarify that agencies' reviews of existing rules should not be limited to rules for which a regulatory flexibility analysis had been conducted. The bill would also require agencies to develop a plan for the review of all existing rules within 10 years, require more details in agencies' analyses and notifications, and require annual reports to Congress on certain agency "determinations" as part of their reviews. Although some of these provisions address long-standing issues, some provisions seem unclear and some may add time and costs to the rulemaking process. Most notably, though, H.R. 4458 does not address GAO's long-standing concerns about the lack of clear definitions for key terms in the RFA.

Regulatory Flexibility Act Requirements

The Regulatory Flexibility Act (RFA) of 1980 (5 U.S.C. §§601-612), requires federal agencies to assess the impact of their forthcoming rules on "small entities," which the act defines as including small businesses, small governmental jurisdictions, and certain small not-for-profit organizations. Under the RFA, virtually all federal agencies (i.e., Cabinet departments and independent agencies as well as independent regulatory agencies) must prepare a regulatory flexibility analysis at the time that proposed and certain final rules are published in the *Federal Register*. The analysis for a proposed rule is referred to asan "initial regulatory flexibilityanalysis" (IRFA), and the analysis for a final rule is referred to as a "final regulatory flexibility analysis" (FRFA). The act requires the analyses to describe, among other things, (1) why the regulatory action is being considered and its objectives; (2) the small entities to which the rule will apply and, where feasible, an estimate of their number; (3) the projected reporting, recordkeeping, and other compliance requirements of the rule; and, for final rules, (4) steps the agency has taken to minimize the impact of the rule on small entities, including the alternatives considered and why the selected alternative was chosen.

However, these analytical requirements are not triggered if the head of the issuing agency certifies that the rule would not have a "significant economic impact on a substantial number of small entities" (hereafter referred to as a "SEISNSE"). The RFA does not define "significant economic impact" or "substantial number of small entities," thereby giving federal agenciessubstantial discretion regarding when the act's analytical requirements are initiated. Also, the RFA's analytical requirements do not apply to final rules for which the agency does not publish a proposed rule.[1]

The RFA also contains several other notable provisions. For example, Section 602 requires each federal agency to publish a "regulatory flexibility agenda" in the *Federal Register* each April and October listing regulations that the agency expects to propose or promulgate which are likely to have a SEISNSE.[2] Section 612 of the act requires the Chief Counsel of the Small Business Administration's (SBA's) Office of Advocacy to monitor and report at least annually on agencies' compliance with the act. The statute also specifically authorizes the Chief Counsel to appear as *amicus curiae* (i.e., "friend of the court") in any court action to review a rule.

The RFA initially did not permit judicial review of agencies' actions under the act. However, amendments to the act in 1996 as part of the Small Business Regulatory Enforcement Fairness Act (SBREFA) (110 Stat. 857, 5 U.S.C. §601 note) permitted judicial review regarding, among other things, agencies' regulatory flexibility analyses for final rules and any certifications that their rules will not have a SEISNSE. As a result, for example, a small entity that is adversely affected or aggrieved byan agency's determination thatits final rule would not have a significant impact on small entities could seek judicial review of that determination within one year of the date of the final agency action. In granting relief, a court may remand the rule to theagencyor defer enforcement against small entities. The addition of judicial review in 1996 is generally viewed as a significant strengthening of the RFA, and is believed to have improved agencies' compliance with the act.[3]

In August 2002, President George W. Bush issued Executive Order 13272, which was intended to promote compliance with the RFA.[4] The executive order requires agencies to issue written procedures and policies to ensure that the potential impacts of their draft rules on small entities are properly considered, and requires them to notify the Office of Advocacy of any draft rules with a SEISNSE. Also, the order requires the SBA Chief Counsel for Advocacy to "notify agency heads from time to time" of the requirements of the RFA, and to provide training to agencies on RFA compliance. It also permits the Chief Counsel to provide comments on draft rules to the issuing agency and to the Office of Information and Regulatory Affairs (OIRA) at the Office of Management and Budget. The Office of Advocacy published guidance on the RFA in 2003 and reported training more than 20 agencies on compliance with the act in FY2005.[5]

Other Requirements Are Linked to RFA Determinations

In addition to triggering an initial or final regulatory flexibility analysis, an agency's determination that a rule has a SEISNSE can initiate other actions. For example, when enacted in 1980, Section 610 of the RFA required agencies to publish a plan in the *Federal Register* within 180 days that would provide for the review of all of their then-existing rules within 10 years, and for the review of all subsequent rules within 10 years of their publication as a final rule. The Section 610 requirement applies to those rules that the agencies determined "have or will have" a SEISNSE, and the purpose of the review is to determine whether the rule should be continued without change or should be amended or rescinded to minimize its impact on small entities. One way some agencies have decided which rules should be reviewed is by focusing only on those rules for which a final regulatory flexibility analysis was conducted at the time the final rule was issued. However, other agencies view Section 610 as requiring them to review all of their rules to determine whether they have currently a SEISNSE, regardless of their previous determinations.[6] Either way, agencies have considerable discretion in deciding what constitutes a "significant" impact and a "substantial" number of small entities, and therefore what rules (if any) are covered by this requirement.

SBREFA established two new requirements that are also triggered by agencies' determinations under the RFA — e.g., compliance guides and advocacy review panels.

Compliance Guides

Section 212 of SBREFA requires agencies to develop one or more compliance guides for each final rule or group of related final rules for which the agency is required to prepare an FRFA.[7] Specifically, Section 212 requires the guides to be posted in an easily identifiable location on the agency's website and distributed to "known industry contacts," be entitled "small entity compliance guides," and explain the actions a small entity is required to take to comply with an associated final rule. The statute also requires the guide to bepublished not later than the date that the associated rule's requirements become effective. However, an agency does not have to prepare the compliance guides at all if it determines that the rule or group of rules does not have a "significant" economic impact on a "substantial" number of small entities.

Advocacy Review Panels

Section 244 of SBREFA amended Section 609 of the RFA to require the Environmental Protection Agency (EPA) and the Occupational Safety and Health Administration (OSHA) to convene "advocacy review panels" before publishing an IRFA for a proposed rule. Specifically, the agency issuing the regulation (either OSHA or EPA) must notify the SBA Chief Counsel for Advocacy and provide information on the draft rule's potential impacts on small entities and the type of small entities that might be affected. The Chief Counsel then must identify representatives of affected small entities within 15 days of the notification. The review panel must consist of full-time federal employees from the rulemaking agency, the Office of Management and Budget, and SBA's Chief Counsel for Advocacy. During the panel process, the panel must collect the advice and recommendations of representatives of affected small entities about the potential impact of the draft rule. The panel must report on the comments received and on its recommendations no later than 60 days after the panel is convened, and the panel's report must be made public as part of the rulemaking record.[8] However, EPA and OSHA do not have to hold an advocacy review panel at all if the issuing agency certifies that the subject rule will not have a "significant" economic impact on a "substantial" number of small entities.

GAO ASSESSMENTS OF THE RFA'S IMPLEMENTATION

GAO has commented on the implementation of the RFA numerous times within the past 15 to 20 years, and a recurring theme in GAO's reports is a lack of clarity in the act regarding key terms and a resulting variability in the act's implementation. For example, in 1991, GAO reported that each of the four federal agencies that it reviewed had a different interpretation of key RFA provisions — most notably, what constitutes a "significant" economic impact or a "substantial" number of small entities.[9] In 1994, GAO again reported that agencies' compliance with the RFA varied widely from one agency to another and that agencies were interpreting the statute differently.[10] In a 1999 report on the implementation of Section 610 of the RFA and in a 2000 report on the implementation of the RFA at EPA, GAO concluded that agencies had broad discretion to determine what the statute required.[11]

In the 2000 report, GAO determined that EPA had certified virtually all of its rules after 1996 as not having a SEISNSE, and that the rate of certifications increased substantially after the passage of SBREFA. In all of these reports, GAO suggested that Congress consider clarifying the act's requirements, give SBA or some other entity the responsibility to develop criteria for whether and how agencies should conduct RFA analyses, or both. In 2001, GAO testified that the promise of the RFA may never be realizeduntil Congress or some other entity defines what a "significant economic impact" and a "substantial number of small entities" mean in a rulemaking setting.[12]

In 2002, GAO again testified that the implementation of the RFA was still problematic, and raised more questions about how the statute should be interpreted.[13] For example, GAO said, in determining whether a rule has a significant impact on small entities, should agencies take into account the cumulative impact of similar rules in the same area? Should agencies consider the RFA triggered when a rule has a significant positive impact on small entities? GAO went on to say the following:

> These questions are not simply matters of administrative conjecture within the agencies. They lie at the heart of the RFA and SBREFA, and the answers to the questions can have a substantive effect on the amount of regulatory relief provided through those statutes. Because Congress did not answer these questions when the statutes were enacted, agencies have had to develop their own answers — and those answers differ. If Congress does not like the answers that the agencies have developed, it needs to either amend

the underlying statutes and provide what it believes are the correct answers or givesomeother entitythe authority to issue guidance on these issues.[14]

In 2006, GAO again testified that "the full promise of RFA may never be realized until Congress clarifies key terms and definitions in the Act, such as 'a substantial number of small entities,' or provides an agency or office with the clear authority and responsibility to do so."[15] In addition to the areas raised previously, GAO said that numerous other issues regarding the RFA remain unresolved, including:

- how Congress believes that the economic impact of a rule should be measured (e.g., in terms of compliance costs as a percentage of businesses' annual revenues, the percentageof work hours available to the firms, or some other metric);
- whether agencies should count the impact of the underlying statutes when determining whether their rules have a significant impact;
- what should be considered a "rule" for purposes of the requirement that agencies review their rules within 10 years of their promulgation; and
- whether agencies should review all rules that had a SEISNSE at the time they were originally published as final rules, or only those rules that currently have that effect.

Therefore, GAO said "Congress might wish to review the procedures, definitions, exemptions, and other provisions of RFA to determine whether changes are needed to better achieve the purposes Congress intended." Also, GAO said "attention should ... be paid to the domino effect that an agency's initial determination of whether RFA is applicable to a rulemaking has on other statutory requirements, such as preparing compliance guides for small entities and periodically reviewing existing regulations."

Although GAO has consistently called for greater clarity in the RFA's requirements, other observers have indicated that the definitions of key terms like "significant economic impact" and "substantial number of small entities" should remain flexible because of significant differences in each agency's operating environment. Notably, the SBA Office of Advocacy said that "[n]o definition could, or arguably should, be devised to apply to all rules given the dynamics of the economy and changes that are constantly occurring in the structure of small-entity sectors."[16] In its guidance on the RFA, SBA said the lack of clear definitions in the act "does not mean that Congress left the terms completely ambiguous or open to unreasonable interpretations."[17] Quoting the legislative history of the act in 1980, SBA said the diversity of both the community of small entities and of rules themselves makes a precise definition of the term "significant economic impact" virtually impossible and possibly counterproductive. Illustrative examples of "significant" economic impacts cited in the guidance range widely — from $500 in compliance costs to a 2% reduction in revenues if an industry's profits are 3% of revenues. Similarly, the guidance suggests that determinations of whether a "substantial number" of small entities are affected should begin with what it called the "more than just a few" standard, but ultimately does not require agencies to find that more than half of small entities would be affected.

PROPOSED CHANGES TO THE RFA BY H.R. 4458

On December 12, 2007, H.R. 4458—the "Small Business Regulatory Improvement Act"—was introduced by Representative Brad Ellsworth and nine cosponsors, and the bill was referred to the House Committee on the Judiciary and the House Committee on Small Business. On December 13, 2007, the House Small Business Committee unanimously reported the bill. No action on H.R. 4458 has been scheduled by the House Committee on the Judiciary, and no comparable legislation has been introduced in the Senate. Similar legislation was introduced in the 109th Congress (H.R. 682 and S. 1388), but was not acted upon.

H.R. 4458 would make a number of changes to the RFA — all of which are supported by the SBA Office of Advocacy and small business representatives.[18] For example, Section 3 of the bill would amend Section 601 of the RFA and define "economic impact" to include direct economic effects of a rule on small entities as well as any indirect effect "which is reasonably foreseeable and results from such rule." Section 4 of the bill would make several changes to the RFA's requirements for IRFAs, FRFAs, and certifications — adding new analytical or reporting requirements, and adding to the level of detail in existing requirements. (Most of those changes are discussed later in this report.)

Section 5 of H.R. 4458 would amend Section 610 of the RFA and establish new requirements for the periodic review of rules. Specifically, within 180 days after enactment, the bill would require agencies to publish in the *Federal Register* and on their websites a plan for reviewing all existing rules that the agency heads determine have a SEISNSE — regardless of whether the agency published a FRFA under Section 604 of the RFA at the time the rule was promulgated. The plan must provide for the review of all existing rules within 10 years after the enactment of the legislation (although the agency head may extend that deadline by two years if completion of the reviews is not feasible), and for the review of rules issued after enactment within 10 years of their publication in the *Federal Register*. Also, each agency must publish a list of the rules to be reviewed pursuant to the plan, including why the agency determined each rule has a SEISNSE, and must request comments from the public, the SBA Chief Counsel for Advocacy, and the Regulatory Enforcement Ombudsman on the "enforcement" of the rule. Finally, the bill would require agencies to submit reports annually to Congress and, for agencies other than independent regulatory agencies, the OIRA Administrator. The annual report is to include (1) the identification of any rule for which the agency head had "made a determination" regarding whether the rule overlaps or conflicts with other rules, and the length of time since the rule had previously been evaluated; and (2) a "detailed explanation of the reasons for such determination."

ANALYSIS OF H.R. 4458

Some of the provisions in H.R. 4458 appear to address certain long-standing issues of concern regarding the implementation of the RFA. Other provisions appear to add to the number or depth of the analytical and notification requirements placed on rulemaking agencies, and some other provisions seem unclear. But H.R. 4458 may be most notable for what it does not do; it does not clarify what constitutes a "significant" economic impact on a "substantial" number of small entities. Therefore, agencies will still be able to determine when a regulatory flexibility analysis is needed (and, consequently, when related requirements are triggered).

Long-standing Issues

For more than 20 years, courts have ruled that agencies need not prepare regulatory flexibility analyses if the effects of a rule on an industry are indirect.[19] Therefore, for example, if a federal agency is issuing a final rule establishing a health standard that is implemented by states or other entities, the federal agency issuing the rule need not prepare a regulatory flexibility analysis even if it is clear that the implementation ultimately will have significant effect on a substantial number of small entities.[20] Likewise, if a federal agency issues a rule directly regulating how long non-immigrant aliens can remain in the United States but indirectly affecting small businesses in the travel industry, the agency can certify that the rule does not have a SEISNSE.[21] Agencies have also indicated that they do not consider the secondary effects that a rule may have on the cost of compliance with other programs.[22]

By clarifying that the term "economic impact" includes indirect effects that are "reasonably foreseeable and result from the rule," H.R. 4458 might result in more agency rules being viewed as requiring an IRFA, an FRFA, or both.[23] Nevertheless, agencies appear to have substantial discretion in determining what indirect effects are "reasonably foreseeable," because the proposed legislation does not define that term. Also, even when the indirect effects of a rule are foreseeable, in some cases the agencies may not be able to provide much detail regarding those effects in their IRFAs and FRFAs (e.g., when the implementation details are left to states or local governments).

H.R. 4458 would also clarify how agencies' reviews under Section 610 of the RFA should be conducted. As a result, agencies would be required to review all of their rules to determine if they currently have a SEISNE, and could not simply rely on their previous determinations when the final rule was published in the *Federal Register*. Enactment of this change could result in substantially more Section 610 reviews, but with a concomitant increase in time and effort required by federal agencies. Still unclear, however, is what constitutes a "rule" under this requirement (e.g., only the provision published in the *Federal Register* or the entire *Code of Federal Regulations* part that the provision amended).

Additional Requirements

Other elements of H.R. 4458 appear to add to the number or depth of the analytical and notification requirements that the RFA currently places on agencies. For example:

- Whereas the RFA currently requires an IRFA to contain a "description" of the reasons why the agency action is being considered and a "succinct statement" of the objectives of and legal basis for the proposed rule, H.R. 4458 would require a "detailed statement" describing those elements.

- Whereas the RFA currently requires that the IRFA contain a description of "and, where feasible, an estimate of the number of small entities to which the proposed rule will apply," H.R. 4458 would require a detailed description of the type of small entities affected, and would require an estimate of the number of small entities affected or an explanation of why such an estimate is not available.
- If an agency certifies a rule as not requiring an IRFA or a FRFA, H.R. 4458 would require that the statement providing the factual basis for the certification be "detailed."
- Regarding FRFAs, the bill would eliminate the current requirement that the statement of the need for and objectives of the rule be "succinct," and would require that any explanation of why the number of small entities affected is not available be "detailed."
- The bill would also require that the FRFA contain the agency's response to any comments from the SBA Chief Counsel for Advocacy in response to the proposed rule and a detailed statement of changes made to the rule as a result of those comments.

Some public interest groups have expressed concerns that these and other provisions in H.R. 4458 would "add additional layers of analysis to a regulatory process already thick with prescriptive requirements and would further tilt the regulatory playing field in favor of regulated interests."[24] To the extent that agencies strictly adhere to the precise wording of these requirements (e.g., developing a "detailed" statement describing a rule instead of a "succinct" statement), agencies could experience substantially increased rule-development time and compliance costs. However, some of the bill's requirements appear to codify requirements that are currently in Executive Order 13272 (e.g., the requirement that each agency notify the Chief Counsel for Advocacy when the agency concludes that a rule may have a SEISNSE). Therefore, if agencies are already performing these executive order-required tasks, their codification via H.R. 4458 would not appear to add to the time or agency effort required to issue rules.

On the other hand, some other parts of H.R. 4458 appear to place substantial new requirements on rulemaking agencies — perhaps most notably, the requirement that agencies implement a new 10-year plan for the review of all of their existing rules. For agencies like EPA that have taken a narrow view of Section 610 and only reviewed rules for which they had published an FRFA, this requirement would greatly expand the scope of their Section 610 reviews to all rules. As a result, some agency rules issued decades earlier that had never before been reviewed would, under H.R. 4458, be required to be reviewed. However, this requirement would also affect agencies that have broadly interpreted Section 610. Therefore, for example, even though the Department of Transportation is expected to complete a comprehensive, 10-year process of reviewing all of its rules in 2008, H.R. 4458 would require the department to review all of those rules again.

Some Requirements Appear Unclear

Some elements of this new Section 610 process seem unclear. For example, H.R. 4458 states that each agency is to submit a report annually that includes "the identification of any rule with respect to which the head of the agency made a determination described in paragraph (5) or (6) of subsection (d) and a detailed explanation of the reasons for such determination." Subsection (d) lists the factors that agencies are to consider in reviewing rules, with paragraph (5) being "The extent to which the rule overlaps, duplicates, conflicts with other Federal rules and, unless the head of the agency determines it to be infeasible, State and local rules." Paragraph (6) of subsection (d) indicates that agencies' reviews of their rules should consider "The length of time since the rule has been evaluated or the degree to which technology, economic conditions, or other factors have changed in the area affected by the rule."

If an agency determines during its review that a rule *does not* conflict with any other rule, and that the relevant technology and economic conditions *have not* changed since the rule was issued, is the agency to include this "determination" and a detailed explanation of how it reached this conclusion in its annual report? Or is the agency only to include such determinations and explanations for rules that *do* conflict with other rules, or where the technology, economic conditions, or other factors *have* changed? If agencies are expected to provide detailed explanations for decisions in either direction for all the rules they review each year, the agencies' annual reports to Congress and OIRA could be time consuming and voluminous. On the other hand, if agencies are only to provide information regarding rules that they consider in conflict with other rules, or rules for which relevant factors have changed, then agencies will have strong incentives to reduce their reporting burden and conclude that those conditions are not present. Also, the bill indicates that the annual reports, as well as agency certifications that the 10-year review process needs to be extended, are to be sent to "the Congress," but the precise recipient is unclear (e.g., the Parliamentarians or a particular committee). It also seems unclear what "the Congress" is to do with the reports and certifications once they arrive.

Value of Mandatory Reviews

More generally, recent work by GAO indicates that statutorily required regulatory reviews are less frequent, and may be less effective, than reviews undertaken at the agencies' discretion — thereby raising questions about the overall value of statutory review requirements such as Section 610 of the RFA. In a July 2007 report, GAO said most "retrospective reviews" of agency rules between 2001 and 2006 were conducted at the agencies' discretion, not as a result of mandatory requirements such as Section 610.[25] GAO also said that discretionary reviews were more likely to involve the public in the process than mandatory reviews, and were more likely to result in changes to the rules. On the other hand, statutorily required reviews were more likely to have review standards, and were more likely to be documented. GAO recommended that agencies incorporate various elements into their policies and procedures to improve the effectiveness and transparency of retrospective regulatory reviews, and that they identify opportunities for Congress to revise and consolidate existing review requirements.

Bill Does Not Clarify Key RFA Terms

Most notably, however, H.R. 4458 does not appear to address the central criticism that GAO has raised regarding the RFA during the past 20 years — i.e., the lack of clarity and inconsistency in how agencies determine what constitutes a "significant" economic impact or a "substantial" number of small entities. As GAO has pointed out numerous times in the past, unless Congress defines those key terms or requires SBA or some other entity to do so, agencies will be allowed to develop their own definitions, and therefore can determine when a regulatory flexibility analysis is required. In some cases, agencies have concluded that rules imposing direct compliance costs of thousands of dollars per year on thousands of small entities did not represent a "significant" economic effect on a "substantial" number of small entities.[26] With the addition of new requirements that IRFAs and FRFAs be "detailed," agencies will have even greater incentives to certify their rules and avoid conducting the analyses altogether (although this may be somewhat counterbalanced by the requirement that the factual basis of any certification also be detailed). A similar phenomenon occurred in 1996 when SBREFA required that agencies prepare compliance guides, and that EPA and OSHA conduct advocacy review panels, for any rule that the agencies did not certify. At EPA, the percentage of rules that were certified as not having a SEISNSE increased from 78% in the 30-month period before SBREFA to 96% in the 30-month period after SBREFA.[27]

As the previous discussion suggests, when agencies certify their rules as not having a SEISNSE, they not only exempt themselves from the requirements thatthey conduct an IRFA and an FRFA; the agencies will also be able to avoid the related requirements to produce compliance guides and hold advocacy review panels (the "domino effect" that GAO mentioned). Also, agencies will continue to have broad discretion in deciding which rules currently have a SEISNSE, and therefore require review under Section 610 of the RFA. Therefore, the issue of what constitutes a "significant" economic impact and a "substantial" number of small entities affects a number of rulemaking requirements.

As GAO has pointed out in the past, if Congress wanted to address this issue, it could define what a SEISNSE is itself, or it could require that SBA's Office of Advocacy or some other entity define the term. A combination of both approaches is also possible. For example, even if Congress were to establish a broadly applicable "bright line" for when an IRFA or an FRFA must be prepared (e.g., any rule that is expected to have at least a $5,000 annual economic impact on at least 5,000 small entities cannot be certified), more industry-specific standards could be developed below that threshold — similar to the way that industry-specific standards have been developed for what constitutes a "small" entity.[28]

End Notes

[1] Many agencies are apparently aware of this limitation; the General Accounting Office (GAO, now the Government Accountability Office) estimated that in more than 500 final rules

published in 1997 the agencies specifically stated that the RFA was not applicable or that a regulatory flexibility analysis was not required because the action was not preceded by an NPRM. See U.S. General Accounting Office, *Federal Rulemaking: Agencies Often Published Final Actions Without Proposed Rules*, GAO/GGD-98-126, Aug.31, 1998, p. 31.

[2] This requirement, as well as a similar requirement in Executive Order 12866, is generally met via entries in the *Unified Agenda of Federal Regulatory and Deregulatory Actions*. The *Unified Agenda* is published twice each year in the *Federal Register* by the Regulatory Information Service Center, and provides uniform reporting of data on regulatory activities under development throughout the federal government.

[3] U.S. Small Business Administration, *20 Years of the Regulatory Flexibility Act: Rulemaking in a Dynamic Economy* (Washington: 2000).

[4] U.S. President (Bush), "Proper Consideration of Small Entities in Agency Rulemaking," Executive Order 13272, 67 *Federal Register* 53461, Aug. 13, 2002. This executive order essentially formalized agreements that had been in place for more than seven years. In response to a previous GAO recommendation, on Jan. 11, 1995, the SBA Chief Counsel for Advocacy and the OIRA Administrator exchanged letters committing the two offices to work together more closely. Specifically, SBA said it would develop new guidance for agencies to follow in complying with the act, and would provide OIRA with a copy of any comments it files with an agency concerning compliance with the RFA. OIRA said it would consider RFA compliance as part of its reviews under Executive Order 12866, and would include SBA in the process when appropriate. See U.S. General Accounting Office, *Regulatory Flexibility Act: Status of Agencies' Compliance*, GAO/T-GGD-95-112, Mar. 8, 1995, pp. 4-5.

[5] See U.S. Small Business Administration, Office of Advocacy, *A Guide for Government Agencies: How to Comply with the Regulatory Flexibility Act* (Washington: May 2003), available at [http://www.sba.gov/advo/laws/rfaguide.pdf]. The Office of Advocacy had issued similar guidance previously. For example, see U.S. Small Business Administration, Office of Advocacy, *The Regulatory Flexibility Act: An Implementation Guide for Federal Agencies* (Washington: 1998), available from the author.

[6] GAO reported in 1999 that EPA conducted Section 610 reviews only for rules that it concluded had a SEISNSE at the time the final rules were promulgated. The Department of Transportation, on the other hand, interpreted the statute to require a review of all rules. See U.S. General Accounting Office, *Regulatory Flexibility Act: Agencies' Interpretations of Review Requirements Vary*, GAO/GGD-99-55, Apr. 2, 1999, pp. 11-12.

[7] Section 212 was amended by Subtitle C of the U.S. Troop Readiness, Veterans Care, Katrina Recovery, and Iraq AccountabilityAppropriations Act, 2007 (P.L. 110-28, May 25, 2007). This description includes those amendments.

[8] For an examination of how the first five advocacy review panels were implemented, see U.S. General Accounting Office, *Regulatory Reform: Implementation of the Small Business Advocacy Review Panel Requirements*, GAO/GGD-98-36, March 18, 1996.

[9] U.S. General Accounting Office, *Regulatory Flexibility Act: Inherent Weaknesses May Limit Its Usefulness for Small Governments*, GAO/HRD-91-16, Jan. 11, 1991.

[10] U.S. General Accounting Office, *Regulatory Flexibility Act: Status of Agencies' Compliance*, GAO/GGD-94-105, Apr. 27, 1994.

[11] U.S. General Accounting Office, *Regulatory Flexibility Act: Agencies' Interpretations of Review Requirements Vary*, GAO/GGD-99-55, Apr. 2, 1999; U.S. General Accounting Office, *Regulatory Flexibility Act: Implementation in EPA Program Offices and ProposedLead Rule*, GAO/GGD-00-193, Sept. 20, 2000.

[12] U.S. General Accounting Office, *Regulatory Flexibility Act: Key Terms Still Need to BeClarified*, GAO-01-669T, Apr. 24, 2001.

[13] U.S. General Accounting Office, *Regulatory Flexibility Act: Clarification of Key TermsStill Needed*, GAO-02-491T, Mar. 6, 2002.

[14] Ibid., pp. 2-3.

[15] U.S. Government Accountability Office, *Regulatory Flexibility Act: Congress Should Revisit and Clarify Elements of the Act to Improve Its Effectiveness*, GAO-06-998, July 20, 2006.

[16] U.S. Small Business Administration, Office of Advocacy, *The Regulatory Flexibility Act: An Implementation Guide for Federal Agencies* (Washington: 1998), p. 16.

[17] Ibid., p. 18.

[18] Ralph Lindeman, "SBA Advocacy Chief Urges Legislation To Strengthen Regulatory Flexibility Act," *BNA Daily Report for Executives*, Dec. 7, 2007, p. A-28. The Office of Advocacy has supported similar provisions in other legislation. See testimony of SBA Chief Counsel for Advocacy Thomas M. Sullivan, in U.S. Congress, House Committee on the Judiciary, Subcommittee on Commercial and Administrative Law, *Regulatory Flexibility Improvements Act — H.R. 682*, hearings, 109th Cong., 2nd sess., July 20, 2006. Individuals from SBA have also written in support of similar provisions. See Keith W. Holman, "The Regulatory Flexibility Act at 25: Is the Law Achieving Its Goal?" *Fordham Urban Law Journal*, vol. 33 (May 2006), pp. 1119-1137.

[19] See, for example, *Mid-Tex Electric Cooperative, Inc. v. FERC*, 773 F.2d 327, 343 (D.C. Cir. 1985).

[20] For example, when EPA published a final rule establishing national ambient air quality standards (NAAQS) for particulate matter in October 2006, the agency certified the rule as not having a SEISNSE "because NAAQS themselves impose no regulations on small entities." In its cost-benefit analysis for the rule, EPA estimated the cost of installing controls to meet the health standard at $5.6 billion in 2020. See U.S. Environmental Protection Agency, "National Ambient Air Quality Standards for Particulate Matter; Final Rule," 71 *Federal Register* 61144, 61217. In a similar case (*American Trucking Associations, Inc. v. U.S. Environmental Protection Agency*, 175 F.3d 1027 (D.C. Cir. 1999)), affirmed in part and reversed in part, *Whitman v. American Trucking Associations*, 532 U.S. 457 (2001), the U.S. Court of Appeals for the District of Columbia ruled that EPA had complied with the RFA because the states, not EPA, had the direct authority to impose requirements to control ozone and particulate matter consistent with EPA health standards.

[21] This example of a 2002 rule issued by the Immigration and Naturalization Service was cited in testimony by the SBA Chief Counsel for Advocacy in support of H.R. 682 in the 109th Congress. Testimony of SBA Chief Counsel for Advocacy Thomas M. Sullivan, in U.S. Congress, House Committee on the Judiciary, Subcommittee on Commercial and Administrative Law, *Regulatory Flexibility Improvements Act — H.R. 682*, hearings, 109th Cong., 2nd sess., July 20, 2006.

[22] For example, in a 1991 rule, EPA acknowledged that the rule in question may have "trickle down" effects on other EPA programs under the Clean Air Act (CAA), Superfund, or the Resource Conservation and Recovery Act (RCRA), but went on to say that "the purpose of today's action is solely to establish drinking water standards that public water systems must comply with. Consequently, EPA does not consider the cost of secondary impacts which may occur under the CAA, Superfund, or RCRA." U.S. Environmental Protection Agency, "Drinking Water; National Primary Drinking Water Regulations;Monitoring for Volatile Organic Chemicals," 56 *Federal Register*30266, July 1, 1991.

[23] The SBA Chief Counsel for Advocacy said his office's "biggest concern with the RFAis that it does not require agencies to analyze indirect impacts." See [http://www.sba.gov/advo/press/07-38.html].

[24] Ralph Lindeman, "House Panel Approves Measure to Require More Agency Review of Regulatory Burdens," *BNA Daily Report for Executives*, Dec. 14, 2007, p. A-2.

[25] U.S. Government Accountability Office, *Reexamining Regulations: Opportunities Exist to Improve Effectiveness and Transparency of Retrospective Reviews*, GAO-07-791, July 16, 2007.

[26] For example, EPA concluded that one proposed rule issued in 1999 would affect more than 5,000 small businesses and impose more than $100 million in compliance costs in the first year, but EPA still certified the rule as not having a SEISNSE. See U.S. General

Accounting Office, *Regulatory Flexibility Act: Implementation in EPA Program Offices and Proposed Lead Rule*, GAO/GGD-00-193, Sept. 20, 2000. In 1989, EPA certified a rule as not having a SEISNE even though EPA estimated it would impose compliance costs on about 11,000 small public water systems of between $333 million and $439 million per year. See U.S. Environmental Protection Agency, "Drinking Water; National Primary Drinking Water Regulations," 54 Federal Register 27486, June 29, 1989.

[27] U.S. General Accounting Office, *Regulatory Flexibility Act: Implementation in EPA Program Offices and Proposed Lead Rule*, GAO/GGD-00-193, Sept. 20, 2000, p. 16.

[28] SBA size standards may be viewed at [http://www.sba.gov/services/ contractingopportunities/sizestandardstopics/index.html].

CHAPTER SOURCES

The following chapters have been previously published:

Chapter 1 – This is an edited, excerpted and augmented edition of a United States Congressional Research Service publication, Report Order Code RL33862, dated January 3, 2008.

Chapter 2 – This is an edited, excerpted and augmented edition of a United States Congressional Research Service publication, Report Order Code RL34354, dated August 5, 2008.

Chapter 3 – This is an edited, excerpted and augmented edition of a United States Congressional Research Service publication, Report Order Code RL34633, dated September 3, 2008.

Chapter 4 - This is an edited, excerpted and augmented edition of a United States Congressional Research Service publication, Report Order Code RL32240, dated August 28, 2008.

Chapter 5 – This is an edited, excerpted and augmented edition of a United States Congressional Research Service publication, Report Order Code RL32397, dated January 17, 2008.

Chapter 6 – This is an edited, excerpted and augmented edition of a United States Congressional Research Service publication, Report Order Code RL32452, dated August 28, 2008.

Chapter 7 - This is an edited, excerpted and augmented edition of a United States Congressional Research Service publication, Report Order Code RL34355, dated February 12, 2008.

INDEX

B

C

D

E

F

G

H

I

J

K

L

M

N

T